Son of Hope

The Prison Journals of David Berkowitz
Volume I

Morning Star Communications
New York, New York 10026 USA

We want to hear from you. Please send your comments about this book to us in care of the mailing address below, or email us at one of our email addresses. Thank you.

Morning Star Communications
New York, New York 10026 USA

www.morningstar-communications.com

www.thesonofhope.com

Unless otherwise indicated, all scripture quotations in this book are taken from the King James Version.

Son of Hope

A David Berkowitz Book

Compiled and edited by Morning Star Communications, LLC

Copyright © 2006 by Morning Star Communications, LLC

New York, NY 10026

Library of Congress Cataloging-in-Publication Data

Berkowitz, David.

Son of Hope: The Prison Journals of David Berkowitz, Volume I / David Berkowitz.

p. cm.

ISBN 0-97789-962-4

1. Christian Life. I. Title.

2006

CIP

Printed in the United States of America

Interior design and Jacket design by GF Graphics

The Spirit of the Lord God is upon me; because the Lord hath anointed me to preach good tidings unto the meek; he hath sent me to bind up the broken-hearted, to proclaim liberty to the captives, and the opening of the prison to them that are bound;

To proclaim the acceptable year of the Lord, and the day of vengeance of our God; to comfort all that mourn;

To appoint unto them that mourn in Zion, to give unto them beauty for ashes, the oil of joy for mourning, the garment of praise for the spirit of heaviness; that they might be called trees of righteousness, the planting of the Lord, that he might be glorified.

—Isaiah 61:1-3 (KJV)

This book is dedicated to the ones who have inspired me the most by the way they lived before death came to take them suddenly and unexpectedly.

My deepest gratitude to my beloved friend, **Andy Tant**, a fourteen-year-old from Tennessee whom God used to pour words of encouragement and hope into me, and to confirm what the Lord had already placed in my heart.

If Andy had not said to me what he did at a crucial time in my life in 1993, I don't think I would be as involved in reaching out to today's generation of teenagers as I am at present. At age 16 Andy was gone.

And my thanks to **Jeremiah Riordan** who, although we never met, provided me with a good example of strength mixed with compassion. His pitching arm may have been the best the state of Illinois had to offer.

To **Karen Lee Fitzpatrick** of the U.S. Forest Service who died in a tragic blaze on July 10, 2001. Karen was more than hero. She was a bundle of beauty, compassion, and spirituality. As a devout Christian, Karen led by example and by love. Her mother, Kathie, is a special friend who has, for many years, been faithfully sharing my story of redemption with the youth in juvenile detention.

And to **Rachel Joy Scott**. The bullets of Columbine took her life but not her message. Rachel's life speaks for itself through her tears and smiles, and by her message of compassion and forgiveness. Millions have been touched by her story. And as the Scripture says concerning the heroes of the faith, they "being dead" continue to speak (Hebrews 11:4).

Only God could cause those who are now deceased to touch more lives in a positive way in death than if they were alive. This is a mystery. The sovereignty of God. Who could comprehend it? Yet it is true. The end of one's life on earth is not necessarily the end of that individual's usefulness to the Lord.

With all my heart I say, "Thank you, Andy, Jeremiah, Karen Lee, and Rachel Joy. I hope to see you guys soon. Even so, come, Lord Jesus."

—David Berkowitz - #78A1976
Sullivan Correctional Facility
Fallsburg, New York

ACKNOWLEDGMENT

Thank you, Lawrence Jordan, for stepping out in faith. I myself never had plans to put some of my journals into a book. To Myrna Games for retyping my journals. And to Kathi Macias for your many hours of selecting the journal entries, editing them, and so much more.

To Chuck and Lorraine Cohen who had the vision for this project over a period of many years.

To Neil Konitshek and David Campbell for their love, dedication, and devotion to the Forgiven For Life website. They sacrificed and ran the site for years. These men put down a strong foundation before passing on the torch to others, who I pray will be just as dedicated to the task at hand.

And to my God-given legal team of Mark Jay Heller, Michael David Heller, Elizabeth Heller and Peter Toumbekis, Esquires. At the beginning of 2005 I was in desperate need of a lawyer. So I prayed. Then, out of nowhere, Mark Heller wrote to me after not hearing from him in more than twenty-seven years. Yes, I believe in miracles.

And a special acknowledgment to attorney Alan Binger, Richard Delfino, Dan Nicholls, and to my beloved father who has continued to love me. Also to an endless list of dear friends, some of whom have been with me for a long time. You, brothers and sisters, have been shoulders to cry on and pillars to lean on when I was weak.

Lastly, and most of all, to Jesus the Messiah. You are my Lord and King. Without you, my precious Savior, I could do nothing.

—David Berkowitz

CONTENTS

2002

2004

2005

May God bless everyone who is reading this message! My name is David Berkowitz. I am a prison inmate with a life sentence, and I have already been incarcerated for more than twenty-eight years. My criminal case is well known as the "Son of Sam" shootings. It was eighteen years ago, when I was living in a cold and lonely prison cell, that God got hold of my life. Here is my story of hope...

Child of Torment

From the time I was a small child my life seemed to be filled with torment. I often had seizures, rolling on the floor and even knocking over furniture. When these attacks came it felt as if something was entering me. My mother, who has long since passed away, had no control over me. I was like a wild and destructive animal. My father had to pin me to the floor until these attacks stopped. When I was in public school I was so violent and disruptive that an angry and frustrated teacher once grabbed me in a headlock and threw me out of his classroom.

I got into a lot of fights, and sometimes I started screaming for no apparent reason. Eventually my parents were told by school officials to take me to a child psychologist or I would be expelled. I saw this psychologist weekly for two years, but the sessions had no affect on my behavior. During this period of my life I was also plagued with bouts of severe depression. When this feeling came over me I would hide under my bed for hours, or lock myself in a closet and sit in total darkness from morning until afternoon. I had a craving for the darkness, and I felt an urge to flee from people.

A Force Was at Work

Occasionally this same evil force came upon me in the middle of the night. When that happened I felt an urge to sneak out of the house and wander the dark streets. I roamed the neighborhood like an alley cat and then crept back into my house by climbing the fire escape. My parents never knew I was gone, though I continually worried and frightened them with my strange behavior. At times I went through the entire day without talking to them. Instead I stayed in my room and talked to myself. My parents couldn't reach me, not even with all their love. Many times I saw them break down and cry when they saw my torment, but they were unable to help me.

Fighting Thoughts of Suicide

Thoughts of suicide often came into my mind. We lived on the sixth floor of an old apartment building, and sometimes I sat on our fire escape with my legs dangling over the side. When my dad saw me he yelled at me to get back inside. I also felt powerful urges to step in front of moving cars or throw myself in front of subway trains. At times those urges were so strong that my body actually trembled. I can still remember what a tremendous struggle it was for me to hold on to my sanity. I had no idea what to do, and neither did my mom and dad. Besides my weekly visits to the psychologist, my parents took me to talk to a rabbi, teachers, and school counselors, but nothing worked.

My Mother Dies

When I was fourteen my mother was stricken with cancer; within several months she was dead. I had no other brothers or sisters, and so it was just me and my dad. He had to work ten hours a day, six days a week, so we spent very little time together. For the most part my mother had been my only source of stability. With her gone I was filled with anger, and my life quickly went downhill. I felt hopeless, and my periods of depression increased in intensity. I also became even more rebellious and began to cut out of school. My dad tried to help as best as he could, even managing to push me through high school. The day after I graduated, which was only a few weeks after my eighteenth birthday, I joined the Army, hoping to escape my problems and start a new life. But even in the service I had trouble coping, though I did manage to complete my three-year enlistment.

The Force Still Had Me

I got out of the service in 1974, ready to start life again as a civilian, but all my friends had either married or moved away. I was living alone in New York City. Then, in 1975, I met some guys at a party who were heavily involved in the occult, though I didn't learn that until much later. Ever since

I was a child I had been fascinated with witchcraft, Satanism, and the occult, and I had spent countless hours watching those types of movies, including "Rosemary's Baby," a story that particularly captivated my mind.

Now I was twenty-two, and this evil force was still reaching out to me. Everywhere I went there seemed to be a sign or a symbol pointing me to Satan. I felt as if something was trying to take control of my life. I began to read the *Satanic Bible* by the late Anton LaVey, who founded the Church of Satan in San Francisco in 1966. Innocently, I began to practice various occult rituals and incantations, oblivious to the fact that I was playing with fire.

I am now convinced that something satanic had, at some point, entered my mind. Looking back at all that happened in my life, I realize I was slowly but surely being deceived. I didn't know that bad things were going to result from all this, yet over the ensuing months the things I once considered wicked no longer seemed so. I was headed down the road to destruction, and I didn't even know it. Maybe I was at a point where I just didn't care.

The Horror Begins

Eventually I crossed that invisible line of no return. After years of mental torment, behavioral problems, deep inner struggles, and my own rebellious ways, I became the criminal that, at the time, seemed to be my destiny. I now see it as the horrible nightmare it was, and I would do anything if I could undo everything that happened. Six people lost their lives as a result of my actions. Many others suffered at my hand, and will continue to suffer for a lifetime. I am so sorry for that.

In 1978 I was convicted for my crimes and sentenced to about 365 consecutive years, virtually burying me alive behind prison walls. When I first entered the prison system I was placed in isolation. I was then sent to a psychiatric hospital because I was declared temporarily insane. Eventually I was sent to other prisons, including the infamous "Attica." As do many inmates, I found life in prison to be a struggle. I have had my share of problems, hassles, and fights. At one time I almost lost my life when another inmate cut my throat. Yet through all this, though I didn't realize it at the time, God had His loving hands upon me.

Hope Was Coming

Ten years into my prison sentence, feeling despondent and without hope, I was walking the prison yard on a cold winter's night when an inmate named Rick came up to me. He introduced himself and began to tell me that Jesus Christ loved me and wanted to forgive me. Although I knew he meant well I mocked him because I didn't think God would ever forgive me or want anything to do with me.

Still Rick persisted, and we soon became friends. We often walked the yard together, and little by little he told me about his life and what he believed Jesus had done for him. He kept reminding me that no matter what we had done, Christ stood ready to forgive if we were willing to turn from the bad things we were doing and put our full faith and trust in Jesus Christ and what He did on the cross—dying for our sins.

Rick gave me a *Gideon's Pocket Testament* and asked me to read the Psalms, which I did every night. It was during those times that the Lord quietly and gently melted my stone-cold heart.

A New Life Begins

One night as I was reading Psalm 34 I came upon verse 6, which says, "This poor man cried, and the Lord heard him, and saved him out of all his troubles." At that very moment in 1987 everything seemed to hit me all at once—the guilt from what I had done, the disgust at what I had become—and I began to pour out my heart to God. In my cold cell on that dark night I got down on my knees and cried out to Jesus Christ.

I told Him I was sick and tired of doing evil. I asked Him to forgive me for all my sins. I spent a good while on my knees praying to Him, and when I got up it felt as if a very heavy but invisible chain that had been around me for so many years was now broken. A peace flooded over me. I did not understand what was happening, but in my heart I knew that my life was going to be different.

Almost Two Decades of Freedom

More than eighteen years have gone by since I had that first talk with the Lord, and so many good things have happened in that time. Jesus Christ has allowed me to start an outreach ministry right here in the prison, where

I have been given permission by prison officials to work in the "Intermediate Care Program" (ICP Unit) where men who have various emotional and coping problems are housed. I can pray with them as we read our Bibles together, and I get the chance to show them a lot of brotherly love and compassion.

I have worked as the Chaplain's clerk, and I also have a letter-writing ministry. In addition, the Lord has opened ways for me to share my testimony with millions via CNN's "Larry King Live" on television, and on Dr. James Dobson's "Focus on the Family" radio program.

There Is Hope for You too

One of my favorite passages of scripture is Romans 10:13, which says, "For whosoever shall call upon the name of the Lord shall be saved." Here it is clear that God has no favorites. He rejects no one, but welcomes all who call upon Him. I know from personal experience that God is a God of mercy who is willing to forgive. He is perfectly able to restore and heal our hurting and broken lives. I have discovered from the Bible that Jesus Christ died for our sins, even though He Himself was without sin. He took our place on that cross. He shed His blood as the full and complete payment God required for our wrongdoing. Romans 3:23 says, "For all have sinned, and come short of the glory of God," but Romans 6:23 promises, "For the wages of sin is death; but the gift of God is eternal life through Jesus Christ our Lord." These passages make it clear that everyone has sinned. Some of us did so more than others, but all have done wrong. Therefore, we must all make the decision to acknowledge our sins before God and be sorry for them. We need to turn from our lives of sin, as well as believe that Christ is the Son of God.

Here's Your Chance

Friend, here is your chance to get things right with God. The Bible says in Romans 10:9-10, "That if thou shalt confess with thy mouth the Lord Jesus, and shalt believe in thine heart that God hath raised him from the dead, thou shalt be saved. For with the heart man believeth unto righteousness; and with the mouth confession is made unto salvation." So believe in your heart that these words from the Bible are true—and then tell someone of your decision. Please consider what I am saying. I beg you with all my heart to place your faith in Christ right now, for tomorrow is promised to no one.

You see, I am not sharing this message simply to tell you an interesting story. Rather, I want you to taste the goodness of God, just as I have in my own life, a man who was once a devil worshipper and a murderer, so that you will know that Jesus Christ is about forgiveness, hope, and change.

I was involved in the occult, and I got burned. I became a cruel killer and threw away my life, as well as destroyed the lives of others. Now I have discovered that Christ is my answer and my hope. He broke the chains of mental confusion and depression that had me bound. Today I have placed my life in His hands. I only wish I had known Jesus before I committed those terrible crimes, for then they would not have happened.

With Love in Christ,
David Berkowitz

1998

"My Spritual Journal"

It is now officially Rosh Hashanah on the East Coast. According to the Jewish calendar, this is Tishrei 1, the first day of the Jewish New Year, and the entry point to another chapter of the history of God's people.

Yesterday I was praying and reading from the book of the prophet Daniel, and the Lord revealed to me that as of sundown on the Jewish New Year (today) I would enter the "most intensified period of spiritual, mental, emotional, and even physical warfare" that I have ever experienced during my eleven years as a Christian.

God is merciful. I am keeping this journal—a task that is long overdue—in order to record, remember, and pass on to others all that will transpire in the days to come. I am, according to the instructions given to me by the Lord God Almighty, to keep this journal until the day I die, or until the day I vanish into the heavens. All the awesome and even frightening events that will take place in this world are already recorded in the Bible. Many will see in the days ahead that the Holy Scriptures will be a spiritual roadmap to show people the way to hope, deliverance, and victory, even as the world and society as we know it begins to crumble around us.

> *"My Spiritual Journey"*
> *I am keeping this journal in order to record, remember, and pass on to others all that will transpire in the days to come.*

1999

NO JOURNAL ENTRIES
MADE IN 1999

2000

"My New Year's Prayer"

Father God, I come to You in Jesus' name. I ask You to use me for Your glory and honor, and to make me a source of blessing and encouragement for people who are troubled, lonely, confused, and hurting.

I pray that my life will no longer be a source of pain and hurt to others like it was in the past.

I pray I can be a light in the midst of the spiritual darkness that is in this world.

Father God, please continue to use me as an instrument of hope, healing, and encouragement.

"Lord, I have tried many times in the past to keep some kind of spiritual journal, and I failed to have the discipline to do it. Please help me to be more disciplined and faithful in doing this. I pray that whatever I write will be anointed and approved by You.

"I know that You have always loved me and never rejected me. You have showered me with Your abundant grace and mercy, and You have spared my life from Satan and from my own self-destructiveness time and time again. I thank You for this!

"Lord, I thank You, too, for choosing me, even before I was in my mother's womb, to one day be able to know and serve You. I pray that my life will no longer be a source of pain and hurt to others like it was in the past. I pray that, as the new creation I am today in Christ Jesus, I can continue to be a light in the midst of the spiritual darkness that is in this world. I pray also that You will keep me as the salt of this earth, and that I will be Your sweet fragrance as I live among the prisoners and guards in this place.

"Father God, please continue to use me as an instrument of hope, healing, and encouragement. I ask you, God of Israel, that Your divine forgiveness through Your Son, Jesus, be fully manifested in my life for all to see, that they may know that You are a forgiving God, full of compassion and mercy.

"Lord, there is so much more I want and need to pray for and about. But this shall suffice for now. Amen!"

"Words of Encouragemant"

I thank God for the opportunity to write this personal journal and to make it available to as many people as possible, so that others might be encouraged to place their faith and hope in the Lord. I also thank God for this chance to share what is happening in my life today, though I am not doing it to impress people, for many will neither care nor believe me. Jesus had the same problem, though on a much larger scale, of course. Multitudes of people saw all the miracles He did while He walked this earth, yet they refused to believe in Him. Now, today, after witnessing the miracles He has done in my life and in the lives of so many others, they still refuse to believe.

> *I am not doing it to impress people, for many will neither care nor believe me.*

In any event, here is my life today, with all its struggles and victories, regrets and hopes, and the daily challenges I must face, as well as the blessings God grants me. Through it all, my faith is in Him, and I believe my best days are yet to come. My prayer is that the Lord would allow whatever I write to be something that will bring clarity and hope to all who read this journal. May the Lord Jesus use my words to encourage others. Amen!

"Prison Life"

There is absolutely no glamour to committing a crime and coming to prison. If people, especially teenagers, knew what awaited them in places like this, they would think twice before breaking the law.

Prisons are places of chaos and misery. One may get the impression that the guards do a good job of controlling the situation because there are few riots—and thank God for that. But the reality is that, internally, prisons are almost always out of control because so many of the inmates are restless.

> *Prisons are places of chaos and misery.*

There is so much tension inside these walls, so much nonsense going on, oftentimes with seemingly endless hours of wild screaming and crazy behavior, and all kinds of wheeling and dealing. To put it simply, prisons are hell on earth. If not for the grace of God in my life, I would have lost my mind long ago.

"Encouragement from the Scriptures"

Moreover the word of the Lord came unto Jeremiah the second time, while he was yet shut up in the court of the prison, saying… "Call unto me, and I will answer thee, and show thee great and mighty things, which thou knowest not."

—Jeremiah 33:1, 33:3

I love the above verse from the book of the prophet Jeremiah because it is so full of hope. Today the Lord greatly encouraged me with this very scripture. I love the way the Lord gave it to the prophet while he was still shut up in the king's prison. Even in the most difficult and trying times of our lives, the Lord comes through with an uplifting word and a promise of better things to come if we will just continue to trust in Him.

Though I am in prison, my prayer is that the Lord will yet open doors for me to reach a generation of young people, many of whom do not understand spiritual things. They do not know the Lord, and they have no understanding of the forces that are at work, even now, to try to destroy them.

"A Time of Renewal and Rebirth"

There seems to have been so many spiritual battles going on since the beginning of this year. I thank God, however, for the little periods of respite.

I awoke this morning with a deep feeling of hope and expectation. Serving the Lord is never in vain, no matter how many people come against me, no matter what kinds of mental games they try to play. My job is to pray for them and to show them compassion.

As I looked at the calendar in my cell I realized the month of March is already here. This means spring is near, a time for change, for rebirth, and for a spiritual re-awakening after the long winter. I have great hopes that in the year to come God will use my life and my testimony, which is really His testimony, to have a positive impact upon others. I live only to serve, for if I cannot serve others and serve the Lord, my life is meaningless and I may as well roll over and die.

"Letter from a Satanist"

This afternoon I received a letter from a man in Rhode Island named Mike, who said he is a "Satanist." Whether or not he really is I have no way of knowing, but he did confess to it. Mike sounded intelligent and nice, and he asked my opinion on a few things.

Usually it takes me a little time to respond to my letters, as I often have a fairly large pile. However, after reading Mike's letter and breathing a brief, silent prayer, I sensed the Lord's leading me to write back immediately with a short and kind response, one typewritten page in length. In my letter I simply discussed some of my past experiences, and then explained to him what Christ has done in my life up to this point.

In addition to sharing a little about the Lord, I told him plainly that the Bible reveals that Satan is a thief who comes to "steal, kill, and destroy" (John 10:10). I also shared the second portion of this verse, which says that Jesus Christ has come to give people an abundant life of forgiveness, hope, joy, and peace, as well as a personal relationship with Him. I then gently but firmly explained the nature of the devil, including the fact that he hates and despises humanity; that he has no love for anyone, including his own followers; and that when he is done using a person to further his own ends, he will discard that individual like a piece of rotten garbage.

To deliberately align oneself with and follow after such a being has to be the most foolish act against one's life and soul. I included in my letter a pamphlet of my testimony, and I will continue to pray for Mike.

"Dealing with My Enemies"

I know with absolute certainty that Almighty God has redeemed and forgiven me. He has called me out of spiritual darkness and brought me into His marvelous light. The Lord has also anointed me to share with others about His goodness and mercy, and to proclaim His promise that no one is beyond the reach of His love and forgiveness. I believe God wants me to demonstrate, as much as is possible, His love for everyone—yes, even to my enemies and to those who, for whatever reasons, hate me. And there truly are people who despise my very life. They continually curse me in their hearts, and are forever looking for ways to hurt me and somehow destroy my Christian testimony.

Several years after I became a Christian, God revealed to me that there would be many people who would try, through ignorance, prejudice, and bias, to fight against me in every possible way. These people have worked very hard and have made many efforts to hinder my attempts at doing good to others and making my amends to society. Some of these enemies have been media people, while a handful have been former police officers and other law enforcement personnel. None of these people know me today; none of them really knew me before, back when I committed my crimes. Some have been total strangers, and a few were former prisoners who sought to cash in on having done time with me in the past.

In addition, there are myriad Satanists and practitioners of various occultic arts who have written hateful things about me. Obviously they now see me as a threat to their evil ways. But my trust and confidence is in the Lord: "The Lord is on my side; I will not fear: what can man do unto me?" (Psalm 118:6).

"Twenty-Three Years Ago Today"

Today, when I returned to my cell at the end of the work day, I sat down on my bunk and began to give thanks to the Lord. You see, it was twenty-three years ago today, on August 10, 1977, that I stood on the brink of eternity. It was the night the police officers surrounded me with their guns drawn.

I could have been shot dead right on the spot. If any one of those officers had opened fire, which could easily have happened on that dark street, I would have gone straight to hell. At the time I was a demon-possessed, tormented, lost, and evil man who hated Jesus Christ. But the Lord in His mercy protected me because He knew there would come a day when I would repent of my sinful life, accept His forgiveness, and believe the gospel.

It was in 1987, ten years after my arrest, when the Lord began to soften my heart. It had been a long gap in between, with even another brush with death in 1979 when an inmate slit my throat with a razor blade. That time I could have died right there on a cellblock tier in the infamous Attica Prison. But once again, God was merciful.

Now, here I stand today in the year 2000, praising God and thanking Him for protecting and delivering me. I know I am so undeserving of His mercy, but with each day, not only am I grateful, I am also learning that God's mercy is like His love: It cannot be measured.

"Praying for Laborers"

And Jesus went about all the cities and villages, teaching in their synagogues, and preaching the gospel of the kingdom, and healing every sickness and every disease among the people. But when he saw the multitudes, he was moved with compassion on them, because they fainted, and were scattered abroad, as sheep having no shepherd. Then saith he unto his disciples, The harvest truly is plenteous, but the labourers are few; Pray ye therefore the Lord of the harvest that he will send forth labourers into his harvest.

—Matthew 9:35-38

I thank the Lord daily for all He has been doing in the prisons. I thank Him also for Christians who have been faithful and willing to answer His call. When Jesus walked this earth, He went everywhere touching hurting lives with the love of God. His heart was moved with compassion when He saw the scattered multitudes—multitudes of people with multitudes of problems!

In the above passage the Lord said something that touched me deeply. He looked at His disciples and told them to pray for more workers for the harvest field. This is amazing to me because, as the Lord, He could have done it all Himself. He could have called battalions of angels to come forth, appear on the scene, and then go out into the world to carry on all these works of compassion. Instead He looked upon His human disciples, just as He looks upon us today, and told them to do the work of reaching out to hurting humanity, and to pray for still more workers to come along and do the same. How humbling this is to realize that God has chosen weak mankind with all our sins and failings to carry out such incredible tasks.

"A Word from God"

Yesterday's Saturday evening service was awesome! I received a wonderful filling of the Holy Spirit, and the Lord really moved in our midst. It was one of the most anointed services we've had in a long time.

The message was about Paul and his apostleship and how the Lord used him to evangelize the Gentiles. At the end of the service the visiting minister from New Jersey was told by the Lord to call some of us up front to the altar to receive prophetic words. I was the first one called, and of course I had no idea what would be spoken over me. The message from the Lord was that I was to start writing, and from that moment forward God was going to begin to open many "great doors" for me to share my written testimony. Terrific! I was jumping up and down in my spirit. This was a very happy moment for me after such a long time of waiting, and after such a seemingly endless journey through the wilderness of disappointment and discouragement.

The minister then asked me to lift my hands in the air. When I did, she anointed my hands with oil and told me to "start writing." She said the testimony would go "throughout the world." Well, North Pole, here I come! (Ha!)

I left the chapel so energized that I still feel wound up, and I could hardly sleep last night. Now I know how Elijah the prophet felt when he ran from Beersheba to Mount Horeb in forty days on only one meal (see 1 Kings 19:7, 19:8).

"Small but Powerful"

Today's message comes from Psalm 66:18: "If I regard iniquity in my heart, the Lord will not hear me." This one little verse is really powerful, and the Lord cut me deeply with it. As we read in Hebrews 4:12, God's Word is like a "two-edged sword."

Iniquity, or sin, and a personal relationship with the Lord just do not go together. Sin and salvation do not mix. They are like oil and water. We have to make a choice: one or the other. These are some of the insights God gave me as I pondered this message while in my cell today. In fact, this verse alone was powerful enough to bring me to my knees in repentance, crying out for forgiveness, and then allowing the Lord to cleanse and renew me. Many times we do not need to hear a long sermon to bring conviction to our heart. Today it took just one verse from the Bible for the Lord to do His desired work in me.

In the Gospel accounts of the life of Jesus, we see that He was able to completely communicate what He needed to say with just a few well chosen but powerful words. This is a good lesson for me, particularly as I launch out into the ministry of writing that God has called me to fulfill.

"The Pain of Pruning"

The time seems to be passing so quickly. In less than one month the year 2000 will be history. I pray for this nation and for our churches. Perhaps the Lord will give us a little more time to repent and to turn away from the sins that displease Him.

Lately I have been doing okay in some areas, while in others I have been struggling. I have strong faith, so this is not the issue. It is that, for now, God's hand of chastening is resting upon my life. God's Word says that when we as true Christians are bearing fruit, He will "prune" us so that we can bear even more fruit. And if you've ever been through a season of pruning, you know that it is painful. When God talks about pruning us, he is referring to the ongoing development of the "fruits of the Spirit" in our lives (see John 15:1-15). The Lord wants to make us sweeter so that our lives can be a blessing to others. A fruit tree grows its fruit for others to enjoy; it does not grow fruit for itself. Therefore, these "fruits of the Spirit" that the Bible refers to are produced for others to be able to taste the goodness of God through our lives.

For that reason I am now experiencing great internal pain. Jesus is doing an "inside job" on me. And while this may be painful, in the end it will make me into a better Christian—more holy, more yielded to Him, and more loving.

"Sin Kills"

The time is passing so quickly. Last year at this time many were worrying about "Y2K." But Y2K was never the problem; the problem was then and still is now only one thing—sin. It is sin that is killing our nation, wreaking havoc in the Church, and hurting and destroying our families and even our very own lives.

This is what the Lord was showing me today and what I am putting down in my personal journal. This morning God sent me to Isaiah 58 and 59, and then He really opened up these passages to me. It is time to scream "Sin!" It is time to cry out that sin is being practiced among God's people, and these sins will eventually ruin us. However, there is still time for us to repent and turn away from our sins and to get closer to the Lord.

I too need to turn away from sin, for it is surely going to kill me if I keep doing the things I've been doing. But God is merciful. He wants us to be holy and obedient, and to be spiritually prosperous. He wants our lives to be as "well watered gardens," full of joy, peace, and hope. Yet, as is often the case, our sins are standing in the way of our spiritual progress. They are quenching the Holy Spirit in us and separating us from a close relationship with Jesus Christ. As I said, these sins—regardless of what they are—will eventually damage each of us and cause the Church to be robbed of power and sacred anointing. The light of hope will be weakened in us unless we, by the power of the Holy Spirit, stop practicing sin.

Sin always kills! (See Psalm 66:18; 1 John 1:9.)

"Brothers in Christ"

God has a great sense of humor. Only the Lord can put a former Ku Klux Klan leader and a Jewish guy like me together as brothers in Christ.

Earlier last year I began to receive mail from a man from Alabama named Roger White. Roger loves the Lord and is always happy to share his testimony with anyone who will listen, but he was once an influential figure within the ranks of the Klan. Then God got hold of him and turned his life around. Today he and his wife, Jill, attend many all black and mixed race churches where he openly shares his story. God has completely changed this man's heart, and Roger has nothing but love for African-Americans, Jews, and everyone else. It has been a real joy to get his letters, which are always so full of energy and encouragement.

Several weeks ago Roger asked for my prayers because active members in the Klan have been threatening him and his family. A large church in New York City, as well as others, is also praying for him in this regard.

In addition to his own story, Roger likes to share my testimony when he speaks at various churches. His wife, who ministers at a local youth shelter, also shares my testimony with the teenagers. Wherever they go and wherever they speak, however, they find that it's the same old story all across America, even in rural Alabama where they live. Teens are caught up in drugs, gangs, depression, peer pressure, feelings of hopelessness, broken and dysfunctional homes, and parents with struggles of their own. And at the root of each of these situations is the same old problem: Sin! There's sin in the cities, and there's sin in the suburbs. Sin is wherever people are because sin resides in our hearts and is a part of our fallen nature. Only through Jesus the Messiah can that sin be taken away.

"No Sin too Great"

But God hath chosen the foolish things of the world to confound the
wise....
And the base things of the world, and things which are despised....
—1 Corinthians 1:27, 1:28

I am so thankful and happy that the Messiah has chosen me to be one of His witnesses and a minister of His grace. If it were up to mankind, I would not have been chosen; I would have been rejected and thrown into the deepest, hottest hell. But God who delights in showing mercy has come to earth to save sinners. The central theme of the Holy Bible is that man is a sinner in rebellion towards God. However, the Bible also teaches that the Lord loves people so much that He came to earth to die for our sins and to pay the penalty for our wicked deeds so that we might be forgiven and restored to fellowship with Him.

Wherever there is hatred, Jesus comes to bring love. Wherever there is racism, Christ comes to bring brotherhood. Wherever there is pain, the Lord comes to bring healing. And wherever there are sinners, Jesus Christ comes and offers His forgiveness. No sin is too great, no deed so wicked that it cannot be washed away by the blood of the Savior. And no life is so hopeless that it cannot be given a new start.

"One Bucket at a Time"

Another year is almost here, and once again the Lord has brought me safely through. I have no complaints, for He has been more than faithful. God has been blessing the services and Bible studies at this prison, and I have a born-again chaplain who loves the Lord. Earlier today, in addition to our morning worship service, we had a special baptismal service in the afternoon. All the new Christians were baptized, and each got the chance to share his testimony with everyone else just before being immersed in the water.

I had tears of joy in my eyes as I listened to these young brothers give the glory to God. Each man was thankful for all that Christ had done in his life. I too was thankful for what God is going to do with each man in the future as they stay faithful to Him.

During the service I had my hands full because I was one of the volunteer "mop men." We have a full-size baptismal tank, and there was water all over the place. I had to help mop the chapel, as well as the corridors leading to the men's room where each inmate had to go to change his clothes. Then, to top it off, the siphon pump that was supposed to empty the tank into a distant utility sink broke down. The chaplain and I, plus a few other inmates, had to get buckets and empty the tank one bucket at a time. It took several hours and was a lot of work, but it was fun. I had a good time praising the Lord, working, and fellowshipping with the brethren. We also sang many songs together and rejoiced in all the Lord had done.

"Hugs for the Savior"

As this year closes out I've been spending time thanking the Lord and meditating on all the good things He has done for me these past twelve months. There were many trials of my faith, and many victories as well. There were also some personal losses of several dear friends, Christians who were a real blessing to me. They prayed for me often, helped with the ministry, and gave my spirit a lot of encouragement when I was at my low points.

Two of those very special people were my Christian brothers Pat Cicala and Dick Williams, and my dear sister in Christ Angela Hewitt, all of whom went home to be with the Lord. I am so grateful to each of them and so thankful for their love. I am a better man and a better Christian because of these three, and I look forward to the day when we will all meet again around the throne of glory.

While the passing of our friends and family may be painful for us, I know that our loss is heaven's gain. Those who have gone on ahead of us have already experienced a joyous homecoming. The Lord was right there behind the veil to greet each one as they stepped into eternity (see Psalm 116:15). For Pat, Dick, and Angela, their trials, troubles, and struggles are all over.

I can't wait for the day when I too will be able to see my Messiah face to face, to look into Jesus' eyes and tell Him that I love Him, to thank Him personally for all He has done for me, and to give Him a great big hug. He truly is the King of kings, and Lord of lords. Not many people are so privileged as to be able to hug a king, but Jesus is a King who will gladly receive our hugs.

"Worth It in the End"

There is one particular inmate the Lord has called me to help and encourage. His name is Michael, and he has no one. Long ago abandoned by his family, Michael is doing a lengthy sentence for setting fire to a youth detention center, causing the death of another young resident.

Michael has been a wanderer on this earth since his youth. Presently he is assigned to the Intermediate Care Program Unit because of his emotional problems and his anger. But since the Lord directed me to befriend him, I have come to find out that he really is a nice person. Michael is not a Christian (yet), but I know God is working toward that end. I too have been working one-on-one with Michael for more than a year now. This morning he was in church, which is the best place for him. We sat together as we always do when he attends. Thus far he only comes on Sundays, but it's a start. And today he actually behaved himself. Sometimes he acts up in church and makes strange noises, and I find myself praying, "Lord, give me patience!"

This past Friday, however, I found Michael in the recreation yard. It was bitterly cold outside, and we had to keep moving to stay warm. He was in one of his foul moods, and he lashed out at me again and again. What anger! It's obvious he is really hurting inside.

I spent the afternoon talking to him about Jesus Christ. Though I saw no outward response, and in spite of the abuse he sometimes heaps upon me, it will all be worth it when Michael finally surrenders to Christ and is saved and delivered from his sins and his demons. Man truly is a sinner, but Christ is a wonderful Savior. Amen!

2001

"A New Year a New Millennium"

As I begin this New Year, I pray that, with God's help, I will continue to touch lives with His love, grace, and compassion. I pray with all my heart that someone will be encouraged by what I say, either by video, radio programs, or my writing.

It is my calling, just like that of any Christian, to spread the Good News that Jesus Christ forgives sins and heals brokenhearted souls. He sets captives free, and He still reaches out to the outcasts and to those who think they have no hope. I pray that God will continue to use me and that the enemy of my soul, Satan, who is always seeking to destroy me and to somehow discredit my testimony, will be bound and thwarted in his efforts by the power of God. I also pray and thank God for all my Christian brothers and sisters who, through letters of encouragement and prayers, have given so much of their time and effort over the years to help me.

> *I am continually amazed and grateful for God's mercy toward me.*

I am continually amazed and grateful for God's mercy toward me. Looking back over the year 2000, I see so much that has been accomplished to further the gospel. And yet I believe that the best is yet to come, for I know God isn't finished with me yet. Hallelujah!

"Reaching Out to the Victims"

"To every thing there is a season, and a time to every purpose under the heaven..."

—*Ecclesiastes 3:1*

One thing I hope to see accomplished and something I have been fervently praying for is the healing of those I have hurt in the past, the victims of my crimes. They are the survivors of that horrible tragedy. God knows I would do everything within my power to go back and change things, to have prevented what happened, but of course I cannot.

Yes, I have so much regret, grief, shame, and sorrow over my past actions. Jesus Christ knows this, and I am fully confident in His promise that He has forgiven me totally and completely. I therefore no longer have to be eaten away by these feelings. The Lord has given me His peace. It is not something I deserve, but the Bible assures me that God's peace is available to all who place their trust in Him, and that includes me. Furthermore, Christ has shown me over time how to take the painful feelings of regret, grief, shame, and sorrow and turn them into something positive. In every TV or radio interview I have given since the "Inside Edition" program of 1993, I have always expressed my remorse and sorrow for what I have done, and I thank God for the opportunities to do this. In every way possible I have publicly expressed my shame, sorrow, and regret. This year I hope to be able to reach out to some of my victims, as the Lord makes a way, and privately express my apologies to each family and to ask for their forgiveness. A minister from a large church in Brooklyn, New York, has offered his help in reaching out to those crime victims. This is a sensitive

> *Yes, I have so much regret, grief, shame, and sorrow over my past actions. Jesus Christ knows this, and I am fully confident in His promise that He has forgiven me totally and completely.*

and delicate thing that not only requires much prayer, but also much wisdom. I had hoped to do this several years ago, but many things came along to stop me, such as the "Summer of Sam" movie and the monstrous media publicity that went with it. Old wounds were reopened, so all I could do was keep waiting.

So far I have already written to one party, and my letter was well received. This is a miracle, and I truly believe God went before me to open their hearts. It does not mean they have forgiven me, but it is a start. And even if no one but Jesus ever forgives me, I will still be thankful for the chance to have shared my sorrow and remorse with them. I know this is the right and honorable thing to do.

"1975-77"

After spending some quality time in prayer this morning, I now want to add more thoughts to what I had expressed in yesterday's journal entry. I have total and complete gratitude in my heart for the mercy and forgiveness God Almighty has shown to me. Looking back upon that tragic time of 1975 through 1977, I cannot offer any excuses for my actions. I do know that in many ways I was not in my right mind, and that I was living in utter torment, under strong satanic influences and powerful delusions. All my thoughts were twisted and illogical. The good became bad and the bad became good. It is impossible to comprehend this without understanding the teachings and ideas that come forth from Satanism.

I was under gross deception. Yes, I knew right from wrong in the legal sense. But I was in such a weakened state of mind that there was nothing left in me to offer resistance. I was at a point where I did not care anymore. My feelings were gone, my emotions had died, and so I went along with the forces that had been reaching out to me for so long. It was as if an evil hand from the unseen realm was engineering everything that happened. There were so many ways that the bad things seemed to supernaturally fall into place. I was totally sold out to the belief that this was my calling in life.

> *I cannot offer any excuses for my actions. I do know that in many ways I was not in my right mind, and that I was living in utter torment, under strong satanic influences and powerful delusions.*

Looking back from the vantage point of today, as I sit in my little prison cell and contemplate my life, I am so disappointed with myself for sinking so low. I feel stupid for having allowed myself to be controlled by thoughts that I am now convinced were not all my own. I know some people will see this as a cop-out or as being in a state of denial. They can think what they want, of course, but over time, as God began to heal my mind,

I started to understand these things.

> *I know some people will see this as a cop-out or as being in a state of denial. They can think what they want, of course, but over time, as God began to heal my mind, I started to understand these things.*

What I am saying is not crazy stuff. Any Christian who understands the things of and about God will tell you that what I am saying is correct. Even Dr. Billy Graham will state that the Spirit of God is fully capable of speaking to a person's heart and mind. Christians throughout the world will attest to hearing the voice of God speak to their spirits and also, at times, being able to know the mind of God.

In any event, over time God has spoken very clearly to my mind, and He has indeed revealed these things to me. Thanks to Him, I now have a better understanding of what happened and how this "Son of Sam" tragedy all came about. It is too painful to dwell upon, and I seldom think about it anymore. I am only going over these things now for this journal so that others may better understand the powers of darkness and, even more important, appreciate God's powers of love, forgiveness, healing, and hope.

I want to end today's entry with a short prayer:

Lord, I ask you to continue to bring healing into the lives of those I have hurt in the past. Touch them with your love and help them to cope with the pain, loss, and grief that never seem to go away. Thank you, Father God. In Jesus' name, amen.

"Jack Died Today"

"Rejoice with them that do rejoice, and weep with them that weep."

—Romans 12:15

Jack died today. He was in his forties and had been in prison for maybe fifteen years. The cause of his death was AIDS. I watched this stubborn, strong-willed man waste away, his skin covered with gross-looking, brownish-colored open sores. As far as I know, this "jailhouse lawyer" and fighter was not a Christian and, during our many talks, he always insisted that his help was coming from the Hindu goddess Kali, as well as the Virgin Mary and his Santeria powers.

I met Jack several years ago in the "Big Yard." He used to watch us Christians walk around with our Bibles. During the warmer weather this open yard was a place for some of us to meet impromptu. Whenever a Christian showed up he hung out with the other brothers. Of course, inviting some unsaved men to pal around with us was the common practice. And so, here came Jack.

I worked for several years in the chapel as a clerk, and Jack, who worked as a porter in the same building complex, often dropped by for friendly discussions. Naturally I witnessed to him many times, and so did other Christians. But Jack was stubborn, convinced he could solve life's problems and lick AIDS by "thinking positive." He did go to a number of our services, however, sometimes on Sundays and at other times when various ministries would come in. I just wish I had some kind of confirmation in my heart that Jack turned to Christ and received Jesus as his Savior before he died, but I don't. I had watched him get sicker as time went on. There were weeks when I would not see him

> *I witnessed to him many times, and so did other Christians. But Jack was stubborn, convinced he could solve life's problems and lick AIDS by "thinking positive."*

because he was in the hospital. He went on many medical trips for treatments, battling his sickness every step of the way.

Last week I heard that Jack had once again been admitted to the prison hospital. As with many who have this virus (nicknamed "The Monster"), he made his trips back and forth to the hospital, becoming sicker and weaker each time, until finally he made the last trip, from which he did not return. Quietly, a few corrections officers went into his cell in the housing unit where he lived and packed his things. This is how everyone knew that Jack would not be back.

Jack was well liked and respected among the inmates, so everyone in the prison was talking about his death. When I got the news I wept silently for him, and I will remember to pray for his family, whoever they may be. Within the next several days or weeks one of them will have to come and claim his personal property, which is now in temporary storage. They will also have to claim his body for private burial. If no one comes to claim him, Jack will be buried in our potter's field. Every maximum security prison has one because not every inmate gets out of prison alive, and not every inmate has a family. In fact, even some who do have families refuse to claim the remains, due to lack of money or interest.

I hope my friend Jack is not of those who end up in potter's field. I hope he gets a decent burial, but most of all I hope to see him in heaven one day.

"Six Months to Live"

I cannot even begin to tell the public how much misery and self-inflicted suffering I have seen over the years. Prisons are places of broken dreams and lost hopes, where the high price tag each convict pays for committing crimes is painfully obvious. I am surely an expert in this area, now having spent almost half of my life incarcerated.

Today I was once again in the infirmary where I took my wheelchair escort to pick up his daily medications. While I was waiting in line another inmate named Jim, with whom I took a required behavior modification-type class several months ago, came up to ask for my prayers. Jim, who is in his fifties, did not look healthy at all, and as soon as he shook my hand he started to cry. I thought he was going to tell me he had received bad news from home, but instead he told me had received bad news from the doctor just a few weeks earlier.

The doctor told Jim he had six months to live. I was stunned. He had seemed fine when we attended that class together. But a lot can happen in a few months. Now the once happy-go-lucky guy who loved to tell jokes while we were sitting in the classroom was dying of hepatitis. His liver was no longer functioning and he was being poisoned by toxins.

I have never seen Jim in church before. When I would see him in the hallways, he was often carrying around the latest lusty novel. But now he was asking for a Bible—funny how bad news can serve as a wake-up call. Suddenly the game is over and it's time to get serious about life—and death.

My heart went out to him. We were only able to speak for a few minutes because he had

> *I have never seen Jim in church before. But now he was asking for a Bible—funny how bad news can serve as a wake-up call. Suddenly the game is over and it's time to get serious about life—and death.*

already picked up his medicine and the rules are that, once you pick up what you need at the medicine window, you do an about-face and walk out the door. But he did manage to linger long enough to tell me what was going on, and for me to promise that I would pray for him and to urge him to come to the chapel so all the congregation could pray in his behalf.

Jim lives in a different cellblock than I do, so I don't see him often. But I have put him on my prayer list and will try to send over some Christian literature like the *Guidepost* or the Billy Graham *Decision* magazines, which we have in abundance in the chapel.

> *Please, Jesus, touch this man's life. Grant him a desire for repentance and the faith to believe the gospel. Help him, dear Lord.*

"One Last Trip"

"For the wages of sin is death…"

—Romans 6:23a

Today I happened to see an inmate who was with me when I was living in Clinton Correctional Facility in the tiny town of Dannemora, New York, near the Canadian border. I've been gone from Clinton for nearly fourteen years now, and I really did not know this fellow very well even then. He was just a familiar face. But I do recall that for a while we lived on the same tier. When I saw him today, I scarcely recognized him. He was rail thin and looked like a concentration camp survivor. That's when I realized he had AIDS.

So far it seems he is talking normally and managing okay, but I know he is one bad cold or flu attack away from death. I've seen it so often over the years. Someone who is HIV-positive gets a bad cold, which quickly becomes pneumonia. He has trouble breathing and goes to the infirmary. Because he is HIV-positive he is quickly admitted, and then never seen alive again. When pneumonia hits, it's almost always the knock-out punch.

When the HIV-positive inmates start getting their array of sicknesses, most bounce back again and again because of the available medical treatments. But each time they go into the hospital, they lose a little more weight, which they almost never regain. With each bout of sickness, they get thinner and thinner, until they look like the prisoner who passed me in the corridor today. I could tell from looking at him that it's almost over. He's got one trip left. I just pray that if I see him again I will have the opportunity to tell him what Jesus Christ has done for me—and can also do for him. This dying man needs to know that God has something wonderful to give him—the gift of eternal life. It's free, and it will last forever.

"…but the gift of God is eternal life through Jesus Christ our Lord."

—Romans 6:23b

"We Must Be Born Again"

This morning at about 11 o'clock I took my wheelchair escort down to the infirmary to see the doctor. While in the waiting area I again ran into Jim, the man who told me last week that the doctor had given him six months to live. Today Jim told me he is down to five months. Personally, I think it looks as if he's down to about two.

I thank God for the several minutes I was able to speak with Jim today. When I saw him last week, he didn't look nearly as bad. Today his face is noticeably sunken in, his ankles are swollen, and his stomach protrudes far beyond his waist, as if he were trying to hide a basketball under his sweatshirt. Even before the hepatitis began to destroy his liver, Jim was on the slim side, though by no means thin. Now he looks sickly and pregnant, with a bleak yellow coloring to his skin. He was also groaning in pain.

Naturally our conversation centered around the health of his soul and the importance of receiving Christ as his Savior. Jim told me that the Catholic priest had already given him his last rites. When I told Jim that Jesus Christ loves him and died for his sins, he insisted he already knew that, having been raised in Catholic schools. I was gentle and never pushy, but I did encourage him to pray to God and to ask Jesus to help him. I also assured him that in this afternoon's prayer meeting in the chapel, the brothers would lift him up in our prayers. He seemed to appreciate this, but I could see I was up against a big stronghold when it came to his unwillingness to repent and fully trust in Jesus. Jim needs to be born again, as we all do, and I need to do a lot more praying on his behalf.

"From Garbage to God's Glory"

I just got back from this morning's prayer meeting, which was very spiritually fruitful. I have been strengthened and encouraged in my mind and soul to continue to press on by God's power.

Every Tuesday afternoon from 1:00 to 3:35, and every Wednesday morning from 8:45 to 10:25, we have prayer meetings in the chapel with a handful of Christians who do not have specific work or progress assignments at these times. Our chaplain supervises each meeting. I can make it most Tuesdays after I drop off my escort at his classroom. On Wednesday mornings, when I do not have to take my escort any place, such as the hospital, I have free time to go to the prayer meetings, although I am still "on call" for him.

Those society casts off as useless garbage are the very ones the Lord is willing to take, clean up, and use for His glory.

It would probably blow people's minds if they could see a crew of convicted felons gathering with a prison chaplain to fervently pray for every imaginable concern. We pray for our own church, as well as others. We pray for inmates and their families, and the guards and their families. We pray for America and for our nation's leaders. We also ask for mercy for other nations, for those who are living on Native American reservations, and for kids who are in every possible form of sin and bondage, from drugs and poverty to loneliness and suicidal thoughts.

I thank God that those society casts off as useless garbage and refuse are the very ones the Lord is fully able and willing to take, clean up, and use for His glory.

"Resisting the Enemy"

For I the Lord thy God will hold thy right hand, saying unto thee, Fear not; I will help thee.

—Isaiah 41:13

Where would I be without the Lord's help? What would my life have come to if Jesus Christ had not intervened? I am quite certain I would be dead, very possibly a case of suicide. Surely if I were alive at this time without God in my life, I would be a bitter and sour man, angry at the world, hating others, hating myself.

So often I realize how helpless I am without the Lord. I am really like a little child tagging alongside his father. Yes, God is holding my hand. Forget being a macho man! Without God I am nothing. In my own strength I could never have survived all these years in prison. Moreover, although I know the Lord has healed my mind and filled my life with peace, the fact is, I am still in recovery. There are terrible memories buried beneath the surface. Maybe it is best that for the most part they stay buried, but from time to time, the bad memories do resurface.

I am still learning to forgive myself, though I have completely and fully renounced my affiliations with Satan. This is not as easy as it sounds because the devil, who is a spirit being, is very active in this world and he never stops his relentless attacks. Every Christian recognizes and knows this truth. We must daily resist this deadly enemy and draw near to God, for the closer we are to the Lord, the further we are from the devil.

"A New Heart"

It's been on the news all weekend. The young man who was convicted of killing comedian Bill Cosby's twenty-seven-year-old son, Ennis, in Los Angeles in 1997 has confessed that he is indeed guilty of the crime. Michael Markhasev, now twenty-two years old and doing life without the possibility of parole for the slaying, wrote a letter to the district attorney asking that his appeal be stopped.

The news reports all say that the folks from the D. A.'s office in this California city are "stunned" by this turn of events and by Mr. Markhasev's seemingly genuine repentance, confession, and actions. Personally, I am not stunned at all. Once again we see a splendid example of what Jesus Christ can do in someone's life. The February 10 issue of the Long Island *Newsday* quoted a portion of Mr. Markhasev's letter as follows: "More than anything I want to apologize to the victim's family. It is my duty as a Christian and it is the least I can do after the great wickedness for which I am responsible."

I remember this tragic case. The slaying of Ennis Cosby was a terrible loss. He was a talented and beautiful human being. Surely his family misses him more than words can ever express. But what is evident to me is that, while in prison, Mr. Markhasev clearly had an encounter with Jesus Christ. Someone shared the gospel with this young Russian man, and God touched his heart. Thanks to some caring Christian who is unknown to the public— perhaps another inmate or a chaplain—not only did Mr. Markhasev ask for forgiveness for his sins, but he stepped forward in holy boldness and courage to "do the right thing," as he said in his letter to the district attorney, and also to apologize to the Cosby family. And thanks to Jesus Christ and Michael Markhasev, the Cosby family can now get on with their lives. The Court of Appeals can also take a major case off its overloaded calendar, and the taxpayers in the State of California will save a tremendous amount of money in legal costs.

Plain and simple, this is a miracle! While the D. A.'s staff is puzzled, all this should be easy to understand for anyone who is a Christian. God reached down and touched a troubled young man in a maximum security prison and gave him a new heart. I am proud to call Michael Markhasev my brother. He did the right thing, and Christians everywhere need to pray for him, as well as for the Cosby family.

"Fulfilling Our Calling"

Earlier this morning I had a handful of chores to do, such as cleaning my prison cell and washing a pile of shirts. Like many inmates, I have to wash most of my clothes by hand in a small bucket, wring out each item, and then find a way to dry them, all inside of my little cell.

By ten o'clock I was finished with my inside chores, so I went to the recreation yard to get some fresh air. While outside I teamed up with two other inmates to do some ice breaking. The guards stationed in the yard have a small utility room with snow shovels and ice breakers, so we were able to get the tools we needed.

It felt good to be breaking up the ice while my friend, Billy, shoveled it away. Then the other man, James, and I took turns throwing down fresh rock salt. After more than an hour of doing this I returned to my cell at 11:45, feeling invigorated and refreshed. It was about fifteen degrees outside at the time.

> *We Christians need to fulfill our God-given ministries and not neglect them.*

After lunch I read Colossians 4. Verse 17 really impressed something in my spirit: "And say to Archippus, Take heed to the ministry which thou hast received in the Lord, that thou fulfil it." I realized that I could put my own name in Archippus' place as an admonishment and exhortation from the Lord to fulfill all that He has called me to do, to stay faithful to my ministry, and to make sure I do not slack off. God wants me to complete the work He has for me.

The apostle Paul was encouraging Archippus to get back on track and stay there. We Christians likewise need to fulfill our God-given ministries and not neglect them, whether that involves witnessing to others and praying for them, breaking up ice, or doing laundry. Whatever we do, we must do it in service to God. Through the reading of Colossians 4:17, I felt as if Paul had spoken those very words to me today.

"Jesus' Lost Sheep"

During this morning's prayer meeting in the chapel, the Lord quietly showed me that He loves His children far too much to ever let any of us go. Even in His Word the Lord promises that, if necessary, He will leave the "ninety-nine" sheep in a safe pasture and go off to seek the "one" who is lost. Every one of His little lambs means something to Him.

I was really touched as I meditated on Luke 15:1-10 today. Christ is burdened for the lost and backslidden. He is grieved when one of His children wanders off. But Jesus doesn't stop at just being sad—He does something about it. Our lost state stirs Him into action. He earnestly begins to seek those who have strayed away, and He does not rest until He finds them. Even then He doesn't make them walk back to safe pasture on their own strength. Instead He carries them to make sure they make it back into fellowship with the rest of the flock.

I also did a lot of crying during this morning's prayer meeting. Lately this seems to be happening every time I get on my knees. I am amazed at the contrast that exists within the Christian life. Weeping and rejoicing, joy and pain, are all intertwined together. Our lives have a mixture of all these things. What a wonderful mystery!

"Keep Loving and Serving Him"

The Lord will give strength unto his people; the Lord will bless his people with peace.

—Psalm 29:11

During my time of prayer this morning the Lord reminded me to keep loving and serving Him, even when things don't seem to be going my way. The Christian's faith is established in adversity. Our faith is strengthened, and it grows and matures during the trials and difficulties of life.

The Lord spoke to my heart that the adverse circumstances and situations that pound against our inner spirits actually serve to keep us humble and broken before Him. Humbled and broken people are the only ones God can truly speak to and use. The proud and the stubborn get set aside. It is the meek who shall inherit the earth, for their dependence is totally upon Him. And it is only those who truly "mourn" who will be comforted by Christ.

> *The Christian's faith is established in adversity.*

The Lord reminded me to trust in Him for everything—to never doubt, to obey Him, and to rest in His love. Jesus assured me that He will strengthen me as needed, and that my life shall always be overshadowed by His peace.

"Love Letters From Tennessee"

I am always thanking the Lord for allowing my life to be a blessing and a source of encouragement to others, especially young people. I am so thankful for the amazing ways the Lord has used the various pamphlets containing my testimony, which have been published by an

> *The hundreds of responses I have received over the years to these ministry outreaches have brought me so much joy. I bow my heart in deepest humility for all He has done with my life.*

assortment of ministries. I am likewise thankful for the radio interviews the Lord permitted me to give, and for the videos that have been made. God had His hand upon all of these endeavors, and He did it all Himself.

The hundreds of responses I have received over the years to these ministry outreaches have brought me so much joy. I bow my heart in deepest humility for all He has done with my life. So here I would like to share some of the letters I received from students at a Christian high school in Nashville, Tennessee. They were inspired to write after watching one of the testimony videos. I will share just a few, although all of them were great. I felt their love as I read their words:

> "I just wanted to write and say that we prayed for you today. We watched your video in class and it really encouraged me. I can see how God is working in your life and how He has used your ministry to speak to other people. You are a true servant of the Lord and I hope that one day I can reach other people like you have. May God continue to bless you."
>
> —Danielle

> "I think it's so awesome the way God has changed your life around the way that He has. People have always told me that God takes the bad and uses it for good. That is so true. You have touched so many lives

and given so many people hope. You are a living example of how God can change a person. Thank you so much for your video testimony..."

—Kristin

"I am proud . . . [of the] change in your life. You will be in my prayers every day..."

—Cory

"I want you to know that your testimony really encouraged me! Keep up the awesome outreach! Just remember you may be the only Jesus that those inmates will ever see. Have a great day!"

—Britt

"We watched your video in our Bible class and it was very encouraging. I really admire your strength of character and the way you have hope even in prison. Your life is a great example of the way God can change peoples' lives. We are praying for you."

—Catie

"I heard the news that you were feelin' the blues when you found the Lord that loved you. All I got to say is I hope you have a great conversion ministry in prison... I hope that many turn to the Lord because He is the only one that can save them."

— Alan

"When I heard about how much you've changed it really inspired me to change my ways and bad habits. To me just thinking about all you've been through and done, but now you've come to know God... I just want to encourage you to keep it up because as of yesterday you have made a significant change in my life."

—Megan

"My Bible class watched your video the other day and many were touched by it. You were once a confused and lost man, but now you have found the Lord and there is such a peace about you. I hope you continue to keep trying to help other inmates find the Lord. You have been forgiven and now you can go on with your life of peace and happiness. Hang in there, man!"

—Mark

"I think it's really great that you've turned your life around the way you have. It really lifts my spirits to see someone work for the Lord the way you are and be so dedicated to it. It's people like you who give me hope for the people whose lives are off track. Thanks a lot for spreading God's word!"

—Lindsay

"You have a very spiritually inspiring story: It's amazing just how willing God is. I really admire your courage throughout your daily life and only pray that I can be as faithful as you. Being in a Christian school, it's a little easier. I pray that things will continue to go well with you. Thank you, David."

—Justin

"I saw the video of how your life got changed once you went into prison. You seem very sincere about ministering to other prisoners about the Lord. I would just like to encourage you to keep up the good work. I wish I had the ability to witness to people about Jesus… This letter is meant for you not to get discouraged about witnessing. Because of you and your testimony, many people will get to spend eternity in heaven. Second Chronicles 15:7 says, 'Be ye strong therefore, and let not your hands be weak: for your work shall be rewarded.' See ya in heaven!"

—Christie

"Rachel's Tears"

I want to end this month by talking about a special book that touched my heart and gave me a great deal of inspiration. I have read it through twice, and I occasionally open it up at random to read several pages again and again.

The name of the book is *Rachel's Tears: The Spiritual Journey of Columbine Martyr Rachel Scott* (Thomas Nelson Publishers, Nashville, Tennessee, 2001). It was written by Rachel's parents, Beth Nimmo and Darrell Scott. As many of you may know, Rachel was one of the thirteen people who lost their lives on April 20, 1999, when two other students entered the Columbine High School in Littleton, Colorado, and opened fire on their classmates. Both of the gunmen also died.

> *People all over the world have come to Christ as a result of the powerful witness raised up from the ashes of this tragedy.*

Though many know the facts about this tragedy, few know the reasons. But once again, God's hand of love has moved in this situation, and He has already brought many good things out of this sad event. For one thing, Rachel's parents, through God's gentle guidance, have turned their grief into positive channels. It was also so obvious to me that Rachel's writings, included in *Rachel's Tears*, are anointed by the Holy Spirit. Since that fateful April day in 1999, many other students at Columbine, as well as people all over the world, have come to Christ as a result of the powerful witness raised up from the ashes of this tragedy. *Rachel's Tears* is a huge part of that witness, and one of the most important books ever published. I encourage others to read it, and to visit the website: www.racheljoyscott.com.

"Jim Is Dead"

As I walked into the chapel this Sunday morning to attend our worship service, one of the prison chaplains called me aside and gave me the news that Jim had passed away. As you may remember, I've mentioned Jim before, but I haven't seen him since February 2.

I believe it was by God's hand that we met in the corridor that day so I could speak with him once more. It was obvious at the time that Jim was very sick and his death was imminent. I tried my best as a Christian to share the gospel with this dying man, to encourage Jim, and even to plead with him to repent and to believe in Jesus. Other Christians had been doing the same, so spiritually, at least, I know he was not neglected. All the brothers gave him lots of love.

The day I last saw Jim I said a prayer and placed him in the hands of the Lord. I had seen him deteriorating a little each time we met, and although I had expected his death, the news still hit me hard. After thanking the chaplain for being concerned enough to tell me, I went into the worship service, where I prayed for Jim's family. Like me, Jim was a convicted felon, but I knew he had an elderly mother, as well as others, who loved him and would grieve his passing.

I am not going to give a glowing report that Jim got born again at the last minute and that he died with a smile on his face, though I certainly wish I could. I thank God for the stories I sometimes hear about deathbed conversions. However, in Jim's case I simply do not know if he finally turned to Jesus for salvation. But if I happen to see old Jim when I get to Gloryland, I am going to be very happy. All his suffering will have been worth it in the end if God somehow used Jim's sickness to get his attention and bring him to his knees (see 1 Corinthians 15:50-58).

"Niagara Falls"

When I spoke to my Christian brother Robert Alexander, who happens to be a former New York State Department of Corrections' employee and is now a town justice as well as a minister, he gave me some great news. "The Choice Is Yours" video had been seen by about 6,000 teenagers during a large youth evangelism conference sponsored by Youth For Christ, and was held in the Niagara Falls Convention Center in the city of Niagara Falls, New York.

Every year some of the leaders of Youth For Christ's western New York region conduct a four-day conference and seminar for teens. This is a very big event that is sponsored by many churches. It is an all-out effort to encourage teenagers who already believe in Jesus Christ to grow in their faith and to mature in their knowledge of the Lord. In addition, it is also a time to evangelize those who may be there as guests but who do not yet know Jesus as Savior and Lord.

This past youth conference was held from December 27-30. "The Choice Is Yours" was shown during one of these days. I knew about the conference ahead of time, but I waited until now to say anything until the official victory report had come in from Brother Alexander.

I do not know how many kids got born again as a result of watching the video, or even in what capacity the video was used. But whatever happened, I give God all the praise because He did use it and, according to Brother Alexander, the youth responded in a positive way. He also said that the Youth For Christ's staff was "very pleased with the results."

"Zero Tolerance"

Perhaps one of the biggest tragedies I see happening today with the prison system is the number of young people coming into the system with long sentences. We are living in an age of "zero tolerance." It is obvious to me that it has become politically correct to show as little mercy to criminals as possible—sometimes no mercy at all! But when a young man aged fourteen to eighteen comes to prison with a sentence of twenty to sixty years or more, with virtually no hope for an early release, his life is basically over. Unless something radical happens to give him hope and a reason to remain positive, over time he will most likely settle into a state of despondency and hopelessness. In addition he will probably be forced into joining a violent prison gang. If he does so it will probably be for one or more of the following reasons: fear and protection; peer pressure; a need for companionship; a need to belong to a group to replace the missing family unit; a need to have a higher status in the prison's hierarchy, for even in prison no one wants to be thought of as an outcast.

All these reasons are nothing more than forms of duress, but he joins nonetheless, for to be alone is to be unprotected. To have no gang affiliation is to increase the potential of being victimized. No one wants to spend years being bullied and pushed around, raped, robbed, or tormented. So eventually the young man joins a gang. He takes his vows and does his acts of violence, including assaulting other prisoners and even the staff, in order to "make rank" and impress the gang's leader. Furthermore, he will be doomed to spend what was supposed to be the most productive period of his life living in a cell. He will work tirelessly and fight constantly to keep his reputation, and he will most likely live a life of rebellion, anger, and complete defiance to all authority.

These things will be this young man's unhappy lot in prison. With such a lengthy prison sentence, there is literally no escape. He will be locked in a vicious cycle with no way out and no end in sight. I am not saying all this to sound negative, but from what I have seen over the years, this is pretty much how it will be. Over time even his family, if he has one, may forget about him as they go on with their lives. The letters and visits, if he ever got any, begin to diminish. As the years pass this young man may become just another forgotten soul buried behind the walls and wires.

This is why it is so important to have active and well established Christian programs and people-loving ministries coming into the prisons, juvenile detention centers, and training schools, for it is in these seemingly hopeless and depressing situations that God can do His greatest works. I know the gospel is still the "good news" no matter where it is being shared, and that Jesus is still able to heal the brokenhearted and set at liberty those who are being held captive by the power of sin and the crushing oppressiveness of this world's system. A young person who gets introduced to Jesus Christ and then begins to have a personal relationship with Him can receive a level of hope and peace, as well as a sense of purpose, that gangs and crime cannot give, whether that young person is in prison or not.

> *One thing the Bible has taught me is the unfathomable worth of every human soul. While the effects of the violent crimes a young man commits can never be reversed nor can the damage be undone, God can still come and work a miracle. He can save that prisoner's soul and change his heart.*

Of course, there is also the need for these young people coming into the prison system to get an education. It is imperative to teach them how to read and write better, as many of them have already dropped out of school altogether. But this is for the professionals and experts to figure out. As for me, my prayer is that prison and youth-centered ministries will continue to be welcomed into these facilities, and that these ministries will flourish. One thing the Bible has taught me is the unfathomable worth of every human soul. While the effects of the violent crimes a young man commits can never be reversed nor can the damage be undone, God can still come and work a miracle. He can save that prisoner's soul and change his heart.

While many in society trumpet "zero tolerance" on crime at all cost, and while severe punishment is sometimes deserved, Jesus Christ still wishes to impart mercy. He has a plan to bring redemption and salvation to our castaway youth, and that plan includes active prison ministries comprised primarily of lay people. These ministries need as much prayer, support, and encouragement as possible, for their labor of love is never in vain.

"A Home for Michael"

At three o'clock I decided to go to the recreation yard and spend almost an hour walking around and getting some fresh air. While there I ran into my friend Michael, whom I wrote about on December 31, 2000. Michael is very mentally ill, and many times he's right on the edge of being out of control. Occasionally he crosses over that edge and becomes angry and abusive, especially with the prison staff.

Today, thank God, Michael was in a jovial mood, telling jokes. He was full of energy and just seemed to want to keep walking around the recreation yard's perimeter, so I joined him. I know God put Michael into my life so I could befriend him, for he is a man who has no real friends. God also put Michael in my life so I could share with him the good news about Jesus Christ.

> *I see this as "spiritual warfare" because there is something inside Michael that does not want to see him healed and delivered.*

Since Michael was not in a hostile frame of mind today, I was able to relax a little and share with him about my life as a Christian. There are times with Michael when I am able to take out my little Gideon's Pocket Testament and read a few Scriptures to him. Today was one of those days. There are other times, however, when I pull that little Bible out of my pocket and he starts cussing and getting belligerent. I see this as "spiritual warfare" because there is something inside Michael that does not want to see him healed and delivered.

Thankfully today he promised to be in church this Sunday. But as I mentioned in my December 31 entry, even in church Michael can sometimes get out of control. He makes odd noises and basically disturbs the worshippers, yet the other prisoners are learning to be tolerant of him. Frankly, I am still learning to be tolerant, too. Yes, Michael does stretch my patience. But I know that when Michael finally puts his faith in Jesus Christ, it will all be worth it. After all, if it takes putting up with a little abuse to make sure Michael gets to heaven, then I am more than willing to endure the temporary hardship.

On his better days, Michael can be a very warm and friendly person, with a great sense of humor. I view him as someone for whom the Savior has a very special love. Besides, I don't think Michael could survive out in the streets. Quite honestly, he probably would not be welcomed in many churches, because who is going to put up with a wild, ranting man bouncing up and down on a church pew while the sermon is being preached? But here, in the prison chapel with the Christian brothers, Michael has found acceptance and love. He has tasted God's compassion, and he has a home.

"A Day of Answered Prayers"

This morning I had to go to the infirmary because the man I escort in a wheelchair had to pick up some medications and get some treatments. When I first entered the building I was disappointed to find the waiting area so crowded. There were at least thirty to thirty-five inmates ahead of us waiting to see either the nurses for "sick call" or to see the doctor.

The waiting area resembles a big fish tank. The front wall and entry door, as well as one long side of the room, are walled with Plexiglas. This way everyone can be watched at all times. In some ways it resembles a bus station with rows of backless wooden benches. There is a large clock on the wall over the exit, which many of the men stare at as if trying to intimidate the clock's hands into moving faster.

When an inmate arrives at the entrance to the hospital, he first has to report to the Officer's Station, and then he is let into the waiting area through an electronically controlled door. At this point the inmate must take a seat until he is called to talk with someone on the medical staff. Since the waiting room was so crowded today, I thought for sure I would be stuck in this poorly ventilated and noisy room for most of the morning.

I pushed my friend's wheelchair to an open spot alongside the wall, and then I managed to find a seat on one of the benches. And, yes, I did get stuck in the waiting area for a long time. Yet I knew as soon as I sat down that God had me here for a purpose, because while I was there I got to see two of my recent prayers answered!

First, I had been praying for a particular Christian brother who has been going through some personal struggles, and he had been showing some signs of losing his faith. During the past week or so he had been on my heart, and I was specifically lifting him up in my prayers. Now, lo and behold, I ended up sitting right next to him. This became a great opportunity to encourage him and to remind this struggling brother about God's precious promises, as well as God's love and faithfulness to His children. We had a good time fellowshipping, and I definitely saw the Holy Spirit beginning to stir his heart. I promised to keep him in my prayers, and urged him in a loving way to "keep on with the Lord," to pray, and to read his Bible.

Then, as he left to see one of the nurses, another inmate came and sat down next to me. This time it was Stewart—we call him "Stu"—who, when I last saw him, was under "disciplinary status" for a violation of some rules. He was being escorted by a guard at the time, and so our conversation had been very limited, though the Lord used that brief encounter to cause me to pray for him. Now the Holy Spirit had orchestrated another meeting. Stu, who has AIDS, was sitting right next to me, and we had plenty of time to talk. I told him how much I had been praying for him, and that I wanted to see him get touched by the Savior.

> *This time Stu listened politely, though he made no outward response. Another seed was sown, however, for most assuredly the Lord ordered my steps today, and He answered my prayers.*

Stu began to confess his struggles and temptations. He told me of his weaknesses, and I assured him that his temptations and struggles were actually very common. But mainly we just rapped. I don't go around preaching at people. I simply talk with them one-on-one, sharing God's love and, sometimes, very clearly warning them of the consequences of rejecting such an awesome salvation.

This time Stu listened politely, though he made no outward response. Another seed was sown, however, for most assuredly the Lord ordered my steps today, and He answered my prayers.

"20/20 News Program"

Today I had the privilege of doing an interview with correspondent Arnold Diaz of ABC's "20/20" news program. I approached this occasion prayerfully and carefully, the Lord seemed to open the door, and there were many good confirmations that I had made the right decision. But the fact is that I won't know for sure until the program is aired, even though the interview went well and Mr. Diaz, though intense in his questioning, was also very fair. The subject of this program is crime-related memorabilia, including items that frequently turn up for sale bearing the ugly moniker "Son of Sam" or some of my correspondence, and how these things often end up on sites such as eBay.

Before I gave my personal consent to do this interview, I was visited by Candace Hewitt, one of "20/20"'s producers. I openly shared with her my hopes, concerns, and even fears about doing such an interview. In turn, she was very sensitive and honest. I had, in my spirit, an "inner witness" that I was doing the right thing by granting it. But what really encouraged me to be a part of this project was that the director of the City of Houston's Crime Victims Office, Mr. Andy Kahan, asked me to do it. Andy and I have been corresponding for some time about the subject of crime memorabilia, and my heart has truly warmed to this man. I feel honored that such a person would ask for my help. In addition, the "20/20" staff tried to obtain permission for Mr. Kahan to come to the prison to participate in the interview. As it turned out, however, the New York State Department of Corrections did not grant permission for him to attend the filming session because of a rule that "no third parties are allowed to be present during media interviews with prisoners."

Nevertheless, this interview enabled me to share my faith in Christ and to publicly apologize for the crimes I had committed. I also got the opportunity to explain how all these crime-glorifying products (everything from serial killer trading cards, to calendars, to sweatshirts) are not made by the convicted felons themselves. These tasteless products are made and marketed by ordinary people who, without any human sensitivity or compassion, have decided that making money is more important than any pain and suffering that crime victims have to endure when they see all this junk producing profits. I likewise shared that seeing the making and selling of such things is also very painful for me, and that this also causes me grief and guilt. I just hope and pray that this program, when it is aired some time in May, will be helpful and informative.

> *Nevertheless, this interview enabled me to share my faith in Christ and to publicly apologize for the crimes I had committed.*

Come to think of it, in a way this situation reminds me of the Lord Jesus when He went into the Temple in Jerusalem. He was angered and grieved by all the open display of greed and moneymaking that were going on in God's holy house. The Lord then took a "scourge" (a whip) and ran through the building driving out the "moneychangers" and turning over their tables. I think many people in America wish Christ would reappear and do the same here, smashing up all the "murderabilia" and putting a stop to this nonsense.

"Mail Call"

Now unto Him that is able to do exceeding abundantly above all that we ask or think....

—Ephesians 3:20

The mail is usually distributed by the cellblock guard at about 4:15 every afternoon, Monday through Friday. There is no weekend or holiday mail service in or out of the prison. In here a corrections officer goes from cell to cell handing each inmate his mail. And so today, as is the routine, I stepped to the front of my cell to receive my letters. I greeted the guard and thanked him. Then I sat down on my bunk to see what came in. Out of habit, I usually scan through each piece first, looking at each return address, and then read them by priority. Some I may choose to lay aside and read later in the day. Others, like advertisements, junk mail, or any silly letters go right into the trash.

> *I found it amazing that he would ask this when it has been one of the biggest cries of my heart that the forgiveness he is talking about would one day become a reality.*

As I thumbed through the half-dozen or so letters I received today, I spotted one that immediately grabbed my attention. In fact, I was stunned. I even started talking to myself out loud, asking why this particular person would write to me. I'm serious! For a minute or so I stood transfixed, staring at the return address and wondering why.

The letter was from Darrell Scott, the father of Columbine High School martyr Rachel Joy Scott. I had not written to him, and I had no idea this man even knew I existed. In addition, it was so ironic because just a few months earlier I had written in my journal how very blessed I had been by the book that Darrell and his former wife, Beth Nimmo, had written together about their daughter. Needless to say, his letter was a big surprise.

Apparently someone had told Mr. Scott that I was encouraged by

Rachel's story. He said he had heard some time ago about my coming to Christ and that he was thankful for what God had done in my heart. This brought tears to my eyes. Only the Lord Jesus could grant all this mercy to me that I would find favor with someone like Darrell Scott. Furthermore, in his short letter he asked if I had been forgiven by any of my victims' families, and if I had developed relationship with any of them. I found it amazing that he would ask this when it has been one of the biggest cries of my heart that the forgiveness he is talking about would one day become a reality. Lord willing, I will write back to Mr. Scott shortly, but the Holy Spirit will have to give me the words, for I don't even know how I would begin.

Yes, once again, God Almighty has done far more with my life for the good than I could ever even think or say. Amen!

"A Glorious Day"

But I have trusted in thy mercy; my heart shall rejoice in thy salvation.
I will sing unto the Lord, because he hath dealt bountifully with me.
—Psalm 13:5, 13:6

These words are so beautiful. Trusting in the Lord, rejoicing in His salvation, singing songs of praise to God for all the goodness He has shown to all of His children...and yet many times we enter into situations and painful trials in which we question everything this Christian life is supposed to be about. Earlier today I had to answer the letter I had received from a dear friend of mine whose twenty-six-year-old son, Mark, died unexpectedly.

My Christian friend Tony is a youth minister on the west coast. He and his wife have been serving the Lord faithfully for many years. He often distributes copies of my testimony and many other tracts to people on the streets of the city where he lives. His letters to me are always full of encouragement, yet his last letter was riddled with pain. His heart was broken as he gave me the news that his dear son was dead. Mark had been a budding evangelist and youth minister. Like his dad, he was a fiery preacher with a burden for souls. Now Mark is in the grave and his dad is understandably asking why.

But Tony did not sound bitter, just very troubled, as he asked for my prayers. He wrote, "David, my wife and I are feeling so much pain...." He asked me to pray for their strength, and then ended his letter with Romans 8:28: "And we know that all things work together for good to them that love God, to them who are the called according to his purpose." I had asked the Lord for wisdom when replying, but when I saw the verse Tony had added to the end of his letter, I realized he was already beginning to understand that God's ways are not our ways; His divine understanding is infinite.

I reminded my dear brother that God is love, and that His plans for our lives do not stop when someone dies. The Bible says that nothing, not even death, shall be able to "separate us from the love of God, which is in Christ Jesus our Lord" (Romans 8:38, 8:39). Tony and his wife have had their struggles in the past, as have I, and I'm sure we will have many more in the future. Yet God is still in control, and Tony's son is definitely in heaven. He has no more temptations to endure, and even the fruit of Mark's labors will live on. I reminded my friend that we Christians are not exempt from suffering. We do not live on a cloud; we live on this earth, in fleshly bodies that are frail. We have not received our new bodies yet, for the resurrection of the just, or righteous, has yet to take place.

> *We Christians are not exempt from suffering. We do not live on a cloud; we live on this earth, in fleshly bodies that are frail.*

I sent Tony my love as I mailed him a card to encourage him, and then I sent a letter in a separate envelope. Lord willing, he will receive both of them next week. I assured my brother that I will keep him in my prayers. I would hope, too, that other Christians who read of Mark's passing will remember Tony and his family in prayer, for the Holy Spirit is an expert Comforter.

I ended my letter by asking Tony to read 1 Thessalonians 4:13-18, which reminds us that we believers in Jesus do not have to grieve as others who have no hope. Yes, we can grieve, for we are but human. But as the ones who have the promise of our dear Savior's return, we do not have to mourn forever. One glorious day, Mark will arise from the grave.

"Come, Lord Jesus"

Four days ago I received a surprise letter from Darrell Scott, the father of Rachel Joy Scott, who lost her precious life in the Columbine High School shooting back in 1999. The Lord answered my prayer and gave me the words to say in response to Mr. Scott's letter, and I mailed my return letter to him this morning—ironically, the second anniversary of the shooting. I told him how grateful I was for being able to read about his daughter's life, and how I found the book he and Rachel's mother wrote to be so inspiring. I also shared with him that I believe the Lord Jesus Christ has given his daughter the desires of her heart because, from reading Rachel's Tears, I can see that she was used by God as a Spirit-gifted missionary, which is what she had wanted to be. I do hope I was able to encourage him and remind him that his life and hers will never be in vain. I also told Mr. Scott that on this day I would be doing my part to pray and fast for the youth of our nation. I would have done this anyhow because this is what I had already planned, and I believe this is what Christ is leading me to do.

> *We believers in Messiah Jesus often need to remind our brothers and sisters who have lost born-again loved ones that Jesus is coming again for His Church.*

I tried to answer Mr. Scott's questions about forgiveness and establishing relationships with the families of my victims. I shared that I would love for the chance to speak to these people, to apologize, to express my sorrow, and to reassure them that I am not even trying to get out of prison and I have absolutely nothing against any of them. I told Darrell Scott that these crime victims have every right to feel anger and bitterness toward me, and to express it openly as some of them have done many times during the past twenty-five years. I also asked Mr. Scott to please pray for these hurting people, and that any suggestions he would have about helping them get over their anger and pain would be greatly appreciated. I then concluded my letter by thanking him for reaching out to me and for caring—and not just for me, but also for those who have suffered because of my past crimes.

The best part was when the Lord had me remind Darrell that he and the rest of his family are going to see Rachel again. This is the Lord's faithful promise for all those who have died (or "fallen asleep," as the KJV Bible words it) in Him, so I asked Mr. Scott to please read 1 Thessalonians 4:13-18. We believers in Messiah Jesus often need to remind our brothers and sisters who have lost born-again loved ones that Jesus is coming again for His Church. He is going to be taking us home to be with Him and with the other believers who have gone on ahead of us. There is indeed a glorious reunion ahead! "Even so, come, Lord Jesus" (Revelation 22:20).

"More on Murderabilia"

I commented on this subject in my April 3 entry, and I also have an "official statement" and some other paperwork on my Web site (www.forgivenforlife.com) regarding the matter of "murderabilia" and the selling of letters, autographs, and novelty-type items for profit. This is something that grieves my heart, though in my case it has been going on since I was first arrested in 1977 and may go on long after I'm dead. Selling crime collectibles is a big thing for some people. With the upcoming execution of Oklahoma City Federal Building bomber Timothy J. McVeigh, scheduled to die by lethal injection on May 16 at the federal prison in Terre Haute, Indiana, you can be sure these profiteers and makers of crime collectibles will be busy hawking their wares. In fact, their new McVeigh-related products are even now in the making or are ready to go to the market.

> *As a nation we need true repentance, as well as a genuine godly sorrow over our propensities for violence and for greed.*

I anticipated this, so this afternoon when I came across a copy of the *New York Times* for Thursday, April 19, 2001, I was not at all surprised to see an article on the front page titled "A City Consumed in Plans for McVeigh's Execution," written by Sara Riner. The article had some comments by Terre Haute Mayor Judith A. Anderson, who said she had been getting a lot of calls from people regarding McVeigh-related products. Mayor Anderson was quoted as saying, "A lot of people have been calling asking if they can sell T-shirts and buttons." Most of these sellers are planning on hawking their merchandise right outside the prison grounds in anticipation of the large crowds that may be gathered there.

I am certainly not trying to be something of a moralist here, as I myself have done so much evil in the past and am so very sorry for this. But it is time for many of us Americans to examine our consciences. We are a nation that has idolized violence and glorified crime. One day we are going to have to wake up and cry out to God for mercy and forgiveness. There are things in our society that are morally wrong. As a nation we need true repentance, as well as a genuine godly sorrow over our propensities for violence and for greed.

I say this ever so humbly, but we need help from the Lord, the One who is the Maker of heaven and earth.

"Pain!"

...the Lord gave, and the Lord hath taken away; blessed be the name of the Lord."

—Job 1:21b

Since my last journal entry of April 30, more heavy trials have come. This has been a painful adventure! One morning last week I awoke from sleep and found my feet horribly swollen. I couldn't walk. I had to crawl to the toilet a few feet away just to urinate. I never felt such pain, and I never felt so helpless.

When I went to bed the night before everything was fine, but when I awoke, the feet that were attached to my legs looked nothing like the ones I went to sleep with. It turned out to be a bad attack of gout, and I ended up being confined to my cell with a week's bed rest. I endured agonizing, foot-throbbing pain day after day, minute by minute, shocked at the doctor's diagnosis. I always thought gout was for old people, and I am only forty-seven!

During this time, however, some amazing things happened. As I suffered, I got closer to the Lord. Something changed inside me, and even my discomfort became a spiritual event. In my distress I continued to cry to the Lord, not with a loud voice, but with pleading whispers and groans. I was physically exhausted from this attack, and I had not slept well during the entire week. Yet when God gave me the strength, I was able to read my Bible. In addition, just after this gout attack began, the Holy Spirit directed me to read the book of Job. I had, of course, read about Job's sufferings many times. But now that I was going through my own trial of pain, the book of Job became more real to me, as the Lord gave me many new insights and much encouragement.

Now, a little more than a week later, I finally have enough strength to

> *As I suffered, I got closer to the Lord. Something changed inside me, and even my discomfort became a spiritual event.*

make a journal entry. I am just getting off my week's medical restriction, and I am learning how to walk all over again. My feet are still swollen, and I still have a fair amount of pain, but there's always a humorous side to every situation, and this is no exception, as some of the guys have been joking with me that I've begun to walk like Frankenstein. Yet for me this has been a time of spiritual renewal. I had a chance to slow down and get quiet before the Lord instead of racing at my usual breakneck pace. Once again my loving Savior has worked out these afflictions for my betterment, and I am also thanking the Lord for my health. We often do not realize how very precious good health is until it is gone and sickness comes in.

Now I am in the process of being renewed physically and spiritually. Looking at this in retrospect, I realize I truly needed to be flat on my back for a week. Thank you, Lord Jesus!

"Mother's Day"

Mother's Day is an interesting time in prison. Almost everyone here seems to have—or once had—a great mom or one or two loving grandmothers. During this morning's worship service my chaplain gave a brief message concerning Mother's Day, and it was a great source of encouragement. You see, most of us feel guilty at being "failures" in the eyes of our moms. Yet there is one thing we can say about almost all our moms: they never stopped loving us, in spite of our rebellion and mistakes.

I lost my mother to cancer in 1967 when I was only fourteen, but I remember that she was always there for me when I got into trouble. And after all this time, I've never stopped missing her. She seems to have been on my mind every moment of each day for the thirty-four years she has been gone. I also miss going to the cemetery to visit her grave in New Jersey, something I used to do several times each year before I got locked up. I would have gone more often if I could have managed it. Being in prison these past twenty-four years has really hurt because I cannot get to her gravesite.

However, God still provides ways for me to honor her memory. Last year and the year before, several dear friends from New Jersey went to the cemetery in my behalf. They visited my mother's grave, and each followed the Jewish tradition of leaving a small stone at the top of her headstone. My friends would have gone again this year except that one of them, my Christian sister Ellen, has been struggling with cancer herself. She doesn't have the strength to drive a car or to stand up for very long.

But under the chaplain's direction this morning, we all joined in prayer for our mothers and grandmothers who are still alive. Some of the men prayed for family members who were sick. A few of them have moms who are in the hospital. One brother has a mother who may not live much longer. One of the worst experiences for an inmate is to have an immediate family member die. Over the years I've seen many men go out to attend a funeral. It is a painful and often shameful event because a prisoner has to go to the funeral home in the armed escort of two guards. The inmate must wear his prison uniform and stay handcuffed, even around his relatives. Although the guards are wearing civilian suits, they are always standing on each side of the grieving man.

> *A lot of anger and grief pours out of the men at times like these, yet I know that God's grace is sufficient, and Jesus is always with those who mourn.*

As a Christian, I've had many opportunities to pray with men who were scheduled to go out shortly to a funeral, or who were just getting back from one. Some cried, some complained, but most just accepted the passing of a loved one as part of life. Almost all of the men I have spoken with, however, expressed guilt at not being the son, brother, or father they should have been.

Several years ago one of the men in our congregation lost his brother to gun violence in Brooklyn. He was off to the funeral a few days later. We've had men lose brothers, sisters, and even children, but most often a parent. Most losses occur as a result of sickness or an accident, though occasionally violence takes a loved one. Whatever the circumstances, to be here and away from family members who are suffering is tough. A lot of anger and grief pours out of the men at times like these, yet I know that God's grace is sufficient, and Jesus is always with those who mourn. Thinking about my own mother on this day, as I do every day, I can say that I still miss her tremendously.

"Blessed Are the Persecuted"

Praying always with all prayer and supplication in the Spirit, and watching thereunto with all perseverance and supplication for all saints.

—*Ephesians 6:18*

The Lord has put a renewed burden upon my heart in the past several days to pray more for my many brothers and sisters who are suffering severe persecution as they serve the Lord in other countries. These people love the Lord and have given Him their very lives. Many are now in prison. Some have already died there. They have lost homes, jobs, property, and even loved ones because they were not ashamed to publicly proclaim Jesus Christ as Lord.

What must it be like to truly be persecuted? I think about this sometimes. What is it like to live the Christian life in places where Jesus is hated and where His servants face punishment and even death at any moment? I do not know the answers to my questions. Yes, I could read many accounts in books and magazines about my persecuted brothers and sisters. But in truth, these are only words. It is one thing to read about something; it is quite another to experience it firsthand. I can read about a Chinese Christian being locked in an isolation cell with rats scurrying about at his feet. I can read about Christians in Arab nations who are publicly flogged for carrying a Bible. But have I felt their pain? No, I haven't. In America we have such a soft and seemingly costless Christianity. It has become a polite, leisure-time religion. Oh, God, in my comfortable Christianity, never let me fail to pray for these dear warriors who have risked all to follow the Holy One of Israel!

I am not putting my persecuted brothers and sisters on a pedestal, for they too are only flesh and blood. I know they have shortcomings and temptations and moments when they fail the Lord. But how I admire their courage and faith! How privileged they have been to shed their blood for Jesus, to taste the blows of angry fists, to know the coldness of a cell or the fear of being discovered for holding a prayer meeting in the woods.

These committed brothers and sisters are great examples for the rest of us, and I believe they are more humble than we are, for their trials have caused them to know the suffering Savior more intimately. They are blessed men, women, and even children, and their rewards will be great. Matthew 5:10 and 5:12 tell us, "Blessed are they which are persecuted for righteousness' sake: for theirs is the kingdom of heaven…. Rejoice, and be exceeding glad; for great is your reward in heaven."

> *These committed brothers and sisters are great examples for the rest of us, and I believe they are more humble than we are, for their trials have caused them to know the suffering Savior more intimately.*

I am not even worthy to stand in the shoes of these committed servants, for I have never suffered as they have. They have fellowshipped in Jesus' sufferings, and they will one day reign with Him (see 2 Timothy 2:12). My calling is to be faithful to pray for them that their faith never fails, that they will be strengthened and encouraged, and that they will always triumph under such trials.

May America one day be so blessed to know this kind of persecution, this fire, this honor. May we know Jesus the way our persecuted brothers and sisters know Him even now.

"Love on Display"

By this shall all men know that ye are my disciples, if ye have love one to another.

—John 13:35

Today several of the Christian brothers and I were talking about the Lord and discussing His Word. We were simply hanging out in the cellblock because it was pouring rain, and no one was going out to the yard in this kind of weather. Each of us had a word to share to encourage one another. What the Lord gave me was John 13:34, 13:35. I said our love for one another and the way we publicly demonstrate God's mercy, compassion, and kindness is our best witness to the reality of the gospel. By living in this love we are actually displaying to the world God's true nature, which the Bible tells us is love. "He that loveth not knoweth not God; for God is love" (1 John 4:8).

We all agreed that, for the most part, much of the world does not get to see God's true nature and character displayed through His followers. One by one, we admitted that each of us is probably guilty at times of not faithfully demonstrating the love of God to this lost generation. We prayed and asked the Lord's help to do better in showing more love to our brothers and sisters in Christ, and to encourage and respect one another. The world sees so much meaningless and empty religion, but what they really need to see is Christians having a loving and joyous relationship with their Lord and with each other. I pray that I and my dear brothers will be more faithful than ever in showing those around us the true heart of Jesus.

"My Birthday"

This is the day which the Lord hath made; we will rejoice and be glad in it.

—Psalm 118:24

Today I turned forty-eight years old. I thank the Lord for His mercy and for bringing me along this far in life, though birthdays are peculiar in prison, as virtually no one celebrates them. Only a few of my closest friends from my church knew about my birthday. I did not want anyone fussing over me. However I did get a lot of cards from Christians on the outside, as well as from my dad, and I'm grateful for their expressions of love.

In prison, almost no one tells others when they're having a birthday. Those who do tend to mention it in a very simple and casual way. No one expects any presents from the other prisoners, although gifts are occasionally given. There have been times I have learned that an inmate who is very poor and has no one on the outside was having a birthday, so I gave him a gift, maybe a deodorant or a shirt I didn't need. I've also given out some food items, like a bag of potato chips or some candy bars. I've seen other inmates do the same for the poorer men. And when an inmate does give one of his fellow prisoner's a gift, it is done with absolutely no fanfare. Usually a man will be handed an item, and then the giver, after saying "happy birthday," quickly walks away.

These are just some of the oddities of prison life. There are no birthday celebrations, no fancy gift giving. For most of us, birthdays are just another day.

"I Absolutely Refuse!"

Now the Lord is that Spirit; and where the Spirit of the Lord is, there is liberty.

—*2 Corinthians 3:17*

As the days march on, I absolutely refuse to let the devil drag me down. I refuse to give up or lose hope. From time to time other prisoners ask me, "Dave, doesn't it bother you that you may never get out of prison, and that you're doing all this time?"

I cannot even count the number of times I have been asked these questions in some way or another. But my answer is always the same. I tell them outright that "doing time" doesn't bother me anymore. While they seem surprised by my answer, I'm not. Not many choose to be in prison, but God has given me a complete peace about it. Sure, I have my regrets at the way I lived my life before I knew the Lord. And yes, I miss my father terribly. I pray for him every day, and I long with all my heart to be able to wrap my arms around him and look into his face and tell him how much I love him. I wish I could take my dad out to a nice restaurant or to a ballgame like other sons can do for their fathers. But I can't, for what's done is done.

> *With each passing day the Holy Spirit is teaching me what this "liberty in Christ" is all about.*

I cannot go back and undo things, as much as I might want to. Neither can I get heartsick thinking about what could have been. Today, thanks to the love and mercy of the Lord, I can have a good life even while incarcerated. The Lord has allowed me to make the best of my situation, to enjoy being with Him and having a sweet relationship with my God. At the same time, there are people on the outside of my prison walls who are miserable. Everything in their lives seems to be going wrong; or they may have so many material things, yet still be unhappy and feel empty inside. That is because the Spirit of God does not dwell in them.

The way I see it, if I have the Holy Spirit living in me, then I have all I need. And because Jesus is my Lord, I will always be all right. God is with me now, and always will be. I know what it is to be in God's presence. I know what it is to be free from guilt and condemnation. With each passing day the Holy Spirit is teaching me what this "liberty in Christ" is all about.

In addition, today I can say with absolute certainty that I *know* Jesus of Nazareth. The One who once lived and grew up in the land of Galilee is now living in me and walking with me. This is true liberty. This is real freedom. This is great stuff! And so, with full assurance because I know the Holy Spirit is with me, I refuse to let the devil drag me down. Amen!

"Another Miracle"

When a man's ways please the Lord, he maketh even his enemies to be at peace with him.

—Proverbs 16:7

Once again I am seeing God's hand of love moving in every situation that happens in and around my life. Yesterday a man who is doing several life sentences for homicides and who always expressed hatred for me sat down next to me and started up a conversation. In the past several years this inmate had made it perfectly clear that he didn't like me. Every time I passed by he had a scowl on his face. A number of times when he was with his friends I heard him whispering my name. In this environment it is fairly easy to identify those who have hatred in their hearts, for it is written all over their faces. This particular inmate's eyes always seemed to blaze with rage whenever I was near.

However, quite a while back the Lord placed it upon my heart to pray for this man. Sometimes I did pray for him, but much of the time, to be honest, I forgot. Quite frankly, I didn't care to be in the same air space because of the angry vibes he gave off. Then one day last year he got "keeplocked" for fighting with another inmate. This means he was confined to his cell for one or more disciplinary infractions. An inmate can be given an infraction for breaking any of a long list of rules, including fighting or carrying a weapon, not making the bed in the morning, or forgetting to carry the identification card each of us is required to keep in our possession at all times.

> *In the years I have known this man, I have seldom seen him smile at anyone about anything. Since yesterday, however, his entire countenance seems to have changed. I know this is a case of the Lord touching an angry heart and softening it.*

When this man got confined to his cell for a thirty-day punishment, the Lord put it on my heart to get him a few food items from the prison's commissary to help him out. When he got those bags of potato chips he thanked me and seemed happy. However, once his confinement was up, he went back to putting on his scowling face and not talking to me. This went on for months and I paid it no mind. This kind of living arrangement is part of the daily life in prison where we are surrounded by both friends and enemies, by those who like us and those who don't. But yesterday, as I was sitting at a table in the dayroom area waiting for my turn to take a shower, he plopped down in the chair right across from me, said hello, and then started talking. He asked me how I was doing and started making small talk.

I couldn't believe this was happening. He actually began to open up to me, and told me a little about his case and that he was never getting out. I said, "It sounds like we're in the same boat." Before long I suggested that he should read the Bible and maybe even consider going to the chapel with me. While he said that he was not ready to start going to church, he did admit that he had been reading his Bible once in a while. I was stunned, and I thought to myself, *This guy is reading the Bible?* I was blown away!

Today he shocked me again by smiling and saying hello to me. In the years I have known this man, I have seldom seen him smile at anyone about anything. Since yesterday, however, his entire countenance seems to have changed. I know this is a case of the Lord touching an angry heart and softening it. Jesus has answered my feeble prayers!

"Setting Things in Order"

Our church is marching on. Several days ago all of us here in the body of Christ at Sullivan Correctional Facility were heartbroken over the transfer of our main chaplain's clerk, who was also one of our dearest brothers. But after coming together in prayer to seek God's guidance, we now have another man to take the position. We prayed for him and he was anointed with oil by the elders. We believe he is Christ's choice, and we are pleased that there were virtually no interruptions with this transition process. Our upheaval was brief.

A few of the brothers asked me to come back and work in the chapel. I thanked them for the offer, but explained that I believe the Lord wants me right where I am, caring for a handicapped inmate and having more time to spend in prayer and Bible study, as well as in writing. Several years ago I was so busy that I probably could not effectively have kept a journal. I first began trying to write a spiritual journal in 1998, but between working in the chapel and being on the go from morning

> *I believe the Lord wants me right where I am.*

until night, I just could not focus on this task. Keeping up with the mail correspondence was enough, plus all the hours of paperwork I had to do as the chaplain's clerk.

However, beginning in the year 2000, the Lord was leading me to slow down. He was opening new doors for me to get involved in other programs and to spend more time in a classroom setting. This lasted for most of 2000. Now in 2001 everything seems to be in place where I can "shut in" and write more. I'm very satisfied and thankful. But for the next few weeks I will be spending extra time in the chapel, in addition to the usual services and Bible studies. This is because I have to help train the new clerk. It is a blessing to serve the Lord and to help my brothers in any capacity the Lord wants me to, and I know that God will give me the strength to do so, because many times (I'm being very open here) I just don't feel like doing all these tasks.

During the past few days I had been reading from the book of Titus in the New Testament. The apostle Paul told Titus, who like Timothy was something of a spiritual son to the elderly apostle, to stay on the Island of Crete and to "set in order" all that was necessary so that the Church could be established in that very lawless and inhospitable territory. Back then Crete was a hideout for pirates and criminals on the run. Because of all the sailors and merchants who passed through the island, it was filled with prostitution and all kinds of vice. But the Lord was moving among the people and many were repenting from their sins and placing their faith in Jesus Christ. In this environment, Titus had to encourage the saints to continue to turn away from sinful lifestyles and to live godly and honorable lives. He had to provide guidance for the local church and appoint elders to govern the congregation and to be leaders by example.

It is no different here in this prison. Even in our chapel things get a little off course and need to be set back in order. This is all part of a Christian's learning process (see Titus 1:4-9).

"Tribute to My Dad"

Like as a father pitieth his children, so the Lord pitieth them that fear Him.

—*Psalm 103:13*

I have such a great and tenderhearted father. I don't think there is another dad like mine anywhere in the entire world. There are times, even at this moment, that I miss him so much I can actually feel an ache in my heart. I thank the Lord that, with all the bad things I have done in the past, and all my failings and mistakes, my dad still loves me. But to be honest, I put my father through hell. I am not only referring to the acts that caused me to come to prison, as horrible as those things were. But from the time I was a young child I had a wild and rebellious streak.

My parents, just simple middle-class Jewish folks, poured so much love into my life. My father had to struggle to make a living working in a little neighborhood hardware store, six days a week, ten hours a day. He would be on his feet all day, and then drag in at night, exhausted. He worked hard, dealt honestly with others, and was always so mild mannered. I don't believe I ever saw him in an argument. Everybody liked my father but, sadly, like so many young people, I did not appreciate him. Looking back, I see that I had not only behavioral and disciplinary problems, but emotional ones too. All of these things caused my parents so much grief. I was living in my own world. I shunned my mother and father and went for days without even speaking to them. And that was no easy task, as we lived in a small three-room apartment in a Bronx, New York, tenement where it was difficult to avoid anyone.

But there were good times too. I remember going to the school yard across the street from our apartment building where my dad and I would sometimes play catch with a softball. He would also fix my bike when he could, and I remember playing Monopoly with him and my mother on an occasional Sunday afternoon. Sometimes Dad took me bowling or for ice cream on a hot summer night. There was a local candy store nearby where we went for ice cream cones, and sometimes we went to Carvel for custard sundaes.

But then there were those dark times when I retreated far into myself. Filled with self-destructive thoughts and struggling with depression, I would flee from my parents. I remember feeling that I would be better off dead, and even wishing that I would die. Sometimes I was completely out of control. My dad believed in discipline, and I got my share of well-deserved spankings. But no matter how my father tried to reach or teach me, this tremendously destructive inner force would win out. Furthermore, there were times I put myself in total isolation. I would lock myself in my room or hide in the closet or under my bed for hours. We lived on the sixth floor, and at times my dad would have to yell at me to get off the window ledge or the fire escape.

> *Like my heavenly Father, my dad's love has been unconditional. He has loved me when I was good and also when I was bad. All these years later my father has stuck by me. Only true love could manage this.*

As much as my parents cared, it was beyond their ability to understand that I was actually thinking of throwing myself down to the ground below. They could not have comprehended my suicidal thoughts or even why I was depressed. It was not their fault. I never shared my feelings with them. My dad would plead with me to open up to him, but I never really did. Yet in spite of all this, my dad hung in there. He tried his best to communicate, and his love for me never stopped. I remember when he took me to my first night game at Yankee Stadium. I had been to day games before, but a night game was something special.

Since I was so emotionally troubled, I had plenty of problems in school. I was very bad in math, especially fractions. Dad tutored me right at the kitchen table. He really pushed me to buckle down and learn because I was so undisciplined at that stage of my life. Without his help and encouragement I never would have graduated high school. Furthermore, my father was with me through my struggles. I remember the times I saw him break down and cry when I was cruel to him, and how he struggled trying to care for me when my mother got cancer in 1967 and ended up in the hospital. She died before the year was over.

Then it was just Dad and me, and he had to work all those hours. I ended up spending a lot of time alone in our little apartment. Actually, I didn't stay home all that much because by this time, at age fourteen, I was staying out late at night and running with a bad crowd. Of course, this caused him more grief. But I was only into myself back then. I was doing many self-destructive things, and I was very immature. I started hanging out on the rooftops with junkies, and also on the street corners with all my friends. Most of the guys who were my age were getting drunk several nights a week. I know my dad still remembers the first time I came home drunk and puked all over the bathroom floor, missing the toilet entirely. He was upset with me, yet no matter how much he begged me to stay home and off the streets, I was set in my rebellious ways and would not listen to him.

However my dad and I eventually moved to a safer neighborhood, the "Co-op City" section of the Bronx. I still had my inner struggles and depressions, but I was doing better emotionally. And still, through all my ups and downs, my great dad continued to try to encourage me. He was patient with my ever-changing moods, and somehow managed to put up with my odd ways. Today I have a lot of guilt about how I mistreated him, and I know he deserved better than me for a son. Nevertheless, today I can truly thank God Almighty for the father I have. Like my heavenly Father, my dad's love has been unconditional. He has loved me when I was good and also when I was bad. All these years later my father has stuck by me. Only true love could manage this.

My dad still writes to me every month, and I write back. Sometimes we speak on the telephone. I have to count my blessings, but I do know, regrettably, that because I am here in prison, I will never get to make up the lost years. Dad is in his nineties now, and I don't know when I will ever see him again face to face. However, I can carry his love in my heart, and this is good enough.

Happy Father's Day, Dad. I love you!

"God's Mercy = Unmerited Favor"

"…God be merciful to me a sinner."

—*Luke 18:13*

After my time of prayer and devotion this morning, the Lord showed me that I need to talk just a little more about His mercy. Basically, God's mercy is His "unmerited favor," meaning there is nothing anyone can ever do to earn mercy or favor from the Lord. The Bible says we are all sinners, and there is no one who is righteous apart from the righteousness that Christ freely gives us. We cannot do good deeds to earn favor with God for salvation. We cannot, through human effort, work our way into God's good graces. Many people believe we can, but the Bible does not teach this at all. The Bible clearly explains that man is a lost sinner and can only be forgiven by placing his faith in Jesus Christ. The Lord Jesus, by His willing death, paid the full price for all our sins. Thus salvation is a free gift to all who come to Christ.

Many people, however, look at the sins of others and see people like myself, with my wretched criminal past, and they think, "Oh, I'm not as bad as that guy." They then falsely think that, because they're "not such a bad person" by their own standards, or because they've never committed a serious crime or taken another person's life, that God somehow sees them as deserving of His mercy, while a more outwardly wicked person would not be. This is a warped and unbiblical view, based solely on pride. These are the people who, regrettably, have a hard time understanding that a murderer or serial killer, or any other kind of criminal for that matter, can be completely forgiven.

Again, I feel it is so important to mention that in God's eyes the entire

> *And since we are all sinners, even though the sins of some are worse by society's standards than others, we must all appeal to God for His mercy so that we may be forgiven and our sins not held against us.*

human race is under sin—condemned to be separated from God for all eternity. Each one of us has done wrong in our lives. We have lied, cheated, gossiped, stolen, and had hateful and impure thoughts toward others. Any one of these sins can damn a person to hell, as surely as the sin of murder. And since we are all sinners, even though the sins of some are worse by society's standards than others, we must all appeal to God for His mercy so that we may be forgiven and our sins not held against us. This puts *all* people on the same plane, and *all* of us are equal before the eyes of the Lord. We are *all* sinners, and therefore we *all* need Yeshua, the Hebrew name for Jesus that literally means "God's salvation."

People who see themselves as deserving of salvation but who cannot believe a murderer can be forgiven are really looking at this subject from their own limited human intellect, not from God's perspective or through His eyes. In a sense, these people are robbing Jesus Christ of His ability to "save...to the uttermost" (Hebrews 7:25). They are saying that God's power to forgive all sin is limited, because in their eyes there are certain sins He cannot forgive. This is an affront to the One who is all-powerful and all-sovereign. These people are actually trying to tell God what He can or cannot do.

Furthermore, by thinking along these lines, people are trying to steal God's glory. Why? Because according to the Bible, God does get a certain amount of glory for Himself when He grants mercy to and forgives the worst of sinners.

So think about what I am saying. No one can merit God's favor. None of us can put himself above someone else. This is what the self-righteous religious leaders tried to do when they looked down in contempt at the woman who was caught in the act of adultery, but Jesus stepped in and set them straight, telling the woman that He forgave her and then instructing her to "go, and sin no more" (see John 8:1-11). Likewise the man who was a tax collector but who begged for God's forgiveness is another example (see Luke 18:10-14). Yes, this dishonest crook understood that his life was an abomination to God, so he beat his chest as an outward act of repentance and cried out to God for mercy. As a result, he was forgiven, while the self-righteous, religious man in this story was not.

Is God any different today? No! Hebrews 13:8 tells us He is "the same yesterday, and today, and forever." He is always merciful, and this mercy is an aspect of His love for all creation. He does not want to see anyone miss the wonderful offer of salvation that Jesus has already paid for. And today Christ is still showing this mercy to all who come to Him, be they repentant "criminals" or so called "good citizens."

> *As it is written, There is none righteous, no, not one; There is none that understandeth, there is none that seeketh after God. They are all gone out of the way, they are together become unprofitable: there is none that doeth good, no, not one.*
>
> *—Romans 3:10-12*

> *For all have sinned, and come short of the glory of God.*
>
> *—Romans 3:23*

"Lenny"

*Create in me a clean heart, oh God; and renew a right
spirit within me.*

—Psalm 51:10

The Lord had something nice for me today. This morning I had the rare opportunity to take time off from my work assignment because the inmate I help care for is in the hospital. He has problems with his heart and will probably be there for a few days. So with the morning off, I decided to go outside to the recreation yard. Though my immediate plan was to do some walking in the fresh air, I quickly discovered several other Christians out in the yard. Before long eight of us were hanging out together, enjoying some fellowship, talking about the Lord, and praying. One man asked me to read Psalm 51, and then we discussed what I had read.

> *The brothers took turns putting their arms around Lenny as we walked. We wanted him to know that he is definitely accepted in our company. None of us is a self-righteous big shot; we're outcasts, too.*

In the midst of this wonderful time of sharing with my brothers, I noticed another prisoner named Lenny, whom I have known for many years. I must admit that I was surprised to see him outside, as he almost always stays in his cellblock. Lenny has been incarcerated for almost eighteen years now. He's doing a fifteen-years-to-life sentence, which means the parole board has already "hit" him (turned him down) twice. Lenny is schizophrenic, but he is still a very decent person. Everyone likes him, and although he can sometimes get very loud as he talks to himself for hours at a time, no one is bothered by him.

Like most mentally ill prisoners, Lenny is a chain smoker. (Nicotine seems to be the drug of choice in prison.) Often other men try to show kindness to Lenny by giving him cigarettes. Knowing what we know about cigarettes today, however, I don't consider these to be an ideal gift. I can't even stand the smell of tobacco smoke, though I've been breathing it in almost continually for many years now. But many prisoners don't know any other way to do something nice for Lenny, since candy is not permitted in the yard, and this facility does not allow inmates to have chewing gum.

Today when Lenny saw me in the yard with the other Christians he came right over and joined us. We all walked around and talked, although Lenny made little or no sense. And yet we had a good time together. The brothers took turns putting their arms around Lenny as we walked. We wanted him to know that he is definitely accepted in our company. None of us is a self-righteous big shot; we're outcasts, too. In fact, some of the other prisoners consider the Christian inmates to be trash and scum. However, we were just too full of the joy of the Lord today to let the attitudes and looks of some of these guys depress us.

"Intercessory Prayer"

I just finished a letter to a friend who was a little downcast because he felt he had no purpose within the Body of Christ. This seems to be such a common feeling because many of us incorrectly believe that ministry is always supposed to be exciting, and that it means traveling all around, preaching, evangelizing, appearing on Christian TV, etc. While these things are part of some ministries, there really is so much more. If I can encourage someone here, let me share something Christ has revealed to me about ministry, which is that intercessory prayer (praying on behalf of other people and situations) is one of the most important ministries of the Church. Intercessory prayer is the oil that keeps the gears of the Church in motion, especially in these end times when the spiritual warfare against the saints is so great, and Christians and their ministries are under attack everywhere. I don't think there is a more effective type of ministry than prayer.

> *Intercessory prayer is the oil that keeps the gears of the Church in motion, especially in these end times when the spiritual warfare against the saints is so great, and Christians and their ministries are under attack everywhere.*

The prayers of God's people can cause the sick to be healed: "And the prayer of faith shall save the sick..." (James 5:15a). Prayer can move mountains or shut up the heavens so that it doesn't even rain, as we see in verse 17 of the same chapter of James: "Elias [Elijah] was a man subject to like passions as we are [he was an ordinary person], and he prayed earnestly that it might not rain: and it rained not on the earth by the space of three years and six months." Not bad! Of course, intercessory prayer is, for the most part, a work and ministry that has no glamour or recognition. Not too many folks are going to see us "praying in secret," as Jesus instructed us to do. But guess who is going to see us? It is the Lord. Jesus says in His Word that when we pray in secret He will reward us openly (see Matthew 6:5-6). This kind of fervent, consistent praying is a behind-the-scenes role, but a vital one. And the Lord has called us to it. Any Christian can pray at least some of the time, and for those of us who happen to have lots of time on our hands, our prayer ministry can be even more effective.

So when I wrote back to this dear Christian friend who felt he had no purpose, I told him that, out of all the types of ministry anyone can do, prayer is the most important. I hope he will realize what a great ministry and calling he has, and what a needful place any of us can fill as intercessory prayer warriors in and for the Body of Christ.

"Updates: Stewart and Michael"

Once again the Lord has been teaching me to have patience and wait upon Him. In many cases and situations, even though the Lord hears our prayers, we don't see immediate answers because God first wants to work on people's hearts and minds. This is especially true in cases where the person I am praying for is heavily bound by Satan and needs a big deliverance or, for whatever reasons, is very far from the Lord. Two men who fall into that category are Stewart (Stu) and Michael, both of whom I have mentioned previously. Stu completed his time and received a "conditional release," which basically means he wasn't paroled but they couldn't keep him here any longer. Now he is back on the streets.

> *In many cases and situations, even though the Lord hears our prayers, we don't see immediate answers because God first wants to work on people's hearts and minds.*

I was able to share the gospel with Stu while he was here, but he thought he was a god, so he didn't seem interested in hearing about the true God. I always showed him kindness, however, and listened to him talk about his life situation. Stu, as I mentioned in an earlier entry, has AIDS. The last time I saw him he had started to look noticeably sick, was losing weight, and was getting that sunken, hollow look that I see so often in those who are suffering with this virus.

Now Stu is out of prison and I wonder about him, especially since he doesn't have much of a family out there. I assume he went the way of most of these men when they leave, which is to be released to a New York City shelter. For the many who have no home to go to, a shelter is all there is. My prayer for Stu is that he comes in contact with some loving Christians with a street ministry or an outreach to the homeless. Maybe through them he will finally open his heart to Jesus Christ.

As for Michael, he made it to the chapel on Sunday mornings a few times during the past several months. I have also seen him in the hallways, and I always greet him and talk to him when I can. But Michael is schizo-phrenic, and for the past month or so, he has gone back to being reclusive. He purposely tries to violate some of the prison rules and gets written up for disciplinary infractions. This is all part of Michael's self-destructive ways. When life gets too stressful or painful for him, he uses this means to shut himself off from people, including inmates and staff. Depending on the types of rules Michael breaks, he is usually confined to his cell for fifteen to thirty days. He loses all privileges, such as being able to go to the recreation yard or watch TV in the dayroom area. Michael, however, instead of being upset and angry as most prisoners are when confined to their cells, loves the isolation. This is not good or healthy. But after all his years in prison, it is the main way he has learned to avoid stress.

I am just going to continue to be hopeful and patient that one day change will come for both Michael and Stu, for I know Jesus Christ truly loves these men.

"Escape from Death"

I was sitting at a table in the recreation area earlier this evening, talking with three other men who, like myself, became Christians sometime during their stay in prison. While each of our crimes and criminal cases is different, there was a unanimous consensus among us that, had we still been out in the streets, we would more than likely be dead by now.

Going over each of our lives (without going into specific details about our cases) we admitted that we had been out of control. We were living reckless lives, taking crazy chances, and daring death to claim us. We all agreed that we could not get out of the mental and physical bondages we were in. On the "outside" our lives were too fast-paced and pressured. We seemed to be on our own individual roller coasters with no way to stop them. Prisons, however, provide lots of time for people to reflect. I have had this same discussion with so many other inmates over the years, some of whom had been drug addicts or alcoholics. Their lives were coming apart, and they were in self-destructive cycles with no way out. And then they were arrested.

> *While none of us wants to be here, and in spite of our prison sentences and present confinement, we realize that God actually used our forced confinement in prison to save our lives.*

While none of us wants to be here, and in spite of our prison sentences and present confinement, we realize that God actually used our forced confinement in prison to save our lives. Because the Lord loved us even when we were in rebellion toward Him, He had to use extreme measures to save fools from their own folly. And He definitely saved a fool like me!

"$$Big Money$$"

Bart, also known as "$$Big Money$$," is a thirty-one-year-old black man who is doing a fifteen-year-to-life prison sentence for the crime of murder in the second degree. He hails from Brooklyn, officially "Kings County," one of New York City's five boroughs. It was his partner, Bart insists, that whacked a drug dealer "several times in the head" with a baseball bat, while Bart was "just there." But Bart did admit to me that he and his partner were definitely trying to rob their victim. Big Money has now been in prison for about seven years.

Bart is an easy guy to talk to because he loves to rap with anyone about anything. Mostly he likes to hang out with his "crew" or play basketball, but every now and then I get a chance to spend a little time with him. This morning I was talking to Bart during the recreation period, as we sat together on top of one of the picnic tables. I was glad for the opportunity to get to know him better, and I quickly learned that Bart had never finished high school. He dropped out in the tenth grade, leaving school with what was probably a fifth or sixth-grade reading level, and opted for the streets instead of an eight-hour-a-day job. Big Money also told me that he never went to a football or baseball game, the zoo, or a wedding. He can't even remember leaving the boundaries of New York City to go on a vacation of any kind, and he's

> *Bart never had a normal American childhood.*

never seen mountains up close. He has never visited the Museum of Natural History or the Statue of Liberty. He's lived in New York his entire life, and yet he has never gone to the top of the Empire State Building. He has never gone to the circus, and he has never played Little League baseball.

In actuality, Bart never had a normal American childhood. For the most part Big Money spent his entire pre-prison life in and around a small one-square mile of territory in the Fort Greene section of Brooklyn. He told me he seldom ventured out of that area except to take the subway to Coney Island during the summer months, when he went along with a few friends "in search of people to rob."

Bart never owned a pet. Before coming to prison he had never watched a "National Geographic" program on TV. He can't remember ever spending time enjoying the simple pleasures of life, such as watching a squirrel scamper up a tree or a bird flying overhead, even though he spent much of his life hanging out in city parks and playgrounds. Bart seems to have no concept of nature or of any kind of life outside his small world of hustling, surviving, and living in the projects.

> *He can't remember ever spending time enjoying the simple pleasures of life.*

Furthermore, Bart never held a legitimate job. He has never cashed a check (at least not legally), or owned a car, or rented his own apartment. Bart has never had a steady girlfriend that he felt he was truly in love with, though he told me he had "shacked up" with a number of women. He has never raised a child, but he admits the possibility that he may have one or more children somewhere.

As our discussion turned to his home life, Bart candidly told me that he has no memory of ever meeting with or speaking to his dad. His mother told him that his father had been around for a little while after Bart was born, but he got into trouble in Michigan and ended up doing "big time" in that state for armed robbery. At some point, Bart remembers, a distant cousin from his neighborhood once told him that his dad did eventually get out of prison, but as far as Bart knows, he never made it back to New York City. A few years after his dad's release, Bart was told that he had died in some big city. He thinks it may have been Detroit or maybe Chicago.

Bart was never a homeless person, yet he was almost never home. His mother always had her door open for him, but he was used to running wild and could not stand living with a handful of brothers and sisters in such a cramped place. His mom, being a single parent with a brood of kids and nothing but welfare checks to support them, could never control Bart, who considered her apartment nothing more than a "crash pad" and a place to get a hot meal when his stomach was empty. It was a little place of refuge and respite from the fast moving life of the streets.

Bart survived, he said, by selling small quantities of drugs (mostly marijuana) to other people in his neighborhood. He was no big-time operator, though he said he sometimes robbed other drug dealers. He would steal whatever he could and occasionally break into parked cars.

In reality, Bart has never lived. And isn't it ironic that the man who nicknamed himself "Big Money" never had much of it. He never made much money stealing things or sticking people up. His takes were always small, although he told me he thought he was a "pretty good criminal." But his dreams of being wealthy, successful, and having "lots of ladies" never materialized, though he somehow has not come to realize this truth himself.

As I listened to Bart, my desire to steer our conversation toward spiritual issues continued to grow. Finally I asked Bart what he felt his purpose was in life, and if he had a vision of something bigger than just trying to survive in the streets and in prison. Bart assured me that when he gets out of prison he hopes to find a good job. Since he has never held a legitimate job in his life, the chances of that happening aren't good, but I didn't tell him that. He also hopes to leave prison with a High School Equivalency diploma, even though he has been in the same pre-GED class for the past three years without making any progress or advancing to the next level. In spite of this, Bart hopes he will someday get married and have kids. He wants a nice home and a few cars. Yet he has no money and lives off the few dollars in prison wages that he makes each week for going to class in the mornings, plus sweeping and mopping the hallways in the afternoons. In total, Bart makes about eighty-five cents per day or $4.25 per week. There is no overtime, and no paid vacations for the man known as "Big Money."

> In reality, Bart has never lived. And isn't it ironic that the man who nicknamed himself "Big Money" never had much of it.

I then asked Bart if he would like to attend the chapel services with me. He said he had gone a few times out of curiosity, but he was not interested at this time. I offered him a Gideon's New Testament, as we get boxes of these as donations, but he declined, explaining that he reads only newspapers and magazines.

Despite Bart's rejection of spiritual help, I thank God for the opportunity we had to talk because I learned that, in spite of his criminal history, Big Money is not a bad person. Surviving in the streets is all he has ever known.

As for his dreams of one day having a better life, they're just that: *dreams.* Will they ever come true? Sadly, there is little chance of that.

"Summer Heat"

Thou shalt not be afraid for the terror by night; nor for the arrow that flieth by day...

—*Psalm 91:5*

We are in the thick of summer now and it is sweltering. During this time of year there always seems to be more tension within the facility. I suppose it is due to a combination of the heat, restless energy among the prisoners, tempers that flare with the rising thermometer, and a change in the prison population. We have a younger and wilder group of men here now. There is always a turnover of inmates in prison, with some who have been here for a while getting transferred, and new prisoners coming in. This means getting to know new men, feeling them out, and seeing what they're about. And for many of the older inmates like me, this means being more cautious around prisoners we don't know.

Prison life is just like that, with men I've come to know moving on to other facilities or being paroled, even as new ones come in. So the process of socialization must start all over again. In this environment, where there is so little trust and so much suspicion, that is no easy task. One thing I have noticed about many of the younger men who are coming into the prison system these days is that they have so much hatred that it seems to seethe right out of their pores. They're noticeably angrier and more frustrated than

> *Prison life is just like that, with men I've come to know moving on to other facilities or being paroled, even as new ones come in. So the process of socialization must start all over again. In this environment, where there is so little trust and so much suspicion, that is no easy task.*

many of us "old timers" were when we first arrived. Of course, only those who have lived in such an environment as this can fully understand what I am talking about, or be able to feel the vibes and tension in the air.

We Christian brothers have been through these cycles before, and we are praying for the peace of this prison. We are also praying that any explosive situations that might occur will quickly and peaceably be diffused. In addition, we are praying that God's love will begin to touch these hard hearts. I've been through many prison summers, and I know, as I meditate on God's promises in Psalm 91, the Lord will keep me safe through yet another one.

"Wanderers"

These men have been wanderers on the earth, reckless, wild, crazy, and out of control. And still they wander, even in here; to and fro, back and forth they pace. For most, time has come to a standstill. That release date is all they see. The time between the start and finish of their prison sentences is just one long blank space.

I have made up my mind that I do not want to be like this. I do not want to live in a "dead zone," killing time, waiting for a prison sentence to expire. And I don't want time to kill me, as it does to some who die of heart attacks, strokes, and sickness before they're due for release. Instead I want to live life to the fullest, in fruitfulness and usefulness, even in here. No wasting time for me. No blank years. No squandering of strength. No futile wishing.

I have made up my mind that I do not want to be like this. I do not want to live in a "dead zone," killing time, waiting for a prison sentence to expire.

You see, in prison many men hide behind macho faces, but alone in their cells at night they cry for mothers at home and grandmothers long dead.

You see, in prison many men hide behind macho faces, but alone in their cells at night they cry for mothers at home and grandmothers long dead. They long for a hug from fathers they have never known.

I too have my tears, sorrows, and regrets, but my dreams are stronger and my hope for the future is too certain to spend my time as a restless wanderer, wishing for things long gone.

"Phil: Lost and Found"

This afternoon I was talking to Phil. He is fifty years old and hails from upstate New York, where he was born and raised in a small town. His mom died when he was in his teens, and like many who are in prison, he struggled with alcohol and other drugs. He ended up pulling armed robberies to support his habit, and he has more than thirty arrests under his belt, most for minor offenses.

> *Phil's worst enemy is his own flesh. He knows the power the "alcohol demon" has had over him in the past. But today his best friend and helper is Jesus Christ.*

When Phil was younger he had many different jobs, primarily as a laborer for construction firms. But his drinking problem caused him to lose one job after another, until he was nearly penniless, living in and out of shelters in the Albany area. It was in this city that he was arrested for his last robbery. Phil has already finished approximately eight years on a ten-year sentence. But, like me, during some point in his incarceration he became a Christian.

Phil and I have had a number of talks in the past, and sometimes I help him write letters because, although he can read, he has trouble writing. Phil's main concern is what is going to become of his life once he's released. We've prayed about this, and I can certainly understand his fears, particularly since his weakness is alcohol. In most communities there are liquor stores and taverns on nearly every corner.

I know it is not going to be easy for Phil when he does leave, but I told him that God wants him to trust in the Lord for strength and guidance. I also told Phil that, in spite of his past failures and even his criminal record, as a Christian he can walk out of these prison doors with dignity, and with full confidence in the Lord. I reminded Phil that, no matter what other people may think of him or what his "rap sheet" may say, he has been completely forgiven by God, and Jesus Christ has promised never to leave or forsake him.

When Phil leaves here it will be a new beginning for him, with a host of new challenges and many struggles. There will be people who will look at him with contempt and disgust because of his criminal record and past failures, things he is sorry for but cannot change. But such is life. Most of Phil's family is gone, either through death or because they disowned him. He does have two older sisters, but they live too far away to be any help to him. But God has His hand upon Phil's life, and Phil is the kind of person the Lord is always reaching out to: broken and empty.

Phil was a lost soul who once was living without hope. He was surviving from day to day by going to the local rescue mission for his meals, and then hanging out on street corners with little chance of finding employment. His life was filled with inner pain. Now, however, as his release date approaches, he is trying to link up with some Christian halfway houses. There really aren't many programs out there, and the few that are have no bed space, so Phil must make his contacts now so that, when that release date finally arrives two years from now, one of these programs may have a bed available.

Phil's worst enemy is his own flesh. He knows the power the "alcohol demon" has had over him in the past. But today his best friend and helper is Jesus Christ.

"Lost Things"

And I [the Lord] will restore to you the years that the locust hath eaten...

—Joel 2:25a

New York is undergoing a record-breaking heat wave. The temperature has been hovering at 100 degrees the past few days, with no end in sight. I am sitting in my cell dripping with sweat because inside this building it is about 110!

Earlier today, however, I was talking with some of the guys. We were discussing our lives, just reminiscing in a very casual way about the situations and circumstances that got us into prison, looking back and thinking about all the years that have gone by, the lost relationships, homes, jobs, etc. As I have mentioned before, I have already spent half of my life in prison. I came to jail when I was twenty-four, and now I'm forty-eight. A few of my friends were discussing their sentences, as well as some of the people and things they lost because of the crimes they committed, and the fact that they had to leave it all behind when they came here.

> *The worst punishment any prisoner can endure is what we inflict upon ourselves, for there is a pain much worse than being confined to a cell.*

Our discussion was really therapeutic, though that was not our original intention. The four of us just started talking, and it developed into something of an impromptu group therapy session.

We then began to talk about punishment. This is a big issue nowadays, especially for the politicians. We inmates are well aware that the public has shifted from their ideas of encouraging rehabilitation to focusing on punishment. There seems to be an emphasis on making it harder for prisoners, taking things away and making life more difficult physically and even mentally. But as the four of us discussed the aspect of punishment, we all came to the conclusion that the worst punishment any prisoner can endure is what we inflict upon ourselves. We have truly punished ourselves far more than the state has, for there is a pain much worse than being confined to a cell, of being deprived of certain freedoms, or of having to eat unappetizing food. There is an ongoing punishment that comes with a guilty conscience. I believe God has placed a conscience in everyone, and in prison, as I know from my own life and from what others have told me, a guilty conscience hurts. There is an inner pain that is so intense, so suffocating, that all the macho role-playing, living in denial, or trying to stay busy cannot silence. This is a pain that can eat away at someone like a cancer, and it stems from a guilty conscience. This pain goes beyond a prisoner having to live with the knowledge that he has hurt someone else, or maybe even taken one or more innocent lives, as I have. Although there is much torment in that knowledge, there is still more. There is the haunting pain of knowing he has thrown away his life and ruined his relationships. Coming to prison has caused men to lose their wives, children, parents, and friends. So many inmates have lost their spouses in divorce. Court orders have severed all contact with their flesh-and-blood children. Parents are left to grow old alone. Now they live with the torment of being marked "felons," knowing that criminal record will follow like a dark shadow, all the days of their lives.

> *A guilty conscience hurts. There is an inner pain that is so intense, so suffocating, that all the macho role-playing, living in denial, or trying to stay busy cannot silence. Finally, a prisoner must sit in a prison cell for ten, fifteen, twenty, or more years, with his conscience whispering to him every day, "Failure! Failure! Failure!"*

Then there is the sickening sense of failure that eats away at a convict. While some may be better than others at denying or hiding it, all prisoners know deep in their hearts that they have failed and betrayed their families. And they know that their lives, to this point, have been a waste. That is an agonizing and punishing thought. In the deepest part of a prisoner's mind, he knows he has not reached his fullest potential; he has not fulfilled the purpose for which he was placed on this earth. Furthermore, he knows that his life, for the most part, has amounted to nothing.

Finally, a prisoner knows he should be working and supporting his family. But now he must sit in a prison cell for ten, fifteen, twenty, or more years, with his conscience whispering to him every day, "Failure! Failure! Failure!" Thus a prisoner is forced to live with such an array of punishments. He has to face a painful reality that must be confronted every time he wakes up in the morning and sees the cell bars, and every night when those cell doors close and the main lights go out.

I know as well as any the pain and anguish of having to face myself in the mirror. I am not talking about a pity party, but rather a sober, self-examination of the destructive, pathological, and antisocial life I led in the past. But I also know that any prisoner who truly desires to change and leave his life of crime and failure behind and become a better person must first face himself and listen to his conscience. In fact, I believe everyone must do this if they want to become Christians, for Christianity begins with a divine call to repentance and restitution. There is a mandate to each of us to do as much good with our lives as possible, and to make amends for the past wherever and whenever we can. And that begins by facing the truth about ourselves.

For a man to choose to confront his own wickedness and to honestly come to terms with himself is painful. Then, to want to change and actually begin the process is difficult. In fact, it is impossible without God's help. Yet it is at this time, when the truth is faced and admitted, that God can truly begin to do a work of healing and restoration in a prisoner's life. Over time many of the good things a prisoner once had can be restored. Repentance is the start of this new beginning, even if the new beginning happens late in life. In the end it will all be worth it.

"Twenty-Four Years"

Today makes twenty-four years since I was first arrested and began this journey of incarceration. In spite of all the hardships of prison life plus other circumstances that brought forth many challenges, this has been an enriching experience. I know that sounds odd. Whoever heard of a convicted felon calling prison an enriching experience? But it is the truth. Christ has given me hope and peace. My heart is settled. My life is going on, and only by His grace.

There is a popular saying about two prisoners, one who looked toward a window in his cell and saw the iron bars, while the other prisoner looked at the same window and saw the blue sky. So prison life, like any other sort of life, is many times a matter of perception. I can spend my days looking back, tormenting myself with thoughts about the past, the things I am sorry for but can never undo or change, or I can focus on what I believe God has called me to do with the rest of my life. As far as I am concerned, there are so many good things to look forward to that there is no point in wasting my time looking back. I know I will be in prison for the rest of my life. I have accepted this, and I have complete peace about the matter. Furthermore, I have never made any effort to seek release, nor have I ever asked any of my

> *In spite of all the hardships of prison life plus other circumstances that brought forth many challenges, this has been an enriching experience.*

Christian friends to campaign for my release from prison. In fact, such a thought nauseates me. May God strike me dead should I ever misuse a Christian brother or sister in such a manner as to have them write a letter, circulate a petition, or do anything along those lines in an effort to get me out of prison. In addition, in the coming months I will be issuing a personal statement regarding the matter of parole. This will all be taken care of properly and decently. I am certain that those I have hurt in the past and who understandably have grave concerns about this matter will be pleased

> *Prison life, like any other sort of life, is many times a matter of perception.*

with the outcome. Once this is done, everyone can move on with their lives. They will not have to worry about this situation ever again.

As this twenty-four-year-anniversary day draws to a close, I am thankful that, for the most part, the news media has been quiet. Another prisoner told me he had heard a brief mention about my arrest on one of those "this day in history" things, but thankfully that was all. However, next year the situation will be much different. A media storm may be brewing, along with lots of misinformation and confusion; hence, my desire to straighten things out as much as possible. Of course, should the Lord see fit to take me, as well as all the other Christians, out of this world through the "Rapture of the Church" before the summer of 2002 arrives, that would be great! But should Jesus not come this year or next, I know He will take me through the coming media storm with my faith intact. Amen!

"Leroy Is Moving On"

This Sunday morning we had our regular worship service, and then in the evening I went back to the chapel for our Bible study and fellowship. During Sunday evenings the meetings are less structured and more informal, which is good because we can all talk and get to know each other better. In a prison setting it isn't easy for defensive barriers to come down so prisoners can learn to trust and open up their lives and share with one another. In the Christian fellowship, however, since we consider ourselves family, we've been able to open up more and also learn how to be more sensitive to one another's needs and situations.

> *In a prison setting it isn't easy for defensive barriers to come down so prisoners can learn to trust and open up their lives and share with one another.*

One of our Christian brothers, a young black man named Leroy who is in his mid-twenties and has been locked up since 1998, came up to me at this evening's service and said he wanted to show me some things he had felt inspired to write. Leroy is a very meek, quiet, and shy person, yet he likes to sing and write songs, even though he doesn't know anything about writing musical notes.

"Brother Dave," he said as he approached me with a smile, "check out my writings."

I was pleased to see that Leroy was making an effort to express himself in this way, since he has little formal education. On paper, to the best of his ability, Leroy had poured out his heart. His spelling and sentence structure wasn't the best, but as I read the six pages he gave me, I saw the big heart of a broken and humble man who loves his God and who strives to make the best of life, in spite of his past failings. My heart went out to Leroy as I read his moving words. He wrote of how, when he was nineteen, he had married a girl from North Carolina who had come to New York City in search of a better life. Both of them were high school dropouts. She was visiting friends in the apartment building where Leroy lived. They met and fell in love, got married, and then realized that neither had a job nor any work experience. Not surprisingly, the marriage between the two immature and impulsive young people didn't last.

Leroy had done his best to write about his failed marriage, and about the woman who had returned to her hometown with less money than when she had left. He wrote about his own struggles with drugs, about getting high out of boredom, and about the wasted years spent hanging out on a street corner along crime-infested Ralph Avenue in Brooklyn. He also wrote about watching the person he had been closest to, his cousin Alfred, getting shot dead when an argument with a neighbor got out of control. Leroy's pain and regret came through loud and clear. But what blessed me the most was when Leroy began to share about his faith in Christ and his love for the Lord. He wrote with joy about how God had blessed his life, for Leroy regularly attends the chapel services here; he tries his best to read the Bible, and he loves to pray. Unlike many who languish here, Leroy is moving on. Though he came to prison for committing a botched burglary and has been classified by the prison system as having a learning disability, he is still making the best of things.

I was happy that Leroy was writing his thoughts and feelings down on paper, and I'm glad that he has made his peace with God. Leroy is a special brother to me, and a prime example of yet another young man that God has saved from the crazy streets and from an empty life.

"Many Walls"

Yesterday I received a letter from a close friend in Los Angeles, who told me he had been able to go into the infamous Terminal Island prison. He was so happy to share with the prisoners in that facility the good news that Jesus Christ loves them. In addition, he had official permission to share his poetry with them. He then told me that the chaplain had escorted him into the lock-down unit to minister and pray with the men who have serious problems. Some have been there so very long and have no hope of release from this special confinement for many more years. I guess the best way to describe this kind of setting is a "prison within a prison." But even in the darkest of places, God has those who proclaim His love and faithfully hold out the Word of hope.

However, my friend also shared his disappointment over the fact that it was very hard to get many of these men to open up to him. After I prayed about the situation, I wrote back to encourage him by explaining that this attitude is quite normal in a prison environment. I told him to keep praying about it, because God can soften any heart. I also explained that, as a general rule, prison inmates are very cautious and guarded people. They have a fear of outsiders, and it takes time to earn their trust.

> *But even in the darkest of places, God has those who proclaim His love and faithfully hold out the Word of hope.*

As I was writing my letter, the Lord spoke these words to my heart: *In prison there are many walls.* I stopped for a few minutes to think about this, and then I realized how true it is. I had never quite seen it this way until the Holy Spirit gave me some clarity. In prison there truly are many walls. Most people think the only walls are those big ones made of concrete that surround the perimeters of many facilities to keep the inmates inside and the public safe. However, as I began to think about what the Lord had told me,

The Lord spoke these words to my heart: In prison there are many walls.

I realized that in every prison there may be hundreds of walls that cannot be seen with the naked eye, yet they are just as real as the concrete walls that encircle the prisons. Some of these walls are the walls of anger, hatred, unforgiveness, bitterness, prejudice, racism, indifference, pride, and suspicion. Fear, of course, is one of the most common walls, and it can be broken down into many smaller walls: fear of assault, fear of change, fear of revealing one's true self, even fear of success. Fear of success is a hard one to imagine, but there are many people who have failed so often that they've grown accustomed to and feel very comfortable with failure. Success and the responsibility that could go with it actually scare them.

In every prison there may be hundreds of walls that cannot be seen with the naked eye, yet they are just as real as the concrete walls that encircle the prisons. But as Jesus said, "The things which are impossible with men are possible with God" (Luke 18:27).

Then there are the walls of myriad different sins. There are lusts and desires that many prisoners do not want to give up, and these walls keep God's Word from entering into their lives. These walls surround their hearts and minds to keep them in spiritual and mental darkness, which is why it is such a challenge for anyone to minister in such a place. But as Jesus said, "The things which are impossible with men are possible with God" (Luke 18:27). As I completed the writing of my letter, I reminded my friend of this scripture and encouraged him to stay faithful to his call. I also asked him to continue to show kindness, love, and compassion, and assured him that in time he will earn the inmates' trust and respect. Finally, I reminded him that the God who called him will also equip him for this ministry, and he will prosper.

"Rest/Unrest"

The month of September is here, the weather has been nearly perfect, and the trees are showing the first stages of changing colors. This month I hope to rest a bit, even as I sense a growing unrest in the world. But I feel the need to be refreshed, both spiritually and physically. As much as possible, I want to spend more time in prayer and reading my Bible. It is time to recharge my spiritual batteries and then, Lord willing, pick up the pace in October after the Jewish holidays.

At the same time, I have this sense of fore-boding regarding Israel and the Middle East. During my prayer time this morning, I wrote down the following message, which I truly

> *God's Word will outlive us all.*

believe God wants me to share as a means of help, encouragement, and even warning for others.

> *There is so much unrest in the Middle East and in Israel. Man is always talking about peace with his mouth but making war in his heart and with his hands. Remember how the Lord said what would be happening in the end times; the Old and New Testaments talk so much about this. Very evil days are approaching for Israel, for America, and for the world. What I am saying is nothing strange or weird. People can scoff at the "Holy Book" all they want, but God's Word will outlive us all.*

"An Urgency"

In these past several days, as the time draws near to the Jewish holiday of Rosh Hashanah, I am getting an ever-increasing sense of foreboding urgency. In fact, in the past week I've been sharing this in letters to some of my friends. I wrote to one friend in New York City, Chuck Cohen, encouraging him not to delay any longer in sharing with others the spiritual messages that God has given to him. Both in a letter and a phone conversation, I urged Chuck to do whatever Christ has called him to do, and to do it quickly. Then, early this morning during my quiet time with the Lord, God increased my sense of urgency by putting the following message into my heart:

> *The world's systems and even the planet itself will be in a state of upheaval.*

It is time now. The hour is late. The world is in desperate need of a message of hope. Our foundations as a nation are cracking, and one day, perhaps soon, people will be hungry for answers. They will be afraid, for the world's systems and even the planet itself will be in a state of upheaval. And many will wake up and realize that Christ is their rock and the anchor of their soul. Remember that we are entering into a period of urgency. So be ready and be filled with the Spirit of God. He is the Spirit of Wisdom and Counsel. Through Christ we can do all things. Through Christ we can do exploits. But we must be ready and our hearts must be still. An army is a professional fighting force. But if their equipment is not in place when the battle begins, all their skills and manpower are worthless. Put everything into place now. Be ready to be used of God.

"A Day of Death"

There is a pall of sadness over the land. Earlier today Death was busy. Terrorists demolished the World Trade Center, bringing down two 110-story skyscrapers in New York City by ramming the twin towers with hijacked passenger jets. Another jet crashed into a portion of the Pentagon in Washington, D.C., and a fourth ended up crashing into a desolate field in Pennsylvania.

It was ironic that I had just turned on my radio when the news was breaking about a plane crash and explosion at One World Trade Center. Earlier today I had taken the inmate that I help care for to the prison's infirmary for his morning medications and treatment. I had just arrived back at my cell about 8:30 and was looking forward to a visit from my Christian brother Jess, who usually comes around 9:00. But at 8:45 I sensed that I should turn on my radio. Even though I am about 100 miles away from New York City, I can get many of the city's stations loud and clear on my little radio. So I tuned to CBS's all news station, as I usually do each day. Their traffic chopper had just arrived at the horrendous scene, and the news reporter on board was beginning to report the first details of the incident. As the minute-by-minute reports began coming in, I knew this was a bad situation and that it could yet get worse. I prayed as I listened.

I doubt that anyone could have imagined all that would follow. As the first fire intensified, eighteen minutes after the first crash a second jet slammed into the other tower. It all sounded so unbelievable. Sadly, the situation continued to worsen.

Shortly after 9:00 I was called to the visiting room to meet with Jess. We had tears in our eyes as we embraced. The prison guards had a TV on in the room, so we were able to watch the events unfold on CNN. Even as we watched in disbelief, we prayed. Word was coming in that police officers and firemen might be trapped in the burning buildings. Minutes later, the first tower collapsed, followed soon after by the second. It all seemed so

> *As we tried to absorb the horror of the attack against our nation, one particular scripture kept coming to my mind, the shortest scripture in the entire Bible: "Jesus wept" (John 11:35).*

unreal. In addition, we heard news reports that another plane had crashed into the Pentagon, and yet another into a field in Pennsylvania. The survivor count for the passengers on board all four jets was zero.

As we tried to absorb the horror of the attack against our nation, one particular scripture kept coming to my mind, the shortest scripture in the entire Bible: "Jesus wept" (John 11:35). I have no doubt that Jesus did indeed weep today. His heart is broken over man's murderous cruelty. And as I sit here this evening in my prison cell, still glued to the radio, I can only be thankful for those who managed to escape from those buildings.

I don't know what the outcome of all this will be, but I do not think that America will ever be the same. I know I won't be. Right now I feel more committed to the Lord than ever before. And right now, I have much more praying to do.

"Days of Sadness"

The World Trade Center in New York City, a chunk of the Pentagon in Washington, D.C., and a patch of desolate valley in a little Pennsylvania town are all in smoldering ruins. The devastation is horrific. The loss of police officers, firefighters, government personnel, and many civilians is mind-boggling.

All the prisoners here have been glued to the dayroom televisions. Each cellblock has two TVs. Those of us who have radios have them on just about all the time. I've been staying up late to listen to mine. Even the prison guards seem to have changed overnight. Most of them have become very aloof to us, though not hostile in any way. They are just distant, almost cold. This tragedy has numbed the nation, and the impact of these terrorist attacks has even rippled into American's prison system.

We inmates are not detached from these events. Some of the men have loved ones in New York City, many of whom work in or near the Trade Center complex. They are anxiously awaiting word, as they are unable to call home due to the phone lines being down. I too have friends who live and work in this immediate area, and I continue to pray for them as I wait to hear of their situations.

> *The chaplains are also putting in some late hours. Instead of going home when their shifts are over, they are staying here in case any calls come in from family members on the outside, sending word to an inmate that a loved one has been injured or killed.*

The chaplains are also putting in some late hours. Instead of going home when their shifts are over, they are staying here in case any calls come in from family members on the outside, sending word to an inmate that a loved one has been injured or killed. Thus far I do not know of any men who have received such news, thank God!

"Exhaustion"

But they that wait upon the Lord shall renew their strength...
—Isaiah 40:31a

The grieving, the pain, the intensity of following all these events beginning on September 11 have taken their toll. Lately I have been so tired and weary. My legs are shaky, and I feel sluggish and weak. I keep reminding myself that Jesus said, "Let not your heart be troubled.... believe [trust] in...me" (John 14:1). But today my body told me in no uncertain terms that I had to rest, so that is what I have been doing. I stayed in my bunk almost all day today. I slept late this morning instead of getting up as I usually do at five or six. Then this afternoon I napped on and off for several hours, which I almost never do. Right now I am up this early evening to make my journal entry, and then it's right back to bed. I have to rest in the Lord and get my spiritual batteries recharged, not to mention that I need to recuperate physically.

> *I do not believe that bullets and bombs will change hearts. Only the message of hope that is found in the gospel can do that.*

Yes, prison inmates grieve too. The loss of lives is horrible. But I know that God is in control, and he will bring good things out of this tragedy. I know it will take the families that lost loved ones a long time to heal, maybe even a lifetime. But God will be there for them, as well as for those who were wounded physically, emotionally, or both. I will never stop praying for the healing of America. Although many are calling for revenge, which is perfectly understandable, I do not believe that bullets and bombs will change hearts. Only the message of hope that is found in the gospel can do that. However, I pray that hearts will not become bitter or calloused because then the enemy will win, for a vital part of each of us will have been destroyed.

Furthermore, I believe the best things that can happen to America after this terrorist tragedy is that we become more loving and kind to our neighbors, more sensitive to those around us, and that we allow mercy to triumph over judgment. We also need to become more humble as a nation, and more thankful to God for our freedoms and for life. For on September 11 we were so suddenly reminded just how brief and uncertain life can be. Tomorrow is promised to no one, so it is vital that we make peace with Christ today. Truly now is the day of salvation.

At this moment, however, I need more sleep.

"Peace and Pain"

The Bible never said that mankind would have a pain-free or trouble-free life on this earth. God never said that in this present world we would live in perfect harmony with our fellowman. And while Christians are encouraged to strive to live at peace with others, we should realize that even with the best of intentions this will not always be possible. Instead, the Word of God makes it clear that all of us will have our share of pain, heartache, and sorrow, but it will be interspersed with periods of joy and good times.

> *The Word of God makes it clear that all of us will have our share of pain, heartache, and sorrow, but it will be interspersed with periods of joy and good times.*

Life is bittersweet. There are moments of grief as well as moments of happiness. During the periods or seasons of happiness we need to be thankful and take note of time, and truly appreciate even the simple things that are so easily taken for granted.

In the Scriptures, the wealthy and successful King Solomon said, "There is nothing better for a man, than that he should eat and drink, and that he should make his soul enjoy good in his labour." He then added, "This also I saw, that it was from the hand of God" (Ecclesiastes 2:24). However, in the verses immediately before this, the wise king said that life would also have grief and sorrow. "For what hath man of all his labour, and of the vexation of his heart, wherein he hath laboured under the sun? For all his days are sorrows, and his travail grief; yea, his heart taketh not rest in the night. This is also vanity" (vv. 22-23). In light of this, I pray that all those who have lost loved ones in the recent terrorist attacks will find peace, solace, and comfort in a personal relationship with God. And I pray that each individual man, woman, or child will come to see God as a loving and compassionate heavenly Father who wants to take up each grieving person in His arms.

Finally, my prayer today is that many will find the spiritual path that leads to hope and healing, and that all who are suffering pain and loss at this time will still find many good things in life to be happy about. Amen! (See John 16:33; Philippians 4:6-7.)

"God Bless You, Mr. Braca"

I have been reading so many different newspapers about the events that began on September 11. Some of the papers I quickly scan because there is simply too much to absorb. With others I read only a select handful of articles that capture my attention.

In the *New York Times* for Saturday, September 22, page B-13, there was a riveting and emotional array of profiles of some of the victims who perished in the World Trade Center disaster. Most of these profiles were very sad. However there was one that stood out and even caused me to rejoice—not in the person's death, but in this deceased Christian's testimony that no doubt lives on.

His name is Alfred J. Braca, a stranger to me. But what I read encouraged my heart. This piece said that Mr. Braca lived in New Jersey, had been married for thirty-three years, and had four children, all of whom I assume are grown. The profile then told how he first met his wife on the Staten Island ferry many years ago. It gave the names of his children, and then went on to say that Mr. Braca, age fifty-four, "was a born again Christian who never stopped counting his blessings." It also said, "He worked as a bond broker for Cantor Fitzgerald, where co-workers nicknamed him 'The Rev' because of his faith." Finally this little piece poignantly closed with the fact that just last month he walked one of his daughters down the aisle for her wedding. I cried when I read that part. However, I have a gut feeling that this godly man, who was very vocal about his faith, may have been able to lead others who were trapped with him to trust in Christ. I can't help but think that he helped many to make their peace with God before their end came. In fact, I imagine that Mr. Braca faced his own death boldly and fearlessly. In my heart I believe he was used by God in the

> *I imagine that Mr. Braca faced his own death boldly and fearlessly.*

last minutes of his life, high above the streets of lower Manhattan, to be a blessing for those who were afraid.

Though a stranger to me, I am proud of this man, and thankful for his faithful witness to his co-workers. I am looking forward to meeting this man in heaven one day, and I have added his family to my prayer list.

"Usefulness/Giving/Helping"

In my entry for Thursday, September 13, I briefly shared that the effects of these terrorist attacks have even touched those who live and work in the prisons. Few of the inmates have been unmoved by these tragic events. The prison guards, of course, most of whom also seem to be volunteer firemen in their local communities, are all involved in blood drives, food and clothing collections, and attending memorials and candlelight vigils in their towns. And all of that is good. However, many of the prisoners are also trying to help.

> *We have been fervently praying for our President and other government leaders, for those who have been hurt or are in mourning, and, of course, for our nation.*

Yes, there are good things happening in prisons. During the second week of this month, our chaplains held prayer vigils in the chapel and encouraged us to attend. Also, in our little prayer fellowship, which meets twice a week, we have been fervently praying for our President and other government leaders, for those who have been hurt or are in mourning, and, of course, for our nation. In addition, many of us wanted to give blood. I wrote a letter to one of the prison administrators here, asking permission to do so, but he promptly replied that the Federal Food and Drug Administration no longer allows this practice because of the high rate of "tainted blood" among prisoners. I know my blood isn't tainted, but I understand their concern. However, the facility's superintendent did grant us permission to form an ad hoc committee to take up a collection for the Red Cross, and nearly all the inmates gave a donation.

I gave five dollars during the direct collection. Then I was able to give ten dollars through a special collection by the "Christian Community." This collection will be gathered together in one lump sum and given over to the ad hoc committee on behalf of our chapel fellowship. The Lord also provided me with enough so that I was able to send out my own $40 donation to the New York State World Trade Center Disaster Relief Fund in Albany, New York.

I thank God for these opportunities to help, even if it is only in giving small sums of money. And I am not saying this to boast, for such a little amount is no real sacrifice. Besides, God should always be the one to get the glory for everything. And yet I feel a burden to mention these things because I think it is important for Christians and even the general public to know that many inmates care. We grieve like everyone else. We pray for the hurting. And, of course, we have our own regrets over our past actions that got us here.

Right now I believe I am speaking on behalf of many thousands of prisoners whose voices never get heard, whose acts of kindness never get recognized. For the most part, people on the "outside" don't have a clue as to what prison life is really like, and how inmates think and feel during times of crisis and great national loss. I hope I have been able to provide some clarity on those issues. Whether the public is cognizant of this or not, Christ is touching the lives of men and women who are incarcerated, and I'm so glad that He is!

"Yom Kippur/Healing and Hope"

I awoke early on this morning of Yom Kippur, the Jewish "Day of Atonement," to pray and talk with the Lord. I still feel a numbness about all that has happened since the eleventh day of this month. And yet, throughout this ordeal there has been one scripture that has been on my mind continually, which is 2 Chronicles 7:14:

> If my people, which are called by my name, shall humble themselves, and pray, and seek my face, and turn from their wicked ways; then will I hear from heaven, and will forgive their sin, and will heal their land.

I believe this passage says it all. And while some will say it is only applicable to ancient Israel, I think it is just as valid for the Church today, for God always has His people throughout the world and in every nation. As Christians we have been called to make intercession for those who are our government leaders and for all those who are in positions of authority (see 1 Timothy 2:1-8). Jesus said to His disciples, "Ye are the salt of the earth" (Matthew 5:13). Then He went on to say in the following verse, "Ye are the light of the world" (5:14). In both instances, He was talking about us. Christ has called His Church to be a blessing to others, and to impact this world in a good way for God's glory. We have been called to "salt" or "season" the world with God's love, and to shine forth the light of God's goodness to a dark and desperate world.

May the Church yield to the Holy Spirit's guidance and press forward with the Spirit's power in a greater way than ever before. A true healing of America must begin with God's people.

"Two Important Questions"

Remember how short my time is.... What man is he that liveth, and shall not see death? shall he deliver his soul from the hand of the grave? Selah.

—*Psalm 89:47-48*

It is now about ten o'clock in the morning. Today I got up early to pray, and then I listened to the news reports that were coming in after the first day of military strikes in Afghanistan. Like many of the inmates here, and like many people in America, I have been closely following these events.

At the same time we prisoners are not exempt from our own personal tragedies and times of solemnity. For instance, this morning just before breakfast one of the food setup workers, whom I've known for years, suffered a massive heart attack and died while unloading a food cart. Chip had been in prison for more than twenty-five years. He was a chain smoker who rolled his own cigarettes, and his cell never seemed to be without plumes of gray smoke. And yet he was a polite, quiet, well-liked man, known among the inmates as an "old timer." Although he was only in his fifties, the many years he had been confined (about the same number of years as my own confinement so far) classified him as an elder in the system.

> *I could only hope and pray that he received Jesus as Savior before it was too late.*

Shortly after breakfast a corrections officer, who happens to be a Christian, came to my cell to ask if Chip had been a believer in Jesus Christ. This guard is a very decent man, and it was obvious that he was shaken up by what happened, especially since Chip had died right in front of him. Unfortunately I could offer no clear answer regarding Chip's spiritual state at the time of his death. I could only hope and pray that he received Jesus as Savior before it was too late.

In addition to Chip's death, we had another incident just yesterday morning when an inmate named Julio called home, only to discover that his mother had passed away the day before. Julio was understandably devastated. Fortunately he and I were able to pray together before I had to go to the chapel for the Sunday morning service. Julio has had some suicide attempts in the past that were serious enough to require medical attention, and even confinement to a psychiatric hospital for a time, so I will continue to pray for him and check up on him whenever I can. Some of the other prisoners are also pitching in to try to help Julio cope with his loss, bringing him coffee or food, and offering words of encouragement and consolation.

> *It is refreshing to know that God's great plan of salvation is available to any and all who want to receive it.*

Between the war in the Middle East and the threat of more terrorist attacks on America, Chip's sudden death, and Julio's losing his mom, this has indeed been a solemn day. With a pall of death in the air, my scripture readings for this morning from Psalms 89 and 90 have been especially relevant, for the Bible teaches that man is born with a sin nature and is therefore spiritually and eternally dead. While this may sound negative and hopeless, it is not. The Lord Jesus came to reveal to us that it is this very sin nature that necessitates what He called being "born again." Only a supernatural new birth can give new and eternal life to those who are dead, and it is that new birth that enables us to have a personal relationship with our Creator.

Through this divine act of being born again, all of our sins are forgiven and removed. This allows us to be put into good standing with God, and to be able to come near to Him, for no sinners can stand in His holy presence. Furthermore, because of this new birth, the eternal death penalty that hangs over every one of us because of sin can be taken away forever. What a blessing! And this is what the well known scripture of John 3:16 is all about: "For God so loved the world, that he gave his only begotten Son, that whosoever believeth in him should not perish, but have everlasting life."

In this world of seemingly never-ending bad news and stories of suffering and sorrow, it is refreshing to know that God's great plan of salvation is available to any and all who want to receive it. The Lord loves His creation.

He cares about our welfare and our eternal destiny, and He wants us to spend eternity with Him in heaven, not with the devil in hell. God gave His sinless Son to die in our place, and He offers complete forgiveness to all who place their faith in Jesus. This salvation is a free gift because it has already been purchased by the precious blood of God's Son.

This brings me back to the thoughts and questions in Psalm 89. Our time on this earth is so short; who will not see death? All of us will see and experience it. Who shall have his soul delivered from the grave and the eternal punishment for sin? All who place their faith in Jesus Christ will know that deliverance, for such people need no longer fear death.

"An Unfolding Miracle"

Today I want to share something very special and deeply personal. I also want to give glory to the Lord for the way He answers prayers, even if it seems those prayers take far too long to be answered. I actually believe that God answers prayers immediately, but it takes time before the results are visible.

Over the years many Christians, including myself, have been praying for Neysa Moskowitz, whose daughter Stacy perished in the last "Son of Sam" shooting back in 1977. Though I have not been aware of any results of those prayers before this, I now know that God has been working on Mrs. Moskowitz's heart all along. I wrote to her in the past, as I believe God directed me to do, and I wrote again last month. Then, just recently, I heard through a mutual friend that Mrs. Moskowitz would like me to call her. I am feeling a bit overwhelmed by that request. This will be a very delicate and difficult situation for both of us. She has pain. I have painful memories. And, quite honestly, I am afraid and very nervous.

> *God is working on this dear lady's heart because He loves her very much.*

It is so hard to explain. I do want to speak with her, to apologize and reach out to her and see her receive God's comfort. And yet I know that, even after twenty-five years, she still has anger, which, of course, is very natural. Nevertheless, slowly but surely, a miracle is beginning to unfold. God is working on this dear lady's heart because He loves her very much. After all, Jesus said that He came to this earth, in part, to "heal the brokenhearted" and to "comfort all that mourn" (see Isaiah 61:1-3). Therefore, by faith, I believe the best is yet to come for Neysa Moskowitz.

"We Know What time It Is!"

Let your loins be girded about, and your lights burning.
—Luke 12:35

This morning we had our regular prayer meeting in the chapel, as we do almost every Wednesday. I had a blessed time with the Lord, and it was good to see about six brothers in Christ, including my chaplain, praying together. There were so many different needs. We know what is going on in our nation and overseas, and we were grieved to hear about the two postal workers in the Washington, D.C., area who were stricken with and recently died from Anthrax. What a waste of lives. This is a dark time, but God is still in control. And as this sort of thing continues to increase, we Christians recognize what is happening—we know what time it is! We cannot know the day or the hour of the Lord's return, but we know it is close. We have no excuse not to be about our Master's business, even if it is simply interceding on behalf of the Church, the lost, or our nation and its leaders.

> *"We have no excuse not to be about our Master's business, even if it is simply interceding on behalf of the Church, the lost, or our nation and its leaders.*

I believe we are living in the Church's greatest hours since the Day of Pentecost, when the Holy Spirit fell upon the 120 or so believers who were praying and waiting upon the Lord. Then, as these believers went forth in the Spirit's power, they "turned the world upside down" (Acts 17:6). It is time for the Church today to do the same.

It is true that we have witnessed the "falling away" of many churches that have departed from the faith. But there are still many more people in this world right now who are open to the gospel. Their world is being shaken in many ways. The foundations so many have trusted in are collapsing. People are fearful. Many are hurting. Surely this must be the perfect season to proclaim Jesus' words of salvation, hope, and truth!

"Thanksgiving"

Surely goodness and mercy shall follow me all the days of my life...

—*Psalm 23:6*

Today is the official Thanksgiving holiday. For me, it was a very blessed and special day, even though, as a Christian, every day is a time for thanksgiving.

I arose early in the morning to say my prayers. Then I sat silently before the Lord in the darkness of my cell, enjoying the quiet. Prison is a noisy, hectic place. From the morning wake-up bell at 6:30 to the nighttime lock-in bell at 11:00, a prisoner's day is a long one. The cellblock is not a place to find peace and quiet. Rather these things must be found within oneself.

But as I sat in the darkness just before the wake-up bell, I thought of all the goodness and mercy the Lord has bestowed upon me, a man so undeserving. Looking back over more than half a lifetime in prison, I can say with confidence that God has been more than faithful. His grace has been sufficient for every situation I've had to face.

> *But as I sat in the darkness just before the wake-up bell, I thought of all the goodness and mercy the Lord has bestowed upon me, a man so undeserving.*

I know, too, that I have failed my Savior so many times. Yet He has still been there for me, holding me steady, guiding my steps—and yes, even chastening me when necessary. But in the end I can say with full assurance that everything in my life has worked out for the good. In my heart I know I am a better person today, and for that God gets all the glory. Christ is the one who changed my heart, and it is what He has done that really counts.

"September 11 Reflections"

The Lord is my portion, saith my soul; therefore will I hope in Him.
—Lamentations 3:24

This morning I reflected on how much the world has changed since the September 11 terrorist attacks on United States soil. These attacks have altered the course of many lives across the nation, not only for those who lost loved ones, but also for many of us who were profoundly affected by the tragedy. In fact, just the other day I was reminded of my own personal significance regarding the date of September 11, for it was on that date in 1998 that the Lord impressed upon my heart to begin this journal.

Actually, I had forgotten all about the sporadic and irregular beginnings of this work, as I seldom reread my own writings. But it was on this date, after spending time in prayer on the eve of the Rosh Hashanah holiday that year, that I was moved by the Holy Spirit to make my first journal entry. Back then, and still today, I felt an urgency to write, to communicate as best I can, certain things on paper, not for my own benefit but to do my part as a Christian to encourage others as they go through life's struggles. It has long been my desire to honor Jesus Christ by showing the world that what He has done for me He will do for anyone, for God is no respecter of persons. I want "God is love" to be the main theme of my writing so others will understand that He is a being of love, mercy, hope, and help for all people.

> *I want "God is love" to be the main theme of my writing so others will understand that He is a being of love, mercy, hope, and help for all people.*

Furthermore, I want to tell others that He is a God of justice who has, in His infinite wisdom, set a limit to the number of days mankind is to rule and manage this planet. God does have a set time, known only to Him, for the culmination of all things that pertain to this present world system.

Judgment will follow the end of this age, and a new heaven and a new earth are promised to those who have repented of their sins and have placed their faith in Jesus Christ. With these scriptural truths in mind, I sense as always the urgency of the times. Events such as the September 11 terrorist attacks and all that has happened since are not only wake-up calls, but also something of markers and warnings posted along life's highway to remind us that the end of the age and the return of Jesus Christ are getting closer.

For those reasons I found it both ironic and startling when a friend from out west wrote to remind me that I had begun my journal writing on a previous September 11. Perhaps even this journal, then, has something prophetic in it. Only God knows.

"Violence"

Lately I have noticed a "spirit of violence" in this place. Just this past week one inmate from my cellblock got clunked in the head with a large rock during a fight in the outside recreation yard. He ended up with several stitches in his head, though it could have been worse. Several days later another man in my cellblock got slashed across the face and was very seriously wounded. Knowing the victim from observation, I would imagine the incident was probably drug related. Some of these guys bring their habits to prison, and this is the eventual outcome.

Over the years I have seen a lot of violence here. Much of it was defensive, as men had to fight off fellow prisoners for one reason or another. However, I can say with assurance that Jesus Christ reminds me daily never to resort to violence to solve my problems. Of course, I didn't always feel this way. It wasn't until I became a Christian that I got rid of my shank (handmade knife).

> *I could easily have lost my life back in 1979, when another inmate slashed me with a razor blade and missed my main artery by a hairbreadth.*

As far as my own experiences go, I could easily have lost my life back in 1979, when another inmate slashed me with a razor blade and missed my main artery by a hairbreadth. There were other times, too, when I could tell by the look in someone's eyes and by his body posture that he was looking for a way to take my life. God, however, had other plans. I have now endured twenty-five years behind bars, and not because of any special skill or old fashioned good luck. I am alive because the Lord is with me, and I am very thankful for divine protection in such an environment as this.

"Continuing Miracle"

Today it happened. The miracle with Mrs. Moskowitz continues to unfold, as once again the Lord has done far above all I could possibly ask or hope for (see Ephesians 3:20). After weeks of prayer and seeking the Lord's guidance concerning His perfect timing, I went to the prison yard, got to a telephone, and called Neysa Moskowitz.

We have already exchanged several letters. She asked me to call her. But I hadn't yet felt it was the right time to call her, though for the longest time I had dreamed of doing such a thing. Ever since I became a Christian I have prayed for the people I hurt by my past actions. I longed for the moment when, by some great miracle of God, I could actually speak with these hurting people and apologize to them, one by one. Now, after twenty-five years, my dream is becoming a reality, at least with one person.

> *I longed for the moment when, by some great miracle of God, I could actually speak with these hurting people and apologize to them, one by one.*

At ten o'clock on this chilly Saturday morning, I dialed her number. Mrs. Moskowitz was home. I started crying and began apologizing as soon as she answered the phone. I told her how my heart went out to her, and she immediately responded with the words, "I forgive you." We spoke for about twenty minutes, and Mrs. Moskowitz said she refuses to be angry anymore because the anger was poisoning her. We had a good conversation and shared a little about our lives. She also talked a lot about her deceased daughter Stacy. We shared many personal things and even had a few laughs, and then Mrs. Moskowitz insisted that I call her again. At the right time, I will. But for now, much healing has occurred for both of us.

"Back at My Old Job"

I'm so happy to be back at my old job, which consists of being an Intermediate Care Program/Inmate Program Assistant. While this sounds like a big jumble, it basically consists of working with the inmates who have special needs, such as emotional problems and learning disabilities. They frequently have trouble functioning and need someone to help them manage their lives, at least up to a point. I have worked at this particular job on and off, alternating between being an escort for prisoners who need to get around in wheelchairs and those who require other physical help. I was also the chaplain's clerk for several years. But out of all my assignments at this prison, working at the E-North Intermediate Care Program has been the most challenging and rewarding.

> *My job is to help these men in any way I can, going from cell to cell to check up on them, talk to them, see if anyone needs anything, and look for signs of depression or other problems.*

Monday through Friday, at about 8:30 in the morning, I leave my cellblock in the general population and head through the corridors to the E-North cellblock at the opposite end of the facility, where I work until about 11:45 A.M. My job is to help these men in any way I can, going from cell to cell to check up on them, talk to them, see if anyone needs anything, and look for signs of depression or other problems. Some of the men need encouragement just to get out of bed, to get dressed and get on their way. A man may need help writing a letter or filling out a form, such as a request for a sick call or a dentist visit. Others need to fill out forms for prison issued clothing, etc. It is a job I truly enjoy, and feel blessed to be able to perform.

"Suicide Patrol"

My daily prayer is that the Lord might lead me to someone who is hurting and depressed, someone who may even be contemplating suicide. I know how quickly the dark demons of death can slip into a prisoner's mind, making life look so hopeless and presenting suicide as the only way out. Over and over again they whisper, "No one loves you. No one cares. There's no hope. End it all. The world will be better off without you." Believe me, I've been there. For years I heard the same evil voice, and felt that dreadful and powerful urge to die. And, oh, how the devil would love to see one more precious soul, beloved of God, plunge its way into an eternal hell.

Oh, how the devil would love to see one more precious soul, beloved of God, plunge its way into an eternal hell.

If I can be used by God to help save a life, that's wonderful. I just want to be there for others when they are in crisis.

How many prisoners throughout the years have already succumbed to this spirit of suicide? How many have given up on life, especially during the holidays when feelings of failure and loneliness seem to press in more intensely than at other times? That's why, when I'm working in the Intermediate Care Program in the mornings, I walk by each cell and check out each face, looking for a sign, an expression, anything that might indicate that an inmate is thinking of taking his own life.

In one sense, of course, I am only another prison inmate. Yet in another, I am a minister who represents Jesus Christ and who is directed by the Holy Spirit. If I can be used by God to help save a life, that's wonderful. I just want to be there for others when they are in crisis, for this is part of what Christianity is supposed to be about.

"Insanity Part 2"

I am in my cell this evening trying to write, while my neighbor, who lives in another cell about five feet away, screams and carries on like a lunatic. It is simply what he does to pass the time.

Most people have no conception of how unstable and unpredictable prison life is. One day the cellblock might be fairly orderly with a reasonable degree of quiet. Then the next day, for no apparent reason, several dozen men will all seem to be hit with a collective insanity. Each one begins to yell and scream and make all sorts of noise, or just act weird. This then develops into a cacophony of harsh, jarring sounds that bounce off the concrete and steel, funnel into ear canals, and quickly enter the brains of the rest of the prisoners.

> The next day, for no apparent reason, several dozen men will all seem to be hit with a collective insanity.

Thankfully I have a pair of headphones, a Walkman, and some Christian praise tapes, so I can at least partially escape the chaos until, one by one, the screamers finally get tired or bored and stop their crazy behavior. Right now I am longing for the late hours when the noise will come to an end and I can have some good quality quiet time. And then tomorrow it is back to my work assignment, plus other chores I have to do, like lots of laundry.

I am thankful though that God has helped me to survive such a chaotic Christmas. I really do love these men and care about them, but I so appreciate God's grace that has kept me sane all these years.

"Wonder"

As this year comes to an end, I remain thankful for all God has done for me and hopeful about what He will do in the coming year. There are many grieving families in America these days, particularly since the September 11 terrorist attacks. But like multitudes of other Christians, I continue to pray that those who are hurting will be able to go on with their lives, and that God will bless them. So many times this year the Lord has spoken to my heart that I am to use every avenue open to me to remind people that Jesus Christ is a God of healing and hope, and that He offers forgiveness to any who ask for it and are willing to repent of their sins.

About eight o'clock this evening I went to the outside recreation yard for a couple of hours. It was bitterly cold, maybe fifteen degrees, but in the quiet of the winter, under the glaring spotlights along the prison walls, I felt the Holy Spirit's warmth. Now, as the midnight hour nears and 2001 draws to a close, I am listening to a music tape by Annie Herring called "Wonder." As I prepare to be ushered into God's presence for a time of prayer, this is just what I need to hear.

> *It was bitterly cold, maybe fifteen degrees, but in the quiet of the winter under the glaring spotlights along the prison walls, I felt the Holy Spirit's warmth.*

2002

"A New Year"

Once again I begin another new year with gratitude in my heart for all that Messiah Jesus has done for me, and for all the spiritual victories He will bring about in the days and months to come. Of course, I know there will be plenty of trials and tribulations, as well.

After re-reading my journal entries for the first several days of 2000 and 2001, I must say that my feelings are pretty much the same this January 1 as they have been in previous years. As always, it is important to acknowl-

> *"A New Year"*
> *I once heard a minister say, "Letting the past swallow up the future is an awful waste of a lifetime."*

edge the sins and mistakes of my past, as I know that my evil actions have affected others and hurt them deeply. But at the same time, God's Word forbids me to beat myself up over sins that God has removed as far as the east is from the west.

I once heard a minister say, "Letting the past swallow up the future is an awful waste of a lifetime." That is absolutely true, so as 2001 becomes a memory and 2002 a reality, I must say goodbye to the past and look with hopeful expectation to the future.

"The Continuing Miracle"

More than once I have mentioned the wonderful work God is doing between me and Neysa Moskowitz, the lady whose daughter Stacy died in the last "Son of Sam" shooting in 1977. I spoke to Mrs. Moskowitz for the second time on December 29 and was able to wish her many blessings for the coming year.

Mrs. Moskowitz is a sixty-eight-year-old widow who lives alone, and whose life has been a string of unending tragedies and losses. She is well acquainted with grief and sorrow, having lost her husband, Jerry, as well as all her children, three daughters, to untimely deaths. In addition, she has several serious medical problems, including a bad back, which causes her periods of excruciating pain. However, I believe that Jesus the Messiah has chosen Neysa Moskowitz for salvation, and I look forward to the day when she will receive Jesus as her Savior.

> *All through the Bible there are examples of God's heart being moved by the sufferings of widows. Mrs. Moskowitz is no exception.*

All through the Bible there are examples of God's heart being moved by the sufferings of widows. Mrs. Moskowitz is no exception. The God of Israel has a good plan for her, and it will come to pass in His time.

"Miracle Move"

It was music to my ears! Shortly after yesterday's lunch meal the correction's officer in charge of the A-North cellblock came to tell me to "pack up" because I was being moved to another cellblock. A number of hours later, at about 5:30 in the evening, I finished loading up a moving cart and was on my way out of what had become a "spiritual war zone" for me. I was moving to another housing unit at the opposite end of the facility, and to a new ministry. I said goodbye to my screaming neighbor, who actually seemed angry that I was leaving. I suppose the devil will now have to think up another strategy of harassment, but until then, I will be living peaceably in the D-North cell block (a.k.a. "housing unit").

> *I had been praying for some time to be able to reach out to these handicapped men more often.*

This move was truly by the hand of the Lord, for once again He is enlarging my territory. I am now living in the housing unit with the inmates who are "sensorially disabled" (hearing-impaired) and/or visually-impaired. Not all of the men who live in this cellblock are handicapped, but many are, and this is the area where I will now be ministering. I had been praying for some time to be able to reach out to these handicapped men more often. This, therefore, will be a great opportunity to make new friends and to share the gospel.

Right now, however, my new cell is in chaos. I still have to unpack my things and do a lot of cleaning. I have been on my hands and knees scrubbing and disinfecting almost all day. When I am through with that, I will need another miracle, which is finding a can of paint. But I don't mind. This move is like a new beginning for me.

"A Cop's Son"

Yesterday I took a ninety-minute training course given by a civilian instructor on how to be a sighted guide—in other words, how to help and escort someone who is blind. With the visually impaired prisoners in my cellblock, it seemed like a good idea. I know that working with the visually impaired is going to be a personal challenge for me, but I'm hoping to be able to take one of them with me to the chapel services once in a while. It is a long walk from the cellblock to the chapel, as these two places are at opposite ends of the facility. I will have to help a blind man navigate through the hallways and corridors, as well as through the crowds of other prisoners who are moving about.

Today I was able to sit down and talk to a forty-two-year-old black prisoner who is doing time for robbery and drug possession. He is not

> *It doesn't matter whether we come from a good home or a bad one, sin is sin.*

one of the blind or hearing impaired men, but he lives in my housing unit. We had an interesting talk about Jesus Christ. Like most of the men here, he is very familiar with my criminal past, so he asked me some questions and I was able to give him a little of my testimony about how Jesus had changed my life.

What really surprised me, however, was when he told me that his mother is a retired New York City police officer who was on the force for twenty-seven years. I couldn't help but notice the irony of the situation. This man is a career criminal, who in his own words spent much of his adult life in and out of prison, while his mom had a successful career in law enforcement. As I have often observed during my quarter-century of being in prison, it doesn't matter whether we come from a good home or a bad one, sin is sin. The Bible explains that we've all been born with a sin nature and an innate propensity to do bad things and to break God's holy laws. Anyone from any background is capable of committing a crime. This is why

> *Anyone from any background is capable of committing a crime.*

the worldwide inmate population consists not only of men and women from the ghettoes of poverty, but also doctors, lawyers, and police officers. Satan is no respecter of persons, anymore than God is. The devil is out to destroy anyone and everyone he can, rich or poor, black or white.

We all need to repent of our sins, and we all need to place our faith and trust in Jesus Christ for salvation, for the Bible tells us in Romans 3:10 that no one is righteous, not even one person. Every human being who has ever lived needs God's forgiveness, and there is no other way to receive it except through Jesus Christ.

"Two More for Hell"

The Bible says that "hell and destruction are never full" (Proverbs 27:20). There is always room for more souls in that place of torment, and earlier today two young men plunged into hell forever. They lived as criminals and drug dealers, and before the sun came up on this gorgeous day, they had already gone to their eternal home.

Ordinarily I am up early on Sundays to pray and have a quiet time of meditation before the 6:30 wake-up bell sounds and the cellblock stirs to life. As a result I seldom listen to the news channels on my radio. Today, however, I decided to turn to the CBS all news station out of New York City. When I did, I heard the news about a violent shootout in the Bronx that left two young men dead and a third man seriously wounded. The report said the men were supposedly selling marijuana out of an apartment on the fourth floor of a tenement building when someone tried to rob them and gunshots were exchanged. In the end, two young men lay dead while the

"Two More for Hell" Others, like the two young men who died today, will end up chilling on slabs in the city morgue.

killers fled into the night. Immediately I began to think about the men who died, though their names were not mentioned. I also thought of their families, of crying mothers and of fathers who had hopes that their sons would grow up and do well in life. Now all they have left is broken hearts and shattered dreams.

I have strong words to share right now, for I believe God's heart breaks when He sees young men and women choosing to commit crimes. He knows the road they are taking will ultimately ruin their lives. Many will waste precious years in prison and end up with criminal records that will haunt them for a lifetime. Others, like the two young men who died today, will end up chilling on slabs in the city morgue.

God offers something so much better. He has a plan and purpose for everyone. God does not want anyone to perish and spend eternity in hell. His desire is that all should repent of their sins and place their faith in Jesus Christ. My prayer today is that Christians will take seriously the call to evangelize and to seek out the lost. Too many are perishing, and hell is still hungry for more. We need a vision of what it must be like for a young person to plunge into hell. We need to see the despair and hopelessness. We need the courage to go into every corner of the world and proclaim the way of salvation. May we have hearts of love that truly care!

The Bible says we are the salt and light of this world. In other words, we can make a difference. We can impact our generation for Christ and see that many are delivered from degradation and death if we are willing to give everything to show others that Jesus is their only hope.

> *My prayer today is that Christians will take seriously the call to evangelize and to seek out the lost. Too many are perishing, and hell is still hungry for more.*

"Baby Faces"

They look more like young Army recruits fresh out of high school and just getting ready to begin basic training than convicted felons facing long prison sentences. Yet this is the type of inmate I see coming into the prison today. In the neighborhoods where they grew up, many lived by a code of violence, and yet, despite the looks of anger and bewilderment on their faces, they seem to have retained some of their childhood innocence and naiveté.

To tell you the truth, this younger generation of baby-faced criminals seems so out of place in here. This is an entirely different generation than my own, but I relate to them because they are traveling down the same road I traveled more than two decades ago. It is the road of sin, sickness, sorrow, misery, and ultimately death. The Bible says, "There is no new thing under the sun" (Ecclesiastes 1:9), so it is no surprise that this road is heavily traveled. In fact, I believe this heavily traveled road of ruin is the broad highway described by our Savior as the one that eventually ends at the mouth of hell.

> *This is an entirely different generation than my own, but I relate to them because they are traveling down the same road I traveled more than two decades ago.*

As the Lord Jesus said, "Enter ye in at the strait gate: for wide is the gate, and broad is the way, that leadeth to destruction, and many there be which go in thereat; Because strait is the gate, and narrow is the way, which leadeth unto life, and few there be that find it" (Matthew 7:13, 7:14). May we dedicate ourselves to prayer that God will use us to lead others away from the broad path of destruction and onto the narrow way that leads to eternal life.

"Talmeek"

It is often a difficult and risky thing to talk about Jesus Christ with Muslim prisoners, who far outnumber us born-again Christians. But this month the Lord has allowed me to share about Jesus with a Muslim prisoner named Talmeek, who lives in a cell near me and is only ten years into a very long sentence. We have become friends, to some degree, and he has been sharing with me many things about his life, especially his struggles and disappointments.

> *I told Talmeek in no uncertain terms that it is Christ who gives me inner peace and a reason to live.*

Talmeek seldom hears from his family, and it saddens him, making him feel like a forgotten man. Yet even in his darkness he is drawn to me because he sees the light of Jesus Christ shining in me. He said he finds it amazing that I am at peace and have such joy, as well as an easy-going attitude, even after being locked up for almost a quarter of a century. He has admitted to me that bitterness is poisoning his soul, and he is feeling very confused and unsettled right now. I told Talmeek in no uncertain terms that it is Christ who gives me inner peace and a reason to live. I have also shown him some of the photos sent to me by some friends in Africa. Talmeek finds it surprising that a white man in prison has friends in Africa. I explained that Christians are really one big family, that our love transcends all human boundaries and colors, and that we are all part of one Body in Christ.

"Sharing with Other Muslims"

Yesterday I talked about my Muslim neighbor Talmeek and how the Lord has allowed us to become friends. I was also encouraged earlier this month when another Muslim named Abdul sat next to me in the class I attend on weekday afternoons. He asked me about the book I had on my desk, More than a Carpenter, by Josh McDowell. This is a classic Christian work, well known to many believers. Josh McDowell specializes in the field of apologetics, vigorously explaining and defending the life and teachings of the Lord Jesus Christ. I felt led by the Holy Spirit to ask Abdul if he would like to have the book. We had been speaking in whispers, and when I asked him this question, he looked around the room to see if anyone was watching. When he was satisfied that

> *I know Abdul will read the book in secret, and I also know God is going to speak to his mind and heart.*

no one was paying attention to us, he said yes. I gave him the book, and he quickly stuffed into his school bag. I know Abdul will read the book in secret, and I also know God is going to speak to his mind and heart. A seed will be planted.

Still another Muslim named Hameed recently came to me and asked questions about what I believe. We had a good conversation, and I was pleased to learn that his sister attends a large evangelistic church in Brooklyn. I know she has been praying for him, and his heart is already being softened.

"Melendez"

I just learned that several days ago a man I knew and had recently spoken to had died from AIDS in the prison's infirmary. His last name was Melendez, though I never learned his first name. He was in his late thirties, and I believe he was from Honduras. Melendez was very poor and always wore the same clothes. He spoke very little English and didn't talk much to anyone, even the many prisoners who speak Spanish. When he first arrived at this facility he went to the chapel on occasion, but then he stopped attending services. When I would pass his cell I noticed he was almost always sleeping. Even when he walked the hallways, he seemed to exhibit a perpetual weariness. Yet he was a nice man, and we sometimes exchanged greetings. And then he disappeared.

> *Melendez died alone.*

I hadn't seen him for months and thought he had been transferred to another facility. I had no idea that Melendez had AIDS. I later learned that one day he was admitted to the infirmary and never got the chance to leave. Melendez died alone. The news of his death made me sad. He had come to America to escape the oppressive poverty in his country, only to die young and be buried in our potter's field.

"Parole"

It was inevitable that someone from the media was going to try to make an issue of my tentatively scheduled parole hearing in June. On Sunday, February 17, the *NEW YORK DAILY NEWS* published a full-page article about it. The reporter had talked to some of the families who were hurt by my criminal actions, including Neysa Moskowitz. This, of course, resulted in an explosion of media coverage. Since the reporter never asked for my opinions on this matter, I will give them here.

The fact is that I have absolutely no interest in obtaining parole, and I have done nothing to try to get it. For example, I have never asked any of my many Christian friends, a number of whom I have known for many years, to write letters of support for me. I have never asked any church or ministry to gather up petitions and signatures to send to a state legislature or to the commissioner of parole or to the governor. And I have never asked any prison officials, including administrators, counselors, correction officers, or civilian staff, to write letters on my behalf or to support me for release. I simply do not believe in doing any of these things.

> *The fact is that I have absolutely no interest in obtaining parole, and I have done nothing to try to get it.*

"More About the Parole"

I have some strong words to say today. Nevertheless, I continue to pray for the healing of the families of those I hurt or killed. I have been doing this for many years, as have other Christians. However, I am sure this recent burst of publicity regarding the hearing is causing my victims much anxiety, aggravation, confusion, pain, and fear. This is not fair to them, but there is nothing I can do about it. I am convinced that some members of the media have no real concern for crime victims. They view them only as people to use for a story, and there is a clever manipulating of emotions when the media wants a certain reaction and response.

> *I am learning to be content with my present circumstances, and God is using me right where I am.*

Though I hope I am wrong, I foresee a media circus. I see my victims boiling with rage and suffering needless worry. I also see media outlets inadvertently working to create fear, anger, and hysteria because they have not informed the general public that I am not seeking parole. Instead the media has created an impression that I am actively seeking release. This is absolutely false, but it has the effect of agitating people and making them angry.

The truth is, I am not getting out of prison. I am learning to be content with my present circumstances, and God is using me right where I am.

"Royce"

I liked Royce as soon as I met him. Because he is almost completely blind and also hearing impaired, he sort of stumbled his way into my cell one day to ask for a cup of coffee. Then he told me he was feeling down and needed a little conversation.

No one can help but like Royce. In spite of the fact that his state-issued green prison uniform always looks as if he had slept in it, he has a perky personality. Most of the time, especially when he has a cigarette in his mouth and a cup of coffee in his hand, Royce remains cheerful and brisk, always ready to joke around. Plain and simple, he is a nice person. Like many of the men in here, he had a bad drinking problem. He also has a hot temper, and when he gets angry he can be mean and nasty. It is quite a sight to see a blind man throwing a tantrum, swinging his fists in the air in a wild frenzy, screaming and cussing too. But other than his tantrums, which usually come about because of the idiots who like to tease him and seldom last very long, Royce is a great guy to talk with.

> *Like many of the men in here, he had a bad drinking problem.*

Lately I have been telling Royce about Jesus and the gospel. Because Royce is blind, a sighted guide must escort him everywhere he goes. However, I haven't been able to take him to the chapel yet because I'm not assigned as his guide. I hope one of these days I will be appointed to him. Meanwhile I'm praying for Royce, and I would love to see him receive Jesus Christ as his Savior and Lord. I believe this will happen in time.

Now that I am living in a cellblock with a number of handicapped men, I can see for myself how they manage and survive. It really is an impressive sight to watch these determined men get around, despite their loss of eyesight, hearing, or both. These humble men have a lot to teach those of us who are blessed with good health.

"The Governor"

What I have done by my criminal actions is inexcusable, and as a result many are still suffering today. However, what some people in the news media have done in recent weeks is also inexcusable. They have given out incomplete information, and in the process reopened many wounds. Even Governor Pataki publicly denounced the upcoming parole hearing, vowing to fight against my release. I respect the governor's position, and I am very impressed by the way he has carried himself while in office. However, this is just another example of media misinformation.

I have decided to write a fairly short, polite, and respectful letter to Governor Pataki to assure him that, contrary to the impressions given by the media, I agree with him that I do not deserve parole, nor am I trying to obtain it. This will give me a chance to express my sorrow over this tragedy and tell him that I am trying to make amends to society wherever possible. I will explain that I always pray for those I hurt, and that I long to see them healed. I believe the Lord will give me the right words, and that this letter will help clarify the situation.

> *I have decided to write a fairly short, polite, and respectful letter to Governor Pataki to assure him that, contrary to the impressions given by the media, I agree with him that I do not deserve parole, nor am I trying to obtain it.*

Furthermore, when the letter is completed, I will send it out by certified mail. I do not expect a response from the governor, as there is no reason for him to reply. But at least I will know the letter has reached his office, and that will be good enough.

"Reconciliation"

O worship the Lord in the beauty of holiness...

—Psalm 96:9a

The Church is alive and thriving behind these prison walls. These men love Jesus, and it is truly glorious to worship the Lord in the beauty of holiness. The Christian prisoners are grateful for their salvation. Jesus said in Luke 7 that those who have been forgiven of many sins love God more than those who have been forgiven of few. Just yesterday during our Wednesday evening Bible class, a man named Julio told how he had led his mother to the Lord by writing his testimony and explaining the gospel to her through the letters he sent to her in Puerto Rico.

> *Jesus said in Luke 7 that those who have been forgiven of many sins love God more than those who have been forgiven of few.*

Julio comes from a dysfunctional family. He had been estranged from his mother for a number of years, and now he is serving a life sentence for a homicide that took place during a robbery. But on October 7, 2000, Julio received Jesus Christ as his Savior right here in the Sullivan Correctional Facility's chapel. Shortly after he felt the need to reach out to his mom and apologize for causing her so much grief. Within the next year she was able to forgive him, and now they are corresponding regularly.

Julio's mother is too poor to make her way to New York to visit her son, but since they are now both sharing a common faith in Christ, God has bonded them closer than ever before. Truly nothing is impossible with God!

"More than Conquerors"

...in all these things we are more than conquerors through him that loved us.

—*Romans 8:37*

O nce again the Lord has given me another opportunity to touch lives and reach out beyond these prison walls. This morning I gave a twenty-five minute interview with a Christian radio station in Fort Wayne, Indiana. The call letters of the station are WFCV AM 1090, and the program is called "More Than Conquerors." The interview seemed to turn out well. Only the Lord knows the outcome, but I pray that people from all walks of life will hear the message of hope. Maybe a prisoner in the county jail or someone confined to a hospital bed will learn that God is willing to forgive the sins of anyone, including a man like myself.

> *Maybe a prisoner in the county jail or someone confined to a hospital bed will learn that God is willing to forgive the sins of anyone, including a man like myself.*

The Lord also had me share some words to encourage the body of Christ not to forget those who are in prison, to share the gospel with their neighbors, and to show love and kindness to everyone. Love is still the best witness, and the Bible says that "God is love" (1 John 4:8, 4:16).

At the end of the program the host and I prayed for the President of the United States and for our nation. As my time to speak was over and I hung up the telephone, I quietly thanked my God for once again giving me the blessed privilege of proclaiming His goodness and mercy to a troubled world.

"A Friend in Ohio"

Brethren, my heart's desire and prayer to God for Israel is, that they might be saved.

—Romans 10:1

I received a warm and encouraging letter from a man who lives in Ohio with his wife and four children. He read my testimony on my Web site and felt compelled to write to me. I am grateful for his encouragement, for my heart has been heavy concerning the upcoming parole hearing and whatever "old stuff" will come out as the twenty-five-year mark approaches.

This man told me that he and his immediate family are all Jews who believe that Jesus is the Messiah. I was happy to hear this because, even though he and I are strangers, in a sense we are already bonded in love, brothers of the "household of faith." He also mentioned that his son is studying to be a Messianic Rabbi.

> *As for Israel and my fellow Jews, I have to say along with the apostle Paul that my heart's desire is to see them come to a full knowledge of who Jesus (Yeshua) is, and to place their faith in Him.*

When I answered his letter I told about my own experiences as a Jew growing up in New York City, "The Bronx." I told him about being raised by loving parents, and while my father was not religious, my mother definitely was. I wrote about how my mother observed the main traditional Jewish holidays, lit candles every Friday evening at sundown in honor of the Sabbath, and diligently kept a kosher home. Just writing about these things brought back fond memories and a deep longing to go back in time and relive those better days. But even then my life was not idyllic, for my youth was a time of emotional pain and troubles. Yet the good memories do live on.

As for Israel and my fellow Jews, I have to say along with the apostle Paul that my heart's desire is to see them come to a full knowledge of who Jesus (Yeshua) is, and to place their faith in Him.

This evening I am going to read Romans 9-11, where Paul gives a wonderful discourse on Jews and Gentiles, and declares that God's salvation is now available to all people through His Son, Jesus. "For whosoever shall call upon the name of the Lord shall be saved" (Romans 10:13). My prayer is, "Lord, please help my fellow Jews and Gentiles everywhere to know You and Your righteousness, which comes through Jesus the Messiah. Amen."

"Victory Ahead"

Today I mailed my letter to Governor George E. Pataki. I sent it by certified mail, with a return receipt card so I will know it reached his office. I believe the Lord gave me the words to say, as it is my desire for all to know my feelings concerning parole.

Speaking of parole, today I was called to meet with a parole officer. She was very honest and open, and it was a pleasure to speak with her. Every inmate must meet with a local parole officer at least two months in advance of the scheduled hearing date. This officer and I talked for over an hour and agreed about wanting the families to know that I am not trying to get paroled. The officer suggested I write a short statement about my feelings and get it to her within a week. She promised to include it with her report, which must be sent to the Office of Parole in Albany.

> *This officer and I talked for over an hour and agreed about wanting the families to know that I am not trying to get paroled.*

Things are going better than I expected and progress is being made. Hopefully these hurting families will soon have the closure they want and need.

"Darrell Scott"

Friday, March 29, was definitely a "Good Friday," for I was blessed and privileged to have a visit from Darrell Scott, who lost his beloved daughter, Rachel, in the Columbine High School shooting rampage on April 20, 1999. Darrell came with two other men, John and Danny. The three of them travel around, sharing the gospel and telling people that God cares about them. Darrell also tells of his daughter's life, her kindness, and her compassion, for Rachel Joy Scott was a faithful witness for Jesus Christ. Even after her death, Rachel's message lives on, touching hearts and giving hope.

We all prayed together and had a warm time of fellowship. I told Darrell I felt so unworthy to meet him, yet once again God has shown His power and sovereignty by bringing Darrell and me together, breaking down the walls between a convicted felon and a man who lost his daughter to gun violence.

> *I told Darrell I felt so unworthy to meet him.*

Darrell Scott has a vision for discipling Christian teenagers to impact this world with God's love. I told him I thought that was a wonderful idea. I know his plans and dreams will come to fruition because we serve a big God. "For with God nothing shall be impossible" (Luke 1:37).

"A Setback"

There has been a setback in my relationship with Neysa Moskowitz. A lot of healing and forgiveness had taken place in previous months, but now things seem to have reversed themselves. Mrs. Moskowitz wanted me to participate in a media project where we would go before a live camera and meet together for the first time. I was tempted to do this for her sake, as the producer was going to pay her for it, though I have no idea how much. I, of course, would get no compensation, nor would I want to. But after much prayer I just didn't feel it was something the Lord wanted me to do. Mrs. Moskowitz was very disappointed and angry at my decision, but in spite of her protests, I had to decline. Now, sadly, Mrs. Moskowitz is livid with anger. She hasn't answered my last few letters and even swears when she speaks of me with our mutual Christian friend, Betty.

> *Mrs. Moskowitz was very disappointed and angry at my decision, but in spite of her protests, I had to decline.*

This is a sorrowful situation, and my heart is heavy because of it. I will continue to pray for Mrs. Moskowitz, yet I feel as if ten years have been lost and we have moved backward to the days when she openly railed against me.

Ultimately God can change any situation, and so I will leave it with Him to do so. I had to do what I believed was right, and I must live to please God at any cost.

"Lies!"

Blessed are ye, when men shall revile you, and persecute you, and shall say all manner of evil against you falsely, for my sake.
—*Matthew 5:11*

No matter what I go through or what I must face from day to day, I know the Lord is with me. Even my painful trials are for a purpose. I may not understand why, but I am not required to know everything. I must simply trust in my God with childlike faith, knowing He has everything under control and I am in His loving care. And so, at breakfast this morning, when I received the news that the media had begun to go after the families of the victims of my crimes and some of the surviving victims themselves, I knew it was for a reason.

I have absolutely nothing against these people speaking out. Naturally they are angry with me, and they hate me very much. I don't blame them for feeling this way because I am the one who hurt them and brought so much pain, grief, and sorrow into their lives. However, what did hurt was when some of them attacked my faith in Christ. The father of one of my victims called me a fake and a phony and publicly alleged that my

> *I believe these victims are being exploited by those who capitalize on their anger.*

Christianity was a sham. Another person said I was playing the role of a Christian in order to get out and kill again.

When I received these reports from concerned inmates who were trying to look out for my welfare, I went back to my cell for a good cry and a long talk with the Lord. Frankly, I don't care if people hate me for my past. I expect them to be angry and to despise me, even as I despise my own criminal actions. But I asked for God's forgiveness a long time ago. I repented of my sins and poured out my heart in remorse to Jesus Christ. I believe, too, that in heaven there are a lot of tear-filled bottles with my name on them.

In any event, before noon the Lord had completely encouraged and strengthened me in my spirit. He took away the pain of rejection and the agony of condemnation that the world spills out in endless supply. Angry people who do not know my heart and who have a burning hatred for me wasted no time maligning me, and this in front of millions of people.

Amazingly, in this dark moment of my soul, the Lord spoke to my spirit and told me to relax. He comforted me with His love and told me there is a big reward waiting if I stay faithful to Him. He encouraged me to maintain my Christian testimony, no matter what others say. These people have spoken falsely, but I forgive them and pray God's best for their lives. Sadly, however, I believe these victims are being exploited by those who capitalize on their anger. I knew eventually this would happen, but I find it ironic that in today's "information age," the media has kept the public ignorant of my true feelings about this upcoming parole hearing, even when my views are readily available on the Internet.

I pray this hearing will soon be over so everyone involved can get on with their lives. Now, however, I must learn to endure the false accusations and lies that have been spoken against me. I love Jesus Christ. He is my Savior and my Lord. The world can mock me, but my life has been hid in Christ. I belong to Him forever.

"Death Sentence"

I was listening to a new program on NPR radio when a report came on about prisoners and AIDS. This report stated that there are currently about 7,100 New York State inmates out of a population of approximately 65,000 that are HIV positive. While a majority of these inmates are not yet considered sick, as they are not showing any symptoms, they still carry the virus. These HIV-infected prisoners, whose lives are prime examples of the devastation of sin, are living under a virtual death sentence. Their poor choices have cursed them, leaving them infected with a deadly virus that has no cure. Some of these men and women will die while incarcerated. Others will get out of prison and return to their old haunts and habits. Many will rejoin the ranks of the homeless, finding their way to city shelters or halfway houses, or settling for the streets, sleeping in parks or under bridges. It is tragic, but when you consider that these people already have a criminal record and a deadly disease, there is little chance they will ever lead healthy, satisfying, or productive lives.

> *I do not see my life in prison as a waste, but rather as a blessed opportunity to speak words of encouragement, to do what Christ has called me to do, to spread His love where there is so much hatred.*

As a Christian, I view this prison as my mission field. The men here have, for the most part, ruined their lives, and they know it. Regret is a constant, tormenting companion. And while many may have no interest in changing, some truly do want a new life. They are tired and burned out from their lives of crime and addiction. Many have lost everything good they ever had, such as wives, children, and jobs. Yet in just such an environment men are open and hungry for spiritual solutions to their bondages. Therefore, it is here that I must work, holding out to them the gospel of hope and peace.

I do not see my life in prison as a waste, but rather as a blessed opportunity to speak words of encouragement, to do what Christ has called me to do, to spread His love where there is so much hatred.

Like St. Francis of Assisi, I have been blessed by God to have the opportunity to bring good things where bad seems to dominate. Where there is sadness, I can bring joy. I can do my part to spread the spirit of forgiveness. I can seek to comfort others as God has already comforted me.

"Parole Hearing"

My parole hearing was today. There were eight other men scheduled to appear before the parole board from the main prison where I am housed, as well as twenty-one men from the minimum security annex just up the road. The two parole commissioners really had their hands full, as they held all the hearings here in the main prison and then went to the annex to meet with the men there.

Last week, after thinking things over and doing a lot of soul-searching, I decided I did not want to attend my hearing. I had wrestled long and hard with this and asked God for guidance, so this was not a hasty decision. However, I felt that by not attending I was clearly demonstrating to the families of my victims that I have absolutely no interest in getting out of prison. I wrote to my parole officer on May 28 and explained my feelings, and she was very understanding, stating that it would not be a problem if I did not go. Every inmate has the option to attend his hearing, and nearly everyone does. I am one of a tiny fraction of prisoners statewide who opted not to go.

> *Last week, after thinking things over and doing a lot of soul-searching, I decided I did not want to attend my hearing.*

I have accepted my sentence, and I am doing my time. There is really nothing more I can do to show my remorse.

"Committed"

As June comes to a close I want to thank God for taking me through every storm and affliction that came my way this month. June has been a month of pruning. I know the Lord Jesus has removed some things from my life that needed to go. I also know this necessary but painful pruning is for the purpose of bearing more spiritual fruit for God's glory. I have committed my life to following Christ, and so I must accept the pain as well as the victory. There is no middle road and no place for compromise. Being a soldier for the Lord, as the apostle Paul said, is no easy task. Yet the Bible encourages us to "be strong in the grace that is in Christ Jesus" (2 Timothy 2:1), and to "endure hardness, as a good soldier of Jesus Christ" (v. 3).

> *Even more important, I know He is holding on to me.*

In this walk many people have rejected me. Many think my Christianity is nonsense. Nevertheless, I have determined in my heart that I will serve the Lord. As the beloved old hymn declares, "I have decided to follow Jesus.... Though none go with me, still I will follow." I want this to be my attitude and my battle cry—that by His grace I will hold on to Jesus, no matter what happens. Even more important, I know He is holding on to me.

I am likewise learning to accept the fact that there will always be people who will hate me because of the past and be indifferent to anything I might say. Still, I humbly thank the Lord for all who have already been encouraged by my testimony, and for all who will be blessed and encouraged by it in the future.

"JayBee"

JayBee was released from this correctional facility during the spring of last year, paroled back to the Bronx where he had lived before coming to prison about nine years earlier. When JayBee got ready to leave, we said our goodbyes, and the evening before his release the Christians in our fellowship gathered to pray for him at the end of a chapel service. Now, slightly over one year later as I was spending some time out in the recreation yard this past Saturday morning, I spotted his familiar face and unique smile just a hundred feet away. JayBee had returned, perhaps to the only safe world he has ever known. Though I was disappointed to see him back, he was happy to see me. He told me he was violated by his parole officer for drinking and for breaking "lots of rules." We walked around the yard together until we caught up with several other Christians, and we all had a mini-reunion.

> JayBee's chances of making it on the outside were just about nonexistent.

JayBee is forty-one years old, though he looks much older. He has been in and out of prisons and mental institutions most of his adult life. He is nearly illiterate, at best able to print his name. When JayBee left here last spring he hoped to rejoin his brother in the Bronx, but it seems his brother wasn't too happy to see Jaybee. Their relationship had never been close, and the nine years prior to JayBee's coming here last time he had drifted in and out of overcrowded shelters, lived in a cardboard box, and eaten wherever and whatever he could. During the long cold winters he had ridden the subways from one end of the city to the other, trying to stay warm, kill time, and survive until the spring thaw. Obviously JayBee and his brother had little contact during that time, and the brother was no more anxious for a relationship now than he had been before Jaybee went to prison

I first met Jaybee at one of our chapel services right after he accepted the Lord a few years ago. He seemed happy and content at the time, and attended all the Bible studies. He often sat next to me and, though he couldn't read, he listened closely and asked questions. Jaybee is a survivor. Unfortunately, he is also an alcoholic. With no outside contacts, no job, and lots of emotional problems as well as his ongoing battle with alcohol, JayBee's chances of making it on the outside were just about nonexistent.

Now he is back, sporting his ever-present two-day stubble and a big smile that shows his crooked teeth. It is obvious he has lost weight, a testament to his struggle to survive while outside the prison walls. But now he is back in the hands of the Christian brothers who care about him, and he seems relieved and content.

"The Parole Board"

Though I did not attend my parole board hearing in June, I have recently been going through a tremendous inner struggle, trying to decide if I should go before the board today. Finally this morning I decided the best and most proper thing would be to appear before them.

I did not go seeking parole. I explained this to the commissioners right away, just as I had done in my March 25 letter to Governor George Pataki, when I wrote: "For if and when I go to this hearing, it will only be to show respect to the parole board, to apologize and take responsibility for my criminal actions, and to basically tell them what I am now telling you—that I do not deserve parole."

I believe the Lord wanted me to go to this hearing and to represent Him there by publicly apologizing for what I did in 1976-77. There were two women parole commissioners present, representing both the governor and the public, as well as several parole or prison personnel. The hearing itself lasted about an hour, maybe less.

> *I believe the Lord wanted me to go to this hearing and to represent Him there by publicly apologizing for what I did in 1976-77.*

Everything went well. While many of their questions were painful and difficult to answer, as they involved my crimes and what led up to them, I had the chance to tell the commissioners what has happened in my life since that time. In response to their direct questions, I spoke of my faith in Christ. This opportunity surprised me, as I hadn't expected the board to ask about my feelings about God. They seemed genuinely interested in hearing what has given me my inspiration and hope, and why I seem to have such a good outlook on life.

"More Media Misinformation"

The media is so predictable. Just as it happened twenty-five years ago, from yesterday morning and all throughout today, virtually every news media outlet on radio and TV (and I also assume in the newspapers, though I haven't seen any of them yet) was abuzz with stories about my parole hearing. And, of course, it is no surprise that, whether through ignorance of all the facts or bias against me, some of the information presented to the public was incorrect.

> *"More Media Misinformation" The parole board was fully aware before the hearing that I was not seeking release.*

All the news I heard on the radio or TV reported that my "bid" or "attempt" to get parole had been denied. What the media did not report was that I had made no such bid or attempt. The parole board was fully aware before the hearing that I was not seeking release, for as I said in my March 25 letter to Governor Pataki, "For if and when I go to this hearing, it will only be to show respect to the parole board, to apologize and take responsibility for my criminal actions, and to basically tell them what I am now telling you—that I do not deserve parole." And that is exactly what I did at today's parole board hearing.

I am saddened to see this "Summer of 77" hysteria back in full force. It hurts to hear the continuous reports about my "bid for freedom" when I made no such bid and those so-called news reports were completely untrue.

"Exhausted"

I am presently going into a recuperation phase to get refreshed and re-energized. But I already feel a tremendous weight off me now that the parole hearing is over. Although I do feel physically and emotionally exhausted from this recent wave of trials and challenges, my heart remains knitted to the Lord's. I belong to Jesus, and He belongs to me.

In my quiet time with the Lord today, the Holy Spirit reminded me that nothing can separate me from God's love. Because I am in the Lord's hands, I have been able to experience a deeper fellowship with Him. Though we all have disappointments and difficulties, hardships and struggles, they will only serve to keep us humble and clinging more tightly to Christ, for it is in these situations that God faithfully provides His enabling strength so we can endure and not give up.

> *In my quiet time with the Lord today, the Holy Spirit reminded me that nothing can separate me from God's love.*

Of course, Satan tries his best to darken our testimony. I know in my own case he works hard at keeping people focused on my past, rather than what I am today. But this is part of the battle. Satan doesn't want us to be free of the past. He wants to keep us prisoners to it, even though God through Jesus Christ has already set us free. And the devil will use anything he can to accomplish his objectives. In my case he uses the media to keep my past in the public eye, hoping somehow to torment me and rob me of my peace. Yet I know what the Word of God says: I am a new creation in Christ. Old things have passed away, and all things have become new (see 2 Corinthians. 5:17). God's Word is stronger than Satan, and His Word will prevail. For me, that is all that counts!

"God Loves All People"

I have been a believer in Jesus Christ since 1987, when the Lord reached into the darkest depths to pull me out of my madness and satanic torment. Psalm 40:1-3 truly describes my life. God has pulled me from the pit and put a "new song" in my mouth, a song of praise and thanksgiving from my heart to glorify Jesus among the nations.

I want to share God's goodness with everyone, but it isn't easy with the spin the media puts on things. I pray more people in the media get saved and become a positive influence in that arena, which would truly impact our nation in a positive way. And besides, Jesus loves them so much. He is not willing that anyone should perish, but that all would come to repentance. God reaches out to prisoners, police officers, politicians, movie actors, and people from all walks of life, including members of the media.

> *They need a touch from my sweet Savior.*

I would also like to ask anyone who reads this entry to please pray for the families I have hurt. Some have already come to terms with what happened and moved on. Most, however, are stuck in the past and very bitter. They need a touch from my sweet Savior. In fact, hundreds of thousands of crime victims in America need this same touch, for we are a deeply grieving nation. Too many have been hurt by violence, and so many are weeping over the graves of loved ones.

America needs a revival and a true spiritual awakening by God's Spirit.

"Update on JayBee"

Today, as I was walking with a crowd of men on our way to the chapel for this morning's service, I heard another prisoner singing a gospel song. When I realized it was JayBee, I waited for him to catch up to me, and then we walked the corridor together. JayBee seemed so happy and content, and I was pleased to see him doing so well, probably better than at any other time in his life.

JayBee had been alone for so long. Now that he's back in prison and among a family of Christian men who truly love him, he has begun to develop into a mature man. He even had on clean clothes this morning, and his whiskers

> *Now that he's back in prison and among a family of Christian men who truly love him, he has begun to develop into a mature man.*

were neat and trimmed. It was a blessing to see him like this. In spite of all the hardships of prison, this place is an oasis of healing and hope for JayBee.

In this facility he has found acceptance among the Christian community. The men are always trying to encourage him. Some of the guys even take turns praying for him. Best of all, he now has the greatest of friends, Jesus Christ, who will never leave or forsake him. And while I do not like to see men confined, in JayBee's case this may be the best option. The streets of New York City are too cold and cruel for such a tender and fragile soul.

"Willie"

The past few weeks have been times of good ministry. I have been able to befriend and share Christ with some non-believers, telling them about the Lord and showing them God's love and care for them. One of those men is Willie, an older black man in his fifties and a veteran whose mind has been damaged by mental illness and years of alcohol abuse. He babbles to himself and walks around in a confused stupor. His thoughts are disorganized, and when he talks he mumbles so no one understands much of what he is saying. Yet when I tell Willie about Jesus, he stops to listen.

Willie is a chronic alcoholic who, while in a bewildered state of mind, stole something and ended up in prison. He was released but quickly violated the rules of his parole and was returned to prison. Willie says he left Sing Sing prison late in the afternoon but didn't get to the parole office before it closed for the day, so he went off to "look for his family." Obviously he was not successful, as he ended up homeless. He wandered around, spending the forty dollars of "gate money" he had received when he was released.

> *When I tell Willie about Jesus, he stops to listen.*

Disorganized in his mind and destitute in his wallet, Willie somehow managed to find his way back to the main parole office in Manhattan. However, he was five days late and could give no satisfactory explanation of where he had been, so he was promptly violated [prison lingo for being reincarcerated for breaking or "violating" a parole rule or regulation], and now he is here with us.

"The Untouchables"

Multitudes of convicted felons, often considered "untouchables," will one day enter into heaven, while many so-called law abiding citizens will not. Why? Because these prisoners heard the gospel—that the Son of God died for their sins and arose from the grave—and they allowed the Holy Spirit to convict their hearts. They repented of their sins and asked Jesus Christ to forgive them, and they not only received forgiveness for all their sins (past, present, and future), but they also received the gift of eternal life and an assurance of eternity with God. While their names may still be recorded on police blotters and in court papers, they are also recorded in God's "Book of Life." And though convicted felons, including myself, must suffer the consequences of our criminal actions—for God is a Being of justice—in His eyes our sins have been forgiven.

It is tragic, though, that so many who are considered by the world to be "good people" see no need to repent of their sins or to place their trust in Jesus. How foolish it must seem to many that the first person Jesus Christ promised to enter into paradise with Him was a thief, dying on a cross next to the Lord. But this thief cried out in faith and with a repentant heart,

> *How foolish it must seem to many that the first person Jesus Christ promised to enter into paradise with Him was a thief, dying on a cross next to the Lord.*

and Christ responded with the most wonderful words a person in this man's condition could ever hope to hear: "Verily [Truly] I say unto thee, to day shalt thou be with me in paradise" (Luke 23:43).

"My Mom Just Died"

Rejoice with them that do rejoice, and weep with them that weep.
—Romans 12:15

My desire is to be a caring and loving Christian who can properly demonstrate and dispense God's love. I want to offer to others a kind word, a smile, and a helping hand. I am sure all Christians desire to do the same.

In this prison environment, the need to touch others with the love of God is so essential. Prison, by its very nature, is a place of pain. There are things a man experiences in this setting that get amplified many more times than if the same things happened to someone on the outside who had the freedom to come and go and be with family members. One of these exceptionally difficult times is when a prisoner gets word that a loved one has died, especially if it is a parent.

> *In this prison environment, the need to touch others with the love of God is so essential. Prison, by its very nature, is a place of pain.*
>
> *All the brothers rallied around Jose to pray with him.*

This is exactly what happened to a precious Christian brother and friend of mine named Jose. He was informed on Sunday evening that his mother had passed away. Her death was sudden and unexpected. Jose is thirty-five years old and was very close to his mom. He was grieving so intensely that I thought he might become unconscious. All the brothers rallied around Jose to pray with him. Some of us wept. I personally felt some of his pain, as I still grieve the loss of my own mother.

Jose lives in my cellblock, so I will spend extra time with him in the days to come. He is a hurting man who is deeply loved by all the Christians here. We will weep with him, and he will not be alone.

"Remembering 9/11"

We had no educational programs or work assignments today, other than the kitchen and food pantry workers who obviously had to report to their jobs. There was, however, a small ecumenical memorial service in the prison's gymnasium with Catholic, Protestant, Muslim, and Jewish chaplains present. I opted not to attend, and instead stayed in my cell most of the day for a time of quiet contemplation, reflection, and prayer.

Concerning last year's terrorist attacks, I still feel heaviness in my heart over the loss of lives. I believe it is my duty to pray for those who lost loved ones or were injured and may yet be recovering physically and emotionally. I am likewise praying for the healing of our nation and for leaders at all levels of government, as directed in 1Timothy 2:1-4. I pray that God will touch their hearts, guide their steps to make good decisions, and grant them continued wisdom to run this country.

> *I am likewise praying for the healing of our nation and for leaders at all levels of government, as directed in 1Timothy 2:1-4*

I also spent a good portion of the day reading various psalms, as well as portions of Isaiah, especially chapter 53. As a Jew who believes that Jesus is my Messiah, I do not know of any other passage of scripture that so clearly portrays Jesus as the humble, suffering servant who carried upon His shoulders the sins of humanity.

Yet in spite of the sadness that has overshadowed this prison on this 9/11 day of memorials and remembrance, my heart still bubbles with joy, simply because I know the Lord and He knows me. His peace is all powerful; His grace is all sufficient.

"Touching Lives"

It is my desire to touch the lives of others with the love of God. This has been my continued prayer, and over time I am seeing this desire being fulfilled. The Lord seems to be directing me to certain prisoners who are very open to talking about God. Mostly, however, these prisoners seem to come to me. The Lord sends those who are hurting and troubled, as well as those who need help and encouragement.

Yesterday, while I was eating my lunch, a man sat down across from me. I could see he was troubled, for grief was written all over his face. He told me his father had just passed away. Ironically he is the fourth man who has lost a parent within the past few weeks. We talked for about ten minutes before we had to finish our meals and return to our cells.

We met again later that day, and then several times today. He seems to be doing much better now. This man is in his forties, and his father was in his seventies. Unfortunately, he and his father were both alcoholics and had a bad relationship. The son had hoped for some reconciliation between them when he got out of prison. Now that would never happen, and he wept as he spoke of this lost opportunity. I prayed for him and told him that God knows he truly longed to make peace with his father. I then encouraged him to invite Jesus Christ into his life. He is not a Christian yet, but he is spiritually hungry. I will continue to pray for his healing and comfort, and that he will open his heart to Jesus.

> *I could see he was troubled, for grief was written all over his face.*

"Full"

Blessed are they which do hunger and thirst after righteousness: for they shall be filled.

—Matthew 5:6

I had a busy weekend, and my spirit feels full to overflowing. A two-day Prison Fellowship seminar just ended late this afternoon. It was a time for the Christians in this prison to be fed the "meat" of God's holy Word.

I thank God for the three members of the Prison Fellowship team who came here to spend the weekend with us (Pastor Don, brother Phil, and sister Sylvia). We spent most of Saturday and Sunday with them, except for the times we had to return to our respective cell-blocks for meals and the regular facility head counts. We only get these weekend seminars about once every two years. I am certainly grateful for the way the Holy Spirit continues to nourish me through God's Word, and through the lives of other Christians like these three ministers. I learned a lot about being a soldier for Christ who is heavily engaged in spiritual conflict against Satan, as well as with an array of demonic powers who seek to destroy men's souls and take people captive in both mind and body. We also learned what it is to be a "peacemaker," touching other lives with God's love. I felt I had to repent for my own lack of love for others.

>
> *We also learned what it is to be a "peacemaker," touching other lives with God's love.*

This was a wonderful weekend of refreshing for my mind and spirit. Tomorrow I return to my daily tasks, mundane chores, and regular work schedules, but I will do so refreshed and thankful.

"Lockdown"

At 6:30 this morning the wake-up bell sounded throughout the facility. This is when the first official body count of the day is taken. Every corrections officer assigned to a cellblock must go from cell to cell to count the prisoners to make sure no one has escaped or died during the night. Each inmate must be awake and standing by his bunk as the officer goes past. It is the beginning of every prisoner's day, though I am usually up earlier, as are the kitchen workers who must be up by five. At 7:30 our cells usually open for the breakfast meal. When the cells were not open by eight, we all knew a facility lockdown was in effect.

> *A lockdown is both a blessing and a curse.*
>
> *It's a little like putting your house together after being hit by a hurricane.*

A lockdown is both a blessing and a curse. It is good for me because I have the whole day to myself. I don't have to go to my work assignment. I can rest, read, catch up on letters or mending or anything else that needs to be done within my cell. The curse, however, is that later on teams of guards will have to search each cell, including mine. Every single piece of property I have and every square inch of my cell will be examined. Nothing is missed.

I'm used to this, and I really don't mind. It is a change from the norm, and every inmate gets the same treatment. The hassle comes when I have to put everything back in its place. It's a little like putting your house together after being hit by a hurricane.

"Lockdown Over"

Late yesterday our lockdown came to an end. It lasted three days, during which all inmates were confined to their cells. I am especially happy now to be able to take a shower. I was also able to go to the chapel this morning for our worship service. It was good seeing the brothers again, as we had missed each other.

My cell got searched just like everyone else's. I had no contraband, but I did lose about a dozen plastic hangers. These were the outdated kind that someone must have decided are no longer permitted. I don't mind, though. I will just get the newer kind when I go to the commissary.

In prison you learn to make do. A certain item that has been permitted for many years—like ball-point pens with a retractable point—can suddenly become "unauthorized" the moment a prison official decides that inmates should not have them anymore. We can still have the standard ball-point Bic and Papermate pens, but not the kind with the top that presses down to bring the point out or back in.

> *In prison you learn to make do.*

Meanwhile, this lockdown and search resulted in a big commotion. Three .22 caliber bullets were found in another cellblock. It was a major find as far as contraband goes. The discovery was even reported in the newspapers and on the radio. No one knows who put the bullets inside of a hollow mop handle, but they were found nonetheless. Thankfully no one got hurt. Now it's back to the normal routine.

"Caught Sleeping"

"…they were all asleep; because a deep sleep from the Lord was fallen upon them."

—*1 Samuel 26:12c*

I'm so happy! It's as if a dark and demonic cloud of death has been lifted. Yesterday I heard the news reports about two men being arrested in connection with the "Beltway Sniper" shootings. It seemed too good to be true, but it was. Now I can thank the Lord that this rampage from hell has come to an end. The Lord answered my prayers and the prayers of many other Christians for the arrest of the ones responsible for these crimes. Many are still praying for the families who lost loved ones.

> *The Lord answered my prayers and the prayers of many other Christians for the arrest of the ones responsible for these crimes.*

Just as the scripture says in 1 Samuel, I believe the Lord caused a deep sleep to fall upon those two men. They slept for hours at an open rest stop along the Interstate, while hundreds of police gathered around their vehicle. These guys did not awaken until it was time for the ordeal to end.

In the Bible there are incidents where God caused people to go into a deep sleep while He accomplished something supernatural. One such story is that of King Saul and his rival, the destined-to-be-king, David. The Lord caused Saul and a battalion of his troops to go into a deep sleep so David and a few of his men could enter King Saul's camp, come right up to him as he slept, and take Saul's spear and water jug.

If God can put an army to sleep, He can surely do the same with two criminals on the run.

"Just One Voice"

Ever since I gave my life to Jesus Christ, He has placed a longing in my heart to reach young men and women with God's message of reconciliation and hope. Many teenagers are presently following the same dark path I once walked. Their lives are without direction. They're oppressed and tormented with all kinds of problems. They struggle with anger and rage, some not even sure why they feel as they do.

Many of our precious youth are headed to one of two places: to jail for breaking the law, or to an early grave because of reckless behavior. America's prisons are filled with young people who threw away their lives by making bad choices. Now they are living with the consequences. Graveyards across this nation are filled with young people who lost their lives to alcohol or other drugs, committed suicide, or were killed in gang fights and drive-by shootings. Large numbers of innocent bystanders died, too, because of kids who made bad choices and crashed their cars or decided to commit acts of violence.

> *Many of our precious youth are headed to one of two places: to jail for breaking the law, or to an early grave because of reckless behavior.*

In the midst of a world in which so many kids are out of control, I want to be a voice of direction and hope for them. I desire to fulfill God's calling upon my life by being just one of myriad voices of concerned Christians who want to point young people down the right path. And if God uses me to touch just one life, then I am thankful for this.

"Wendell Judd"

Wendell Judd, another dear Christian brother, walked out the doors of this prison today. I know Wendell had a smile on his face that went from ear to ear, because I saw him as he made his way down the south corridor for the last time. I was going in the opposite direction, and we stopped to give each other a big hug. I'm looking forward to giving him an even bigger hug when we meet in heaven.

While I am glad he is headed out—Wendell will be living with his sister until he finds a place of his own—his loss will be felt here. Wendell comes from a background of poverty and he had a drug problem, but now this man is on fire for the Lord! Brother Judd has a heart for souls, and he runs after them. He brought so many men to church that one day I nicknamed him the "Church Beacon." He liked this nickname, and it was very fitting. At 6'5" he towered over everyone, and he shone with God's love so much that many prisoners were drawn to him.

> *I'm looking forward to giving him an even bigger hug when we meet in heaven.*

While he was here Wendell completely recommitted his life to Christ. He spent several years with us, and his spiritual growth was good. He sang in the choir and was the lead singer for many of the songs. Before he left he was concerned because he didn't know any churches in the neighborhood where he would be living. So I gave him the address of the Capital City Rescue Mission in downtown Albany, where he will get some hot food, clothing, fellowship, and good preaching. Wendell is so gifted and talented, and he loves the Lord so much, that he will be a blessing to any church he joins.

"A Father's Son"

Last week an inmate shared with me the concerns he has for his son who is presently living with his mother in another state. This father has been in prison for twelve years, so the contact he has had with his son has been limited. Now the father is worried because his son is at a rebellious stage in life. He has begun to get involved with drugs, and he may even have joined a street gang. This hurting father pleaded with me to write to his son, and to pray for him too. I told him I would be more than willing to reach out to his child.

After seeking the Lord's guidance as to when to write and what to say, I sat down and typed this young man a letter. I also included a printed copy of my testimony. Basically, I had a talk with him on paper. I was gentle, but I also kept it real. I told him about my coming to prison when I was twenty-four, and how I have since been incarcerated for more than twenty-five years. I encouraged him to stay in school and to pick his friends wisely. I also told this young man never to take his life for granted. I stressed that life is precious, and if we are not careful, we can throw it away by hanging around with the wrong people, experimenting with drugs, and making bad choices. I gave him a lot of things to think about, and I finished by saying that when he is older he will never regret staying away from drugs, gangs, and trouble.

> *This hurting father pleaded with me to write to his son, and to pray for him too.*
>
> *I thank God for the chance to reach out to young kids on the edge and maybe make a difference.*

I have said these same words to other men's sons, and I thank God for the chance to reach out to young kids on the edge and maybe make a difference.

"Gangs"

Christians need to be in prayer about the gang situation in here, as it is prevalent in every prison. Men are desperate for acceptance, looking for approval from their peers. Lots of guys want a reputation, and the devil is more than willing to give him one as a cold-blooded killer, but at the cost of his soul.

These gangs are like cults. To get accepted you have to prove yourself in a variety of ways. You may even have to shed someone's blood. And once you're a member, you can never get out other than to risk having your own blood shed, or to be forever disgraced by going into "protective custody." So many inmates are getting caught in this web of bondage. Yet we Christians know that Jesus Christ can deliver and protect anyone who calls upon His name. All who want to be rescued from gang membership can be. But it is so much easier to avoid this in the first place.

> They promise power and protection as well as respect, but it is all an illusion.

> The control and influence of these gangs can be overcome by the power of Jesus Christ and His Word.

Prison gangs lure lonely and insecure men. They promise power and protection as well as respect, but it is all an illusion. Being in a gang is like being in a prison within a prison. Not only are these gang members controlled by prison authorities, but also by the ridiculous rules of the gang. This is not freedom. It is just another lie perpetrated by the enemy of our souls who seeks to steal, kill, and destroy. But the control and influence of these gangs can be overcome by the power of Jesus Christ and His Word. Prayer and fasting is needed for all those involved with gangs, whether inside or outside of prison.

"Progress Report"

As this month comes to a close I thank the Lord for all He has done, and for all He will continue to do. Wonderful things happened in November, including the salvation of several prisoners. One of these inmates is a Jew, another was a Muslim. A third man, a Gentile, has since transferred after spending about two weeks here.

The Jewish man, Horace, is growing spiritually. He is reading the Bible and asking a lot of questions about the Scriptures, and he has been bold to discuss his new faith with others. But Abdullah, the man who was a Muslim, has not been back to the chapel since that day he publicly professed faith in Christ. The reason for that is persecution by the members of the mosque he had been attending. Abdullah is only about 5' tall. He is a quiet person, more of a follower than a leader. It is therefore not too surprising that he has not attended our services since.

> *Abdullah is going through a struggle right now, and I have seen this happen before with men who were Muslims but who heard the gospel and placed their faith in Jesus.*

We Christians are praying for Horace and Abdullah. God's Word never returns to Him without accomplishing the purpose for which it was sent. I believe by faith that Horace will continue to grow, and Abdullah will come around in time, though he may remain a "secret believer" for a long while. Abdullah is going through a struggle right now, and I have seen this happen before with men who were Muslims but who heard the gospel and placed their faith in Jesus.

God has His strong hands around both these men, as He does with everyone who has professed faith in His name.

"Son of Suffering"

The Lord has been speaking to my heart that I am now entering into a new phase of ministry. Starting several months into next year God is going to expand the outreach of my testimony for His glory. However, He has also been warning me that I am going to suffer in the process. This suffering will be mental and emotional, rather than physical, and to some extent it has already begun. Even some Christians I have known for years will turn against me. Inexplicable things will happen, and I will face many spiritual struggles. But after a long season of struggles and conflicts, huge victories will be achieved and God's work will be advanced.

> The "Son of Hope" may, for a season, become the "Son of Suffering."

Godly men and women of old have undergone such trials, as have many saints today. I am no exception. Therefore, the "Son of Hope" may, for a season, become the "Son of Suffering." This is not something I want, nor am I looking forward to more hardships. It is simply the cost of following the Lord Jesus, who was the greatest Sufferer of us all. As the Scriptures tell us, He was a "man of sorrows" who was well acquainted with grief. And yet, what is my life but a "living sacrifice" (Romans 12:1)? And God is faithful. He will not allow me to experience more than I can bear. Besides, I cannot tell God what to do or not do. He is the Potter, and I am merely the clay in His hands. I am learning to accept everything that comes my way as His will, for I know that good will be the ultimate result.

"Andy Tant"

It would take an entire book to do justice to this story, but I'll try to condense it as best I can. Six years ago to the day, a kind, loving, brilliant young man left this earth. His name was Andy Tant, and he was only sixteen years old when he stepped into eternity, but while he was here he impacted my life in a very positive way.

Andy was filled with the Spirit of God, and possessed a level of godly wisdom that I have never seen equaled in one so young. I became friends with Andy, whose parents are devout Christians, in 1993. Andy was the editor of his middle school newspaper. He heard my testimony and said it inspired him, so he got in touch with me. We exchanged a few letters and spoke over the phone, and it was hard to believe Andy was only in his teens, for he was mature beyond his years. His level of spiritual insight was exceptional, and he was active in ministry, such as reaching out to the homeless in nearby Nashville.

God used Andy to encourage me to share my story with his classmates, which gave me the inspiration to begin reaching out to other young people. When Andy shared my story with the students and faculty at his school, it was so well received that I knew his generation would be receptive to what I had to say. Then, on a lonely country road on December 8, 1996, my young friend died in a car crash. I was

> *"Go reach them, David. Tell them your story of hope. Bring some light to my generation."*

stunned and saddened, as were many who knew and loved him. But today Andy's voice continues to resound in my ears: "Go reach them, David. Tell them your story of hope. Bring some light to my generation."

With God's help, I will do so.

"Hating God"

This is not a very upbeat message for the approaching new year, but the Holy Spirit impressed it on my heart today after a time of prayer. The world system is beginning to display an increasingly intensifying fury against God. Some people are going wild with rage over something as simple as a Nativity scene displayed outside a public library or in a park.

In the months and years ahead, we need to be prepared for a tremendous onslaught of demonic forces to come against the Church, especially against the leaders, evangelists, and all godly men and women who love Jesus Christ and are truly living for Him. Lying spirits and spirits of anger and confusion are everywhere. Many people want to shove God out of their minds. They do not realize they are opening themselves up to strong delusions because of their continued rebellion against the things of God.

> *The public is being programmed to see evil in God's anointed ministers and their motives, as the specter of open persecution becomes more of a reality.*

Much of society takes joy in hearing stories about ministers who "fall" and commit some sort of sin, but a number of godly men and women are also being accused of things that are not even true. The public is being programmed to see evil in God's anointed ministers and their motives, as the specter of open persecution becomes more of a reality.

Today's Christian must be spiritually prepared for such events and for this kind of spiritual climate. Open persecution has been going on in other nations for years. American missionaries are dying on foreign fields for sharing the gospel and for demonstrating the love of Jesus. Second Timothy 3:12 cautions us not to think such persecution cannot happen to us, right here on the shores of the United States.

"National Enquirer"

I would love to have ended this year with some encouraging reports about God's exploits, but I will have to save that for next year. Right now I have to address an urgent matter because, as I continue on my Christian journey, I recognize that the devil is getting more clever and diabolical in his attacks against my life and my testimony.

This, of course, is no surprise. In fact, I am learning to rejoice in these fierce trials. The devil is mad at me, and that is a blessing because it surely is evidence that whatever I am doing is shaking the kingdom of hell. But recently I learned that a woman who had reached out to me in October, asking for help in dealing with the issue of forgiveness, had

> *The Enquirer article was an attack of demonic ferocity unlike anything I had ever experienced.*

apparently made some kind of deal with the *National Enquirer*, a scandal tabloid.

In response to her initial request for help, I wrote three letters to her, all filled with words of kindness and encouragement. I tried to share the comfort of Jesus with this woman who had tragically lost a child through an act of violence. I do not know all the details of how it came about, but a lengthy story about me, filled with fabrication and falsehood, soon appeared in the *National Enquirer*.

I was devastated. The *Enquirer* article was an attack of demonic ferocity unlike anything I had ever experienced. I was alleged to have written letters to this woman, confessing to unsolved crimes, telling her that I committed my first murder when I was eleven years old, and admitting that I would have the "urge to kill" until the day I died.

The entire article is false and absurd, and I am praying about the situation. But for now, I am simply glad this year is finally over.

Hallelujah!

2003

"New Year's Day"

It doesn't seem like a new year at all. On New Year's Eve my cellblock was very quiet, an entirely different atmosphere than this time last year. Most of the prisoners seem subdued, as if there is a sense of something in the air. It's not the feeling of an impending prison disturbance or anything like that. In fact, I can't really describe it except to say it is some kind of inner knowing that life in America is changing. There is a different attitude in our country now, especially since the 9/11 terrorist attacks. We somehow sense that 2003 may be different for America than in previous years. I know I am being vague, but changes are taking place in society, and knowledge of those changes shows up as uneasiness beneath the smiles and the business-as-usual attitude of the inmates and prison administration.

> *Changes are taking place in society, and knowledge of those changes shows up as uneasiness beneath the smiles and the business-as-usual attitude of the inmates and prison administration.*

Meanwhile, I thank the Lord for seeing me through another year. I have passed through a series of spiritual storms, and no doubt there will be more. I ask the Lord to continue to use my life for His glory, as well as to bless others. And, as always, I pray for the families of the victims of my crimes. They are entering another year without their loved ones, and I am responsible for causing these people so much pain and grief. I cannot change the past, though I wish I could. May the future be better for them.

"Update on Wendell"

On November 15, 2002, Wendell Judd was released and returned to his community in Albany, New York. Like many of those who get out of prison, Wendell was unsure of what awaited him on the outside. The world can be a hostile and unforgiving place. Even families can forget an incarcerated loved one and move on with their lives. Leaving prison is like leaving a time warp and going out into what has become unfamiliar territory to try to rebuild a new life from the ashes of an old one. Few make the adjustment successfully. But we had prayed for Wendell before he left, placing him in God's hands, and the Lord did not disappoint us.

> *We had prayed for Wendell before he left, placing him in God's hands, and the Lord did not disappoint us.*

Those of us here in the church-behind-walls recently received word that Wendell is doing fine. He found a church congregation in the Albany area that welcomed him with open arms. Wendell now has an older Christian man, an elder of the church, to mentor him and hold him accountable. And Wendell is singing in their choir, just like he did when he was here with us. I breathed a sigh of relief at this news, and I thanked the Lord for His faithfulness.

"Thinking About Suicide"

This afternoon I had the opportunity to talk with a man who appeared to be contemplating suicide. He was crying when I walked by his cell. He saw me and quickly tried to avert his eyes, but I had already caught a glimpse of the despair and hopelessness on his face. When I stopped to ask him what was wrong, he cried all the more.

The man's name is "Joe T." and he has been in prison for about fifteen years. He has a history of what is referred to in prison as "cut-ups," or slashings of various parts of his body, and other suicide attempts. Joe came to jail when he was in his late teens, having been charged with murder during what police officially listed as a robbery. But Joe once told me that he knows the guys who actually committed the murder, and they were trying to impress other gang members.

"Today, after talking with Joe for a while, I told the officers on duty that he was showing the classic signs of being suicidal.

Joe grew up in the Coney Island section of Brooklyn, a borough in New York City, at the time when many teens in his drug-infested neighborhood longed to be gangsters. Like many of the young people in his neighborhood, Joe is a high school dropout with an extremely low reading level.

To this day Joe proclaims his innocence. He told me he was only passing by a storefront when the victim was shot to death by another young man. Joe walked off, minding his own business and not wanting to get involved, but the police picked him up a few blocks from the scene of the crime. A witness ultimately pointed to Joe as the gunman.

Today, after talking with Joe for a while, I told the officers on duty that he was showing the classic signs of being suicidal, so they went over to speak with him. After about five minutes they left to make the required phone calls to report the situation to various members of the prison's mental health staff.

While they were making the calls I went back in to speak with Joe. I had already learned that he had given away some of his personal items, like new towels and clothes, to his friends. This is a bad sign and a clear cry for help. I told his friends to hang on to Joe's things until he got his head together. They were glad to do it, as they understood he was very depressed and not thinking clearly. Soon a member of the facility's mental health staff came into the cellblock. I talked with her a bit and filled her in on what I knew before she went to talk with Joe.

Since Joe can't read or write very well I sometimes helped him with letters to his mother or sisters. I know he wants to go home, and his family wants him there. Yet no amount of wishing can get someone out of prison.

As it turned out, after interviewing Joe the mental health staff member determined he would not have to be placed on a special suicide watch. If he had to go this route it would have entailed his being taken out of his regular cell and placed in a special cell in the mental health unit. I'm glad Joe will get to stay here with us, and I will keep my eye on him and stop by to talk and pray with him whenever I can.

"Columbia Space Shuttle"

I was listening to my radio this morning when the first reports came in concerning a possible crash of the Columbia spacecraft. Now, hours later, these reports have been confirmed. I immediately said several prayers for the families of those astronauts, one of whom was from Israel.

Earlier this morning I had been reading the New Testament letter of First Peter, focusing especially on verse 24 of chapter 1: "For all flesh is as grass, and all the glory of man as the flower of grass. The grass withereth, and the flower thereof falleth away."

How true! All mankind's accomplishments, no matter how humanly good and noble, will eventually come to nothing. Looking at things with the perspective of eternity in mind, only what the Lord does will last.

I believe in time much of man's space travels will amount to nothing of eternal value, for we Christians, once we receive our new bodies in heaven, will probably be able to travel to the farthest galaxies. And when God makes His new heavens and a new earth, which the Holy Bible says He will do, I am certain we will be able to transcend all limitations of space and time.

> *All mankind's accomplishments, no matter how humanly good and noble, will eventually come to nothing.*

It is good that man seeks to learn about the universe, and nice that people try to accomplish great feats and seek to make scientific progress for society. But ultimately even these fine things will be meaningless in eternity when all human time comes to an end and each person goes to his or her eternal destiny.

In the meantime, seven brilliant and heroic people lost their lives today. I will continue to pray for their families.

"Update on Joe T."

When I left Joe on Thursday afternoon, he was in the hands of one of the facility's mental health professionals. At the time he was depressed and doing things to indicate that he might hurt himself, including crying and giving things away to some of his friends.

The Office of Mental Health has a Satellite Unit, also known as an "observation unit," though the latter term is not officially used anymore. The word satellite seems somehow more benign and less threatening or intrusive than the word observation. In reality they are the same thing. I imagine just about every maximum security prison in New York State, possibly throughout America, has an Observation/Satellite Unit on its grounds for those inmates who need to be kept on a twenty-four-hour suicide watch. Years ago these special cells were called "padded cells"; now they are more commonly referred to as "strip cells."

> *I imagine just about every maximum security prison in New York State, possibly throughout America, has an Observation/Satellite Unit on its grounds for those inmates who need to be kept on a twenty-four-hour suicide watch.*

The good news is that I saw Joe on Friday, and he was still in his regular cell. But this time he was smiling and joking around, and he seemed to be doing much better. His friends had already given back the property he tried to give them.

"Wives and Children"

It is now evening, a good time to sit in my cell and quietly reflect after a full and busy day of chapel services. As I do so, I find it interesting that some of the most frequently requested prayers from my fellow Christian prisoners is that their wives and children would "get saved." For those family members who have already professed faith in Christ, the request is that they would get "on fire" for Jesus. I find it ironic that God reaches down and touches the hearts of these prisoners, and they fall deeply in love with Him. They serve the Lord with fervor, yet their wives and children on the outside remain indifferent to their loved one's faith.

> *They serve the Lord with fervor, yet their wives and children on the outside remain indifferent to their loved one's faith.*

Today, for example, during this morning's altar call, men with wives and kids jammed the altar, many of them with tear-stained faces, pleading with the Lord to be merciful to their loved ones. Each man stood individually before the altar to stand in the gap for their wives and children. These men weep because their families seem so "worldly minded" and disinterested in knowing Christ, or in serving Him to the fullest. Christian prisoners yearn for their families to get touched by God.

"Lockdown Day 1"

I had a restful day today, both physically and spiritually. Beginning shortly after this morning's breakfast, it was announced that our prison was going into total "lockdown" in anticipation of a possible terrorist attack on the United States. Several days ago President Bush issued a Code Orange, which resulted in the prison staff going into a heightened state of alert. This morning, for reasons unknown to me, this level of alertness was increased. We inmates are now confined to our cells, and we may be here unto this Code Orange comes to an end. I do not know if any other prisons in New York have been locked down, but I do know that all the civilian volunteers who usually come into this facility have been banned from the prison grounds until further notice. These volunteers come in at various time throughout the week to do educational tutoring, teach Bible studies, or conduct other workshops and self-help programs.

> *We inmates are now confined to our cells, and we may be here until this Code Orange comes to an end.*

Right now I feel like the apostle John who was left in isolation on the Island of Patmos, as all our chapel services and Bible studies have been cancelled. But for me this is a time to fellowship more closely with the Lord and to pray more.

"Lockdown Day 2"

This is the second day of our lockdown. I awoke at about six o'clock this morning to find a Styrofoam food tray parked on the "feed-up" slot in the middle of my cell door. There was a cup's worth of dry corn flakes in the main compartment, and a small apple and several sugar packets in the smaller compartments. An eight-ounce Styrofoam cup of lukewarm milk sat beside the tray. This was my breakfast. When a prisoner finds a Styrofoam food tray placed in the slot of his cell door, it is a sure sign his door is not going to be opening any time soon. Knowing I had to face the rest of the day in confinement, I spent most of the morning and afternoon reading and praying, which was nice. I needed this rest anyhow.

> *Knowing I had to face the rest of the day in confinement, I spent most of the morning and afternoon reading and praying, which was nice.*

I have also been listening to the local news station on the radio, and that was how I learned that the prison was under a lockdown, not only because of the statewide Code Orange alert but also because a corrections officer had found a thick law book in the law library that had what looked like a bullet hole in it, a suspicion soon confirmed by the New York State police crime lab. The assumption now was, where there was a bullet hole, there had to be a gun.

In October of last year this facility was closed for a lockdown and search because three bullets were found inside the hollow tubing of a mop handle. A thorough search was made for more bullets, and even for a gun. But after three days the prison was reopened and things went back to normal—until now.

"Lockdown Day 3"

We all knew they were coming; we just didn't know when. They began their intense search for contraband the first day of lockdown, and then around nine o'clock this morning they marched into my cellblock in a long column of twos, looking like Vikings or soldiers ready for combat. The New York State Department of Correctional Services Cell-Extraction Team (CERT Unit) had arrived. Their specialties, in addition to searching for and discovering anything prison inmates are not permitted to possess, are to quell riots and other disturbances, to end hostage situations, to disarm weapon-carrying inmates, and to extract from a prison cell by any means possible any inmate who refuses to come out voluntarily.

> *Being "strip-searched," as it is referred to in jailhouse jargon, is a rite of passage for every prisoner.*

Every guard in this statewide CERT Unit comes with a full complement of protective gear: steel-toed stomper boots, hard helmet with a Plexiglas face shield, rip-proof gloves that look like big bear claws and are used for wrestling a knife or razor out of an inmate's hand, a stab-proof vest that looks exactly like a bulletproof vest, canisters of Mace, a gas mask, handcuffs, and a long black baton.

The guards who belong to this specially trained unit are not known for being gentle or polite. They even wear knee and elbow pads, similar to what football players use, to protect their joints in case they have to scuffle with an unruly prisoner. Not all prisoners are intimidated by the battle-ready appearance of the CERT Unit, and they foolishly fight back.

Now they are here, moving in military-style formation, a battalion of "Darth Vader" look-alikes, coming to let us know who is in charge. First they gathered by the dozens on the ground floor of my cellblock, which they used as a staging area. Then the guards grouped into teams of three. When this was done, they fanned out in front of the individual cells.

Suddenly a three-guard team appeared in front of my cell. My door, made of rows of steel bars, sprang open, and in came two of the guards. The third officer stood blocking the narrow entryway, his baton raised into the air, which is standard procedure. I was immediately ordered to undress. Being "strip-searched," as it is referred to in jailhouse jargon, is a rite of passage for every prisoner. I must have gone through this hundreds of times, not only during these kinds of special searches, but also at the end of every visit, so I know the routine, though I have never gotten used to it. It is very degrading but necessary. Inmates are known for being very clever when it comes to hiding things, and stories abound of all the strange objects that can be found in ordinarily private places.

> *I know the routine, though I have never gotten used to it. It is very degrading but necessary.*

As I took off each item of clothing, a guard would grab and examine it. My pants pockets, the elastic lining of my undershorts, and even my socks were held up to be scrutinized, one at a time, under my ceiling's fluorescent light. Then each sock was turned inside out, and the process was repeated. Finally, as I stood undressed before them, one of the guards scanned my body from top to bottom, front and back, with a handheld metal detecting wand. I was "clean." No contraband was found. Every prisoner gets the same treatment, no exceptions. Nevertheless, I was relieved when the search of my cell was over, as it was an unpleasant experience.

Next, however, came the clean up. Right after the search, my cell looked like a home that had been overturned by a 150-MPH hurricane. Half of my property was piled on top of my bunk. The rest was scattered and crumpled across my floor. Nothing had been left untouched. I spent most of the remainder of the day reorganizing and trying to restore my things to their original places.

The CERT Unit spent several hours in my cellblock, as they also had to check outside the cells, including the dayrooms. After that they moved on to begin this same process all over again in a neighboring cellblock, until every square inch of the prison has been searched.

I had an odd feeling as the last of the Cell Extraction Team left. When I heard the loud slams of the electronically controlled sliding steel doors closing behind them, it felt as if I had been invaded and violated by a foreign army. They left behind a big mess. But at least everyone, including myself, now knew there were no weapons in anyone's possession.

"Lockdown Day 4"

Sometime during the early morning hours, just before the sun came up, one of the prison employees left another Styrofoam food tray in the slot of my cell door, along with another cup of lukewarm milk. The lockdown and search for contraband is not over yet.

This is the fourth day of confinement, and I have most of my property back in order after yesterday's thrashing. No damage was done to my things, but many other men lost various items—not weapons, just odds and ends that the Cell Extraction Unit search teams determined, on a case-by-case basis, should be confiscated.

> *In the midst of all this it seems a number of the inmates go a little stir crazy during a prolonged lockdown.*

In the midst of all this it seems a number of the inmates go a little stir crazy during a prolonged lockdown. For those who don't like to read or who miss being able to watch their programs on the dayroom televisions, the cell time starts getting to them. Some of the inmates have been standing by their cell doors, yelling to their friends, trying to carry on conversations at distances of ten to one hundred feet. Prisons are generally noisy places anyway, but during a lockdown there is nothing for many of these men to do but try to talk to each other by yelling from one cell to another. And if one cannot find something worthwhile to do, like studying for his General Educational Development (GED), he is often left to pace about in his little cell, walking in circles or cleaning the same small area again and again.

"Lockdown Over"

Our lockdown ended late yesterday afternoon. The Cell Extraction Team packed up their equipment and dispersed. Most of them had been mobilized from different prisons all across New York State. This has been quite an ordeal, but it's over, and I think I held up well. During those four days I spent much of my time reading, praying, typing letters, and writing in my journal. I was also able to rest, which was nice. This was a big change from my busy work schedule and all the Bible study classes in the chapel.

> During those four days I spent much of my time reading, praying, typing letters, and writing in my journal.

I was finally able to use the phone for about ten minutes today, and best of all I was able to take a hot shower. Now it's back to my regular schedule and routine.

"Cory"

I live in the general population section of the prison, but Monday through Friday from 8:30 A.M. until 3:00 P.M. I work with the special-needs inmates in the Intermediate Care Program, helping out in any way I can. For the most part, these guys manage very well, but there are some who have serious issues. All of them have been labeled as having some form of coping difficulty, which means they might have limited intellectual abilities or severe emotional problems. As a result, many of them "act out," expressing their anger and frustration in inappropriate ways; others, when under stress, tend to regress into a deeper level of psychosis. Most of these inmates take psychotropic medications to help them function and cope with the daily stresses of prison life.

> *In the midst of all this it seems a number of the inmates go a little stir crazy during a prolonged lockdown.*

Cory is such a person. Most of the time he is quite mellow, but today he surprised me by coming up to me privately and telling me he was hallucinating. He said everything seemed to be closing in on him. The things he said and the way he was behaving made me think he might be contemplating suicide. He had tried it once before, when he took an overdose of various pills he had managed to squirrel away. Cory ended up in a coma for several weeks before he recovered. For the past week he has seemed unusually quiet and subdued. I sensed he was wrestling with something, and now I see my feelings were correct. He was fast becoming depressed, possibly even psychotic.

Mental illness is like a demon that sneaks into its victim and insidiously poisons the mind. Most people who become mentally ill and psychotic do not even know what is happening to them, nor do they realize they are sick. Thankfully, over time, Cory has come to understand that he has a mental illness that sometimes manifests itself in spite of the medications he takes. This is a very positive step on Cory's part, as most mentally ill people remain in denial all their lives. When Cory came and told me how he was feeling, he may have saved his own life. After he confided in me, I gently asked if he wanted me to tell someone about his problem. He told me not to tell any of the guards, but instead to find one of the Intermediate Care Program's trained staff. I immediately went to the office of the counselor assigned to the program and explained about Cory's situation. The counselor made a phone call and started the process to have him committed into the Satellite Unit.

Mental illness is like a demon that sneaks into its victim and insidiously poisons the mind.

I have tried on several occasions to share my faith with Cory. He went to the chapel a few times several years ago, but he never returned because he said he felt "paranoid" in such a setting. Nevertheless, on occasion he reads the monthly Prison Fellowship newsletters and some other popular Christian magazines. I do not know how much longer Cory will be away from the I.C.P. cellblock, but I hope he returns soon. Until then, I will continue to pray for him.

"United States Armed Forces"

It is surprising how many prison inmates at my facility have sons or other relatives serving in the United States Armed Forces. During the past several Sunday morning worship services when my chaplain asked for prayer requests, those with loved ones in the military made their requests known. Then, as the weeks went by, a few of the men personally asked me to pray for their sons. One man reminded me to pray for his eighteen-year-old who had recently enlisted in the Marines. Another stopped me in the hallway to remind me to pray for a son who is in Kuwait.

I personally have several friends in the military. Thomas is presently in the Persian Gulf, and James is stationed in California. Most of James' unit has already gone to the Middle East, and he expects to be shipped out very soon. I also have two friends, a husband and wife, who are both in the Marine Corps and serving in the Asian Pacific. Two missionary friends of mine are in Germany, where they minister to U.S. Military personnel and their families. They told me in a recent letter that many soldiers from the large bases in Germany have already gone to the Persian Gulf.

> *God is a shield and protector to all who place their trust in Him.*

These are troubled times, and there is tension in the air. I know many people with loved ones serving our nation are worried and concerned. But I know, too, that God answers the prayers of His children. I keep thinking of one of my favorite passages of Scripture, Psalm 91, and it reminds me that God is a shield and protector to all who place their trust in Him.

"My Mother's Things"

I am thinking of my mother today, and I want to share a little more about her. Mom was a fantastic knitter. She worked wonders with wool and her knitting needles. Many of her friends and neighbors begged my mom for the colorful afghan blankets she created.

Shortly after my mother died, my dad decided to get rid of almost everything she owned. He also gave away the remaining few of her blankets that, due to her illness, she never got around to passing on to others. However, as my dad began to give away her things, I felt resentful toward him, although I kept my feelings to myself. I now know that at the time I was too immature to understand that this was my

I am glad my dad loved my mother enough to allow her possessions to be a blessing to others.

father's way of getting through the grieving process. It was something he needed to do so he could start a new life.

That was in 1967. Several years later my father met a wonderful widow who had lost her husband to a heart attack. They married in 1971 and have been together ever since. God has blessed their lives, granting them health and happiness, and I am truly glad for them. Furthermore, I no longer hold any resentment toward my dad for giving away my mother's things. I know those who got her jewelry, clothing, cooking utensils, and even her handmade blankets were able to put them all to good use. Otherwise the items she owned would have remained stockpiled in closets and cabinets, collecting dust and going to waste. I am glad my dad loved my mother enough to allow her possessions to be a blessing to others.

"Forty-Eight Hours"

Last night I listened to President Bush's speech, warning Saddam Hussein that he has forty-eight hours to get out of Iraq. At this juncture it seems war is inevitable. I hope it is over quickly with a minimal loss of life. My personal feelings about the Iraq situation are that Saddam Hussein is a very wicked man. He is a ruthless ruler who hates the nation of Israel. Like many of the leaders now in power in the Middle East, he wants to destroy the Jews.

At times God allows war in order to remove from power those rulers who do evil. This is a hard concept for many to understand, but there are many places in Scripture that talk of war being used as a vehicle of chastening and punishment. War is not a good thing, and the Bible never describes it as such. It is, however, a sometimes necessary tool that must be used to overthrow diabolical regimes and remove cruel tyrants from power.

> *God has not been asleep while Saddam was building up his arsenal, or while he was ordering the torture and executions of many of his own people.*

I hate the thought of war, and I don't want to see anyone die. Yet I do believe that whatever weapons Saddam Hussein has hidden away would eventually be used against other countries, particularly Israel. When Saddam Hussein is removed from power, which may be very soon, this will be one less threat against Israel. The Bible says, "He that keepeth Israel shall neither slumber nor sleep" (Psalm 121:4). God has not been asleep while Saddam was building up his arsenal, or while he was ordering the torture and executions of many of his own people. The Lord has been watching Saddam Hussein's every move, and He has been keeping score all along.

"Code Orange"

Ever since the terrorist attacks of September 11, 2001, life in the United States has changed. The prison system has changed too. Ordinarily you might think that those who are incarcerated in correctional facilities in New York State would not be affected by world events as far away as Iraq. That is absolutely wrong. We are very much affected.

Now, because of the war in Iraq and the possibility of more terrorism in America, the entire nation has been placed on a Code Orange alert status by the Homeland Security Department. This heightened level of alertness certainly seems logical and justified at this time. However, it has impacted my life as well as the lives of the other inmates. Effective Tuesday morning, March 18, all civilian volunteers were once again banned from entering facility grounds. Because of this new Code Orange alert, the Christian ministers and Bible teachers are not permitted to come into the prison, so all of our civilian-run services and Bible studies are cancelled.

> *Effective Tuesday morning, March 18, all civilian volunteers were once again banned from entering facility grounds.*

I do not know how much longer this higher level of nationwide security will go on, possibly until the war in Iraq is over, but probably not. But whatever happens, God is watching over us in here. We Christians have been meeting and praying in our respective cellblocks, and all is well at this time.

"Cop Killer"

I have been sharing God's Word with a man who killed a police officer more than twenty years ago. This inmate is known throughout the prison system for his propensity for violence, mostly intense punch-and-drag-out fights with other prisoners. Yet the Lord seems to have arranged it so this man often sits next to me during mealtimes. Today he told me he has begun to read his Bible, and he expressed great interest in the life of Job. He also said that because of the crime he committed he realizes he will probably never be released from prison. Over the years the two people who were closest to him, his mother and grandfather, both died. Now, other than a male cousin, he has no one.

> *I know God is behind the scenes working on this man's heart.*

This afternoon as we were eating, he unexpectedly blurted out that he was sorry for taking the policeman's life. I was stunned. Anyone who knows this man would recognize it was nothing short of a miracle for him to utter such words, for he has been angry and defiant for more than two decades. He has often exhibited high levels of rage against the system, and over the years I have heard some of his threats and seen some of his fights.

Today, however, I looked at his face and noticed his eyes were wet, as if he was almost ready to cry. True, it was only a tiny fraction of remorse, but it was real. And I know God is behind the scenes working on this man's heart. Something is changing inside him. He doesn't realize it yet, but I do.

"War in Iraq"

I am continuing to pray for my nation and for my leaders. I pray for the troops to be kept safe, and for this war to end soon. I also pray for the people of Iraq. Their suffering and pain is more than any of us living in the United States can comprehend.

In the Middle East empires have come and gone. Nations have gone from life to ashes, and then into desert. There have been many wars fought in the land that is now Iraq, and there will still be wars in this region until Christ returns to earth.

With this current war in mind, I have been reading Jeremiah 50 and 51, and I see definite comparisons to the biblical account of the attack on the ancient city of Babylon. These two chapters describe idols being torn down and smashed into pieces. The armies of the nations surrounding Babylon were firing their expertly aimed arrows at the city, causing Babylon's palaces with their palatial ornaments and gardens to be destroyed. Babylon's expansive buildings were being burned and looted, and pulled apart brick by brick. The city's rulers were being thrown into dismay and confusion, and its soldiers were trying to hide, but they were surrounded with no place to flee. They were no match against the armies of the invading nations, and they fell dead in the streets. How similar this all sounds to what is now happening in Iraq. It seems history is repeating itself once again.

> *The armies of the nations surrounding Babylon were firing their expertly aimed arrows at the city, causing Babylon's palaces with their palatial ornaments and gardens to be destroyed.*

"Ministry Opportunities"

Within the past several weeks it seems the Lord has been placing more people in my path, either so I can share my testimony with them or simply to encourage them. God has made ways for me to proclaim His name and to tell people of His goodness, not only here in this prison but also outside these walls.

Today a student in North Dakota will be sharing my story with her professor and classmates. She is a psychology major who asked me to prepare a message for her to pass on to the class. She will incorporate it into her oral presentation and then into her written report. Also, a ministry team of Christian lay people from Times Square Church in New York City will be leaving today for Cuba. A friend of mine gave them 1,000 copies of the "SON OF HOPE" testimony tracts in Spanish to distribute while they are there. I am thrilled and thankful for this opportunity.

> *God has made ways for me to proclaim His name and to tell people of His goodness, not only here in this prison but also outside these walls.*

And then today I was blessed with a wonderful visit from some friends who are involved with youth ministry. Tim and his son, Chad, came to see me, along with Don and his son, Eli, and another young man in his twenties named Tim. They usually come here about once each year, and we encourage each other in our walk with Christ. During our visit of several hours, we talked about what the Lord is doing in our lives, and we also prayed for one another. Visits like this help to strengthen and bolster my faith. Truly my life has come a long way since those dark and sad days of 1976-77.

"The Curse of Release"

This morning Jeffrey left the prison. He had completed the term of his sentence to include his allotted time off the back of his sentence for good behavior, and now he is once again back on the streets. Jeffrey has spent a large portion of his life in between prison terms where, for the most part, he lived on the streets or in dirty, stinky, overcrowded shelters. On the good days, he managed to score small rooms in boarding houses, where he said he did a lot better. But sooner or later his mental illness and alcoholism got out of control and he was evicted. Then he had to start all over. Nevertheless, Jeffrey is a decent human being who regrets his violence and recognizes his illness. But he is in his fifties now, and he is tired of trying. That's what worries me most about Jeffrey's release.

While he was here we had our talks. I suggested he visit a Rescue Mission when he was paroled, and he said he would like to and that he knows of one in the area where he will be living.

> *My prayer is that Jeffrey is able to get into the mission, and that he makes it this time.*

The people at the mission will feed Jeffrey and give him some clothes, and they will tell him of God's love for him. My prayer is that Jeffrey is able to get into the mission, and that he makes it this time. Most of all, I pray that he surrenders his life to Jesus Christ, for without God in his life, Jeffrey will have nothing, for he is a lonely and psychologically fragile man who will be living in a world that has no time for what it considers life's losers.

I know I am not the only one concerned with Jeffrey's situation. Jeffrey himself knows the dangers that await him, and that knowledge was mirrored on his face as he walked out the prison doors this morning. Unlike most of the men when they are released, Jeffrey was not wearing a smile.

"Eddie"

Today I spent about an hour counseling with Eddie, who is presently "keep-locked," meaning he is confined to his cell for a disciplinary infraction. When I spoke to Eddie this morning I could tell he was depressed. He told me he misses his family, especially his daughter who is now five years old.

Eddie got into trouble when he was twenty and wild. He has been incarcerated for four years now and has at least forty-six more to do. I have talked to Eddie about receiving Jesus, but he insists he is not ready, though he has a Bible and always reads the Christian testimonial books I lend him.

I know from being in prison for so many years that, apart from suicide, the most extreme self-inflicted punishment for anyone doing time is the loss of family contact or the increased difficulty in maintaining it. Fortunately Eddie's older sister has custody of his daughter and is helping to raise her, but he has already missed out on four years of his little girl's life. Eddie told me he would love to see his child again, as well as get a visit from his sister. But she has no funds and no vehicle to make the three-and-a-half-hour trip (one way) from her home in upstate New York. As a result, Eddie has no idea when he will see his loved ones again. Thankfully, his sister sometimes sends current photos of his child.

> *Apart from suicide, the most extreme self-inflicted punishment for anyone doing time is the loss of family contact.*
>
> *Now he must grow up in prison.*

Eddie will be released from his "keep-lock" status tomorrow, having completed a seven-day punishment. Usually inmates who break the rules get more cell time than that, so the disciplinary officer who conducted Eddie's hearing must not have considered his infraction very serious.

Frankly, Eddie knows he is in prison because he committed a terrible crime and that he must continue to endure the pain he created for himself.

He was a "wannabe" who tried to join an infamous street gang called "the Bloods," but he is short and soft-spoken and never became more than a follower. It was obvious he had no self-esteem, yet he perceives himself as a gangster. Being simple-minded, psychologically fragile, and wanting to please those he idolized, it was inevitable that he would get into trouble. Now he must grow up in prison.

"Anger"

Earlier this afternoon an inmate who had been showing signs of agitation suddenly jumped another man who was sitting quietly at a table in the E-North dayroom area and began to pummel the man with his fists. The corrections officers quickly responded and broke up the fight, but not before the victim was hit in the head several times, leaving him with some bruises and minor swelling around his face. Unfortunately, an event like this is not uncommon in such an environment.

Although the attacker had been exhibiting some mental and behavioral problems during the past few days, much of the time acts like this are the result of pent up anger. Something seemingly trivial can set off an altercation, but underlying anger is almost always the main cause. In this case, shortly after the incident was brought under control, a handful of guards took the aggressor to the observation area in the Mental Health Unit. He may have to be medicated and held there for a few days, or he may be returned to his cell tonight. Either way, he will receive a misbehavior report for his disciplinary infraction, meaning he will probably lose all his privileges and be confined to his cell for fifteen to thirty days. When his punishment time is over, he will rejoin the other men, unless he violates the rules again or becomes overtly psychotic.

> *Although the attacker had been exhibiting some mental and behavioral problems during the past few days, much of the time acts like this are the result of pent up anger.*

"Fiftieth Birthday"

I will praise thee; for I am fearfully and wonderfully made: marvellous are thy works; and that my soul knoweth right well.
—*Psalm 139:14*

I turned fifty today, though I did not tell anyone. Birthdays are not a big deal in prison, anyhow. Still, I did spend my day rejoicing in the Lord, thanking Him for all He has done for me.

In Bible times, every fifty years the Jews celebrated a special jubilee (see Leviticus 25). These jubilees were important and sacred. When the trumpet (shofar) sounded throughout the land on a fiftieth "Day of Atonement" (Yom Kippur), which always falls on the tenth day of the seventh month in the Jewish calendar, the priests were to proclaim liberty to all those in captivity. Slaves were released by their owners; no one was to remain in bondage. All debts were cancelled, and it was a time for a new and fresh beginning.

> *I am now ready for a fresh start at the age of fifty, and I hope this is the time the Lord will place a new anointing upon my life.*

Looking at this from a spiritual standpoint, I am now ready for a fresh start at the age of fifty, and I hope this is the time the Lord will place a new anointing upon my life. Perhaps, beginning sometime this year, God will start to use me in new and different ways. This is the desire of my heart, for like the prophet Isaiah, each day my voice shouts to the heavens, "Here I am, Lord. Use me!"

"A Close Call"

Every correctional facility is fraught with danger, and no part of any facility is exempt, not even the chapel. This morning my chaplain had a close call when, during the closing minutes of our worship service, an irate inmate known for his propensity to violence and having recently lost his mother to an untimely death, stormed toward the podium. He then stood before the chaplain, fists clenched in defiance, and began to berate and yell at him.

From my vantage point by the back door, which is some thirty feet away, I could see the inmate's veins popping out along the sides of his neck. It was an extremely tense situation, but my chaplain stood quietly with his head bowed in a show of humility, which I believe was very wise in such a volatile atmosphere. This inmate, who is doing a life sentence for a brutal homicide, lashed out ferociously. He stood in front of the entire congregation, accusing my chaplain of not caring enough about his mother's death and not praying enough when she became ill.

> *God was with my chaplain, however, and we are all thankful for the Lord's divine protection.*

No one wanted to see this prisoner become violent. I was praying, and I am sure everyone else was doing the same, including the chaplain. Our visiting minister, Rev. Benjamin Mackey, a former drug addict but now an honest family man and evangelist who comes into our facility to preach one Sunday morning each month, was also praying as he watched this situation unfold. After a loud tirade that lasted about four minutes—although it felt more like twenty—this inmate made an abrupt about-face, marched up the center aisle, and barged out the door, still in a rage. For a moment the only sound was the whispered voices of men in prayer. Finally our chaplain broke the silence and asked us to join together in prayer for this man, which we did.

I know many of us understood this mourning man's grief. He had lost his mother and had not been able to be at her side as she passed into eternity. He is angry at God, not understanding that it was sickness that took his mother, not God. Nevertheless, my chaplain will be required to file a report of this incident, which I am sure by now he has. None of us wants to see this prisoner punished and penalized, but he was out of control and made threatening gestures. He also said many cruel and unkind words to an anointed man of God. My chaplain is a New York State employee, and it is against the law, not to mention a serious violation of prison rules, to verbally threaten with violence or to intimidate an employee.

God was with my chaplain, however, and we are all thankful for the Lord's divine protection. It was almost as if an invisible barrier formed between the chaplain and this enraged individual. This inmate has bulging muscles. He is a weightlifter and plays on a prison football team. He could have hurt my chaplain severely, but God, as always, was in control.

"Father's Day"

Behold, how good and how pleasant it is for brethren to dwell together in unity!

—*Psalm 133:1*

This was a day for the healing of deep emotional wounds and for the spirit of forgiveness to move throughout our congregation, bringing restoration and peace. Last Sunday I wrote about a frightening and potentially explosive situation that occurred when an inmate charged to the front of our chapel and began to yell at the chaplain. This prisoner blamed the minister for the death of his mother, accusing him of not praying enough. The inmate could have gone to solitary confinement for his actions. Instead my chaplain spoke on his behalf, and he was allowed to stay out of lockup. This in itself was a miracle and a direct answer to prayer.

> *This was a day for the healing of deep emotional wounds and for the spirit of forgiveness to move throughout our congregation, bringing restoration and peace.*

Today, however, something even better happened. This man came back to the chapel to attend our worship service, and he received permission from my chaplain to go up front to the podium to address the congregation. He stood before us and humbly apologized for his actions. He expressed his embarrassment and sorrow over his outburst and explained about the pain he had been feeling over the unexpected loss of his mother. Then this prisoner asked for our forgiveness, as well as forgiveness from the chaplain.

He went on to speak for several minutes, taking full responsibility for his actions. When he finished he turned to the chaplain and they embraced. It was a beautiful sight and a tender moment. Christ was honored, and a sense of peace filled the building. Any remaining tension and anger melted away, and the remainder of the service went smoothly as we rejoiced in the Lord.

"Suicide Attempts"

When I arrived at work this morning at the prison's Intermediate Care Program, I learned that two young men had tried to commit suicide over the weekend. Both of them, in unrelated incidents, decided to cut and slash themselves on a rainy Sunday afternoon.

My job is both a ministry and a challenge. I am only in this special cell-block Monday through Friday in the mornings and afternoons, but as a Christian and a caring person, I try to help these men as best as I can, listening when they need to talk or helping them write letters. But even when I am not physically present in the unit, I pray for those who live there.

Fortunately, the first cutting incident was more like a cry for help by a man in his early twenties who is doing several multiple life sentences and will never be released because the arrangement of his sentences exceeds the human life span. The second inmate, however, is in his thirties, and he made a far more serious attempt by slashing his wrists and cutting himself on other parts of his body as well. The correction officers on duty at the time had to wrestle the razor out of his hands to stop him from inflicting more damage.

> *The Bible describes the lives of criminals and those who do bad things as being like a troubled sea full of unrest. It is never calm, never at peace.*

This inmate had to be rushed to the hospital and came very close to dying. Now he will probably spend considerable time at the Central New York Psychiatric Center in the rural town of Marcy, New York, where prisoners exhibiting severe mental problems get committed until their conditions stabilize. Then they are usually returned to the facility where they were housed before the incident.

Shortly after I came to prison in 1978, I made several suicide attempts. As a result, I ended up at the same psychiatric hospital as these two inmates. At the time I had been displaying bizarre behavior and was having difficulties coping with prison life. All this took place while I was confined to an isolation cell at New York State's Clinton Correctional Facility in the tiny town of Dannemora, near the Canadian border. Even though this occurred nearly twenty-five years ago, I still remember my feelings of dread, despair, and hopelessness, as well as a lot of self-hatred. I wanted to die, but God watched over me. Now my days of self-destruction are over, and I recall that juxtaposed with the desire to end my pain through suicide was a deep longing to live. I am certain these two men are experiencing similar feelings.

Interestingly, the Bible describes the lives of criminals and those who do bad things as being like a troubled sea full of unrest. It is never calm, never at peace. And while the sea is in its agitated state, it casts up all the mud and dirt on its bottom, polluting itself (see Isaiah 57:20-21).

Tragically, these men have a history of suicide attempts, as well as other forms of self-destructive behaviors. Neither has any inner peace. I believe that unless they encounter a radical life-changing event, they will probably continue along their downward paths. I like these guys. I care about them, and I hope they eventually get out of prison and succeed in life. However, I regret to say that the way they are now, simply walking out of a prison is not going to change anything for either of them.

> *Tragically, these men have a history of suicide attempts, as well as other forms of self-destructive behaviors.*
>
> *Life is precious, and God wants to give them a new start, as well as complete forgiveness and a personal relationship with Jesus.*

Nevertheless, I will continue to pray for them. If they return to the special unit where I work, I will try to help them whenever I can, telling them God cares about them and will never give up on them. I will also tell them that suicide is a waste. Life is precious, and God wants to give them a new start, as well as complete forgiveness and a personal relationship with Jesus Christ.

JUNE 24, 2003

"Prisoner in Distress"

Yesterday evening my friend Al and I decided to go to one of the prison's recreation yards to get some fresh air. Normally we would have been in the chapel for a worship service at that time, but the ministry team that was scheduled to come in had to cancel, so Al and I found ourselves with some free time on a nice night.

As we walked together we were approached by a prisoner of Jamaican descent. We could tell by the look on his face that he was under a lot of stress. It was only several weeks ago that he first began to attend some of our chapel services. I remember praying for him the first time he came to the altar. Now, as Al and I listened, he told us he had learned that his wife was HIV-positive. In other words, she had been exposed to the AIDS virus.

This inmate had been incarcerated for about six years and has only a few years left on his sentence. Now he fought tears as he expressed his pain over the realization that his wife had been unfaithful. She had confessed to him over the phone that she had slept with another man who, tragically and unknown to her, was carrying the deadly AIDS virus.

> Yet even in these kinds of situations the Lord is faithful and gives wisdom to those who ask for it.

My heart went out to this brokenhearted man. Al and I spent about thirty minutes talking and praying with him as other prisoners passed by in their circular travels around the yard's walking path. Neither of us wanted to give him bad advice or speak within the framework of our limited human understanding. As Christians and ministers, we wanted to give him words of encouragement and genuine spiritual help.

This prisoner was in deep distress, devastated at the news he had received. Yet even in these kinds of situations the Lord is faithful and gives wisdom to those who ask for it. As we prayed and sensed God's words of encouragement for this man, we passed them on to him. We embraced him and shared scriptures with him as well. The best part of this entire incident was that, while this man was certainly hurting, he did not hesitate to tell us that he wants to forgive his wife, who undoubtedly was lonely and needed companionship. They also have two children, and now that she has been exposed to AIDS, the family relationships have taken on a whole new dimension.

I am no marriage counselor, but Al and I told this man to continue to seek the Lord and come to the chapel for fellowship. We promised to continue to pray for him, and as we ended our talk he told us he felt much better. Al made him promise never to lose faith in God because of this setback. As for how he will handle the situation once he is released from prison, Al and I fully trust that God will guide him and give him wisdom. We also promised to keep everything confidential, which is why I have not written anything that would identify this man in any way.

"I Remember"

And he that sat upon the throne said, Behold, I make
all things new.

—Revelation 21:5a

There are some things that are hard to express and painful to remember. Today has been like that, as I reflect on that tragic period of 1976-77. At the same time, I do not dwell on it because it is in the past and there is nothing I can do to change it. I do, however, remember that it was exactly twenty-seven years ago today that I took the life of a young woman who did not deserve to die. Her death was senseless and brutal, and I would give anything if I could undo the crime. But though I can't change the past, I do pray constantly for this young lady's family. Before I went to bed last night I prayed for them, and when I awoke in the night, I got down on my knees and prayed again, asking the Lord to comfort their hearts and ease their pain and grief. I am so very sorry for what I did to devastate their lives.

> *I would give anything if I could undo the crime. But though I can't change the past, I do pray constantly for this young lady's family.*

I am also looking forward to the day when there will no longer be any death or pain, sorrow or mourning or evil, for the Lord Jesus has promised to make all things new. How I long for that day!

"There Is Hope!"

Almost twenty-six years have gone by since my arrest for a string of brutal crimes. God knows the sorrow I have because of what I did, and for the innocent lives that were lost. I would give my own life to undo the damage, but that is not possible. However, in the midst of my own spiritual darkness and demonic despair, Jesus Christ reached out and touched my heart with the most perfect love I have ever known.

> *I am a living witness to the fact that God loves everyone, that we are all precious to Him, and that He wants us all to come to Jesus to have our sins removed.*

God has been merciful to me. It is a mercy I do not deserve and never will. Yet the Lord Jesus invited me to come to Him. He washed away all my sins with His own blood and healed my mind. He has given me a whole new life, even in prison. I know there are those who think they have done so many bad things that God can never forgive them. But that's not true. I am a living witness to the fact that God loves everyone, that we are all precious to Him, and that He wants us all to come to Jesus to have our sins removed.

If you are one who believes God can never forgive you, please think about what I am saying. If God can forgive me, He can and will forgive anyone. All you have to do is ask. Imagine this: God has taken me from being a murderer and has made me into a minister of His love.

Christ wants to change your life too. Talk to Him; share what's on your heart. Be open and sincere, for God already knows everything about you, and He will never turn away or reject you.

"Jumper"

At about 12:30 this afternoon, shortly after the lunch meal was completed, an inmate tried to kill himself by jumping over the railing from the
top tier of the E-North cellblock, the approximate height of which is equiv-
alent to that of a three-story building. This man landed in a heap, with
blood pouring from his mouth and his bones badly bruised, possibly broken. A team of corrections officers placed him on a stretcher and rushed
him to the infirmary, where an ambulance from a nearby town rushed him
to an outside hospital. Later today I heard that several officers who loaded
him into the ambulance said his heart had stopped twice. I began to pray
for this man the moment I heard the news of his suicide attempt—and in
this environment, news, whether accurate or
not, spreads quickly.

> *An inmate tried to kill himself by jumping over the railing from the top tier of the E-North cellblock.*

I know the man who tried to kill himself.
He may already be dead, but I am awaiting
word, and I don't think that an accurate report
on his condition will come for another day or
two. For now, all I can do is pray and trust in the
Lord that he will survive and be okay.

This man had been depressed. He had not heard from his family for
some time, and was concerned that they had abandoned him. He has also
been struggling with mental illness, which is why he was housed in the E-
North cellblock.

This morning I reported to my work assignment at the Intermediate
Care Program, my heart still heavy over yesterday's news. I was also concerned about the men who had witnessed this suicide attempt. I hadn't been
there to hear the sickening thud of soft flesh slamming into concrete, but
these men were. They saw his fall and the pool of blood that spread beneath
him. And so I reported to work, hoping to encourage and comfort those
who had witnessed this horrifying incident.

I felt the tension as soon as I walked through the steel doors that separate the cellblock from the main corridor. A spirit of depression and despair permeated the place, and I understood its source. I know that doing time can bring out the worst in people. The pain that often remains hidden in the heart can be revealed through the daily pressures of prison life. The crushing loneliness and lack of letters from family or the loss of loved ones who die or decide to move on with their lives takes a toll. The demons of pessimism, despondency, and hopelessness hunt for souls in places such as this. In addition, the feelings of guilt and failure can be overwhelming.

But finally the good news arrived. I received word from several different prison guards and civilian staff that the man who tried to take his life will be okay, which is nothing short of a miracle. He has some broken bones, a dislocated shoulder, a possible skull fracture, and possibly a broken or fractured jaw, but he is alive and will recover. After his trip to the emergency room of a local hospital, the prisoner was returned to this facility and has been placed on around-the-clock observation in an isolation room in the prison's infirmary. I was told he is alert and conscious, but also in a lot of pain. Several people told me he is talking and said he is thankful he didn't die. I know God was watching over him. Now, however, it remains to be seen what prison officials will do with him. Although I am sure it will be at least several months before he is completely healed, I do not believe he will be allowed back into the cellblock, for there would be nothing to stop him from trying again.

> *The demons of pessimism, despondency, and hopelessness hunt for souls in places such as this.*

In the meantime, everyone in our church congregation will continue to keep this man in our prayers.

"A Devout Jew"

This morning I had a very spiritually productive time of dialogue and sharing my faith with an orthodox Jewish man named Eleazar, who is in his fifties. Eleazar showed no hostility, only an honest curiosity to know more about my faith in Jesus. I explained to him that, even though I believe in Jesus as the Messiah, I have not changed my religion and I still consider myself to be Jewish. I explained to him that Jesus was Jewish, as were most of His early followers, including nearly all the writers of the New Testament.

> *Even though I believe in Jesus as the Messiah, I have not changed my religion and I still consider myself to be Jewish.*

We also talked about our backgrounds. He told me he is from Colombia, a nation in South America. He and I are both the only children of our parents, although I have a half-sister I didn't meet until I was in my early twenties. After his parents died and he had no remaining close family members, Eleazar decided to come to the United States to start a new life. But having left a small Jewish community in the capital city of Bogota, he ended up getting into trouble in America when he teamed up with some other Colombians who were selling drugs.

Eleazar has now been in prison for eight years. He recently attended a parole hearing and was granted parole, provided he accepts deportation back to Colombia. He knows, however, that because he no longer has any close relatives in his home country and because he is being deported, the authorities will be waiting for him. But since it was his only chance to be paroled, Eleazar opted for deportation.

I believe, too, that had the parole board not had the option of deporting Eleazar by granting him parole and thus paving the way for the Department of Immigration and Naturalization (INS) to get custody of him, Eleazar would have received the standard "two-year hit" that almost all New York State prison inmates get at their first parole board appearance.

But Eleazar has something else working in his favor. He has recently made friends with some influential rabbis within the large Jewish community in Sullivan County. One of these rabbis comes to visit him about once a month and has begun the process of trying to get Eleazar deported to Israel, rather than Colombia.

Eleazar and I agreed that being deported to Israel would be good for him. As a Jew he can, with some outside help, make his pilgrimage to Israel and eventually become an Israeli citizen. He is very excited about this prospect, and I told him I will pray that it happens, for if he is forced to return to Colombia, the results could be disastrous. Since he has no family and no job awaiting him in his country, and because the INS is sending him back for committing crimes while in the United States, it is possible the Colombian police could cause Eleazar to "disappear." But if he is allowed to go to Israel, he will have a chance to start a new life and get back on his feet again. For him this would be a true blessing from God.

"Update on Jeffrey"

In the days before Jeffrey was released from prison in April, I was able to share my faith in Christ with him. I encouraged him to go to a Christian mission, which he agreed he wanted to do, and I have been praying for him ever since.

Today I got a nice surprise. Another inmate told me he had received a letter from Jeffrey, saying he was doing well. It seems he lived in a local park for a while, but was somehow able to work things out with his parole officer, who got Jeff into a boarding home run by Christians. All fifteen residents of the home are required to attend daily prayer meetings and listen to the Scriptures as they are read.

It is obvious that God is watching over Jeffrey. I honestly thought his chances of making it on the outside were slim—and they would have been if the Lord had not intervened.

"Thinking About Mrs. Moskowitz"

Anyone close to me knows how I grieve over the past and how sorry I am for the crimes I committed at a time when my life was out of control and my thoughts were demonic and twisted. God knows I would change things if I could, but the reality is that the pain I caused other people will not go away. Their loved ones will never be replaced. And if I had the opportunity to personally apologize to everyone I hurt in the past, I would gladly do so.

Stacy Moskowitz was one of those victims of my crimes. I have been praying for Stacy's mother, Neysa Moskowitz, for many years, as have some of my friends, and these prayers have not gone unanswered. As I shared in earlier entries, Mrs. Moskowitz and I have had several phone conversations and exchanged quite a few letters. I was even able to send her small amounts of money on three occasions, which she appreciated because she is a widow with limited finances. Not only has she lost her husband and her daughter Stacy, but also another daughter named Ricky Beth, who died at the age of thirty-seven from a terrible disease.

> *God knows I would change things if I could, but the reality is that the pain I caused other people will not go away.*

It is clear that Mrs. Moskowitz has known much suffering in her lifetime, and death has been an unwelcome guest on several occasions.

With the help of some of my friends, I had hoped to bring Mrs. Moskowitz from her home in Florida to New York so we could meet face to face. My friends had planned to pick her up and drive her here. All her expenses would have been paid, and she would have been treated like a queen. Sadly, however, our developing relationship was severed when someone in the media approached her about filming our first meeting for television. Mrs. Moskowitz wanted to okay the filming, but I did not feel it was the right thing to do. I felt it was selfish exploitation on the part of the reporter, and so I politely and honestly expressed my feelings and declined the offer.

Now Mrs. Moskowitz is angry at me again and has stopped communicating with me. After receiving no further response from her, I finally stopped writing, though it saddened me to do so. However, I have kept a log of all the letters I mailed to Mrs. Moskowitz over the years. My first letter was a ten-page typed letter dated July 25, 1998. There were many more after that, since at the time she was responding. When we stopped communicating, I held on to those letters for a long time, as I truly cherished them. But now I have turned them over to an attorney for safekeeping, as I felt they were no longer safe in this prison environment.

I still find it sad that, had a certain media person not come between Neysa Moskowitz and me, we would more than likely have met by now and I could have shared many things with her to ease her mind, as well as confess my guilt. But even now, I am confident that one day this will happen. When it does, our lives shall be better as a result.

Over the years I tried my best, within the limitations of imprisonment, to help Mrs. Moskowitz. I certainly haven't neglected or deliberately ignored her, and I am well aware of her grief and pain. And, of course, I will never stop praying for her. Whether she has kept my letters or what she plans to do with them, I don't know. That, of course, is her business. I only hope she will recognize that they were written in a friendly, kind, and encouraging manner, and that one day God will use their contents to help restore our relationship.

Neysa is a good person, and I wish her the best in life. God loves her, and so do I.

"In Remembrance of 9/11"

This morning from 8:30 to 9:45 we had a beautiful and poignant memorial service in the prison's chapel, which was open to any inmate who was able and wanted to attend. Normally we would not have a service in the chapel on a weekday morning, as we must be at our respective work assignments or in our classes. Today was an exception. I was pleased to join the other men as we prayed for the families who lost loved ones, and for those who were injured during the terrorist attacks of 2001. The Catholic chaplain was in charge of this event. We had an opening prayer, followed by a selection of worship songs. Then the chaplain allowed various inmates to approach the podium, one at a time, to share from their hearts what September 11, 2001, meant to them.

I was so impressed by what each man had to say. This tragedy affected our lives so deeply. A handful of speakers shed tears, as they recounted what they were doing when they first heard about the attacks. Most were concerned for their families, and some knew people who worked in the Twin Towers. One Hispanic man in his late twenties told us about his firefighter brother who spent many days digging in "The Pile" in search of victims. Some said they had experienced an urgency to rededicate their lives to Jesus Christ. Every one of them challenged us not to take life for granted and to make the most of the time we have on this earth.

We remembered the victims of 9/11, and we will not forget them in our prayers.

"A Lost Soul"

"Whoever comes to Me, I will never turn him away."
—Jesus Christ (John 6:37, personal paraphrase)

Today I received a letter from an older Christian couple I have been corresponding with for a number of years. One of the things they shared about was the untimely and tragic death of their grandson's best friend, who was only twenty-three years old. The young man had committed suicide. My friends were trying to make sense of his desperate act. They knew he had been struggling with drug addiction and had been in rehab, though he didn't do well in the program.

> *If young people only knew how much God loves them and how much He wants to embrace and help them, they would run to Him. They would jump into the arms of Jesus, and never again buy into the lie that there is no hope.*

Now, sitting in my cell on this chilly, almost fall evening, I am trying to imagine what this young man's life was like. He must have been depressed. Maybe he felt shame and failure, and believed there was no hope. Perhaps he thought he had tried everything and nothing had worked. Sadly he saw suicide as an option to end his pain. I wish instead that he had placed his faith in Jesus Christ.

I do not know if this young man ever heard the gospel about God's unconditional offer of complete forgiveness for his sins. But I do know this: If young people only knew how much God loves them and how much He wants to embrace and help them, they would run to Him. They would jump into the arms of Jesus, and never again buy into the lie that there is no hope.

Unfortunately, however, multitudes do not know the truth. Perhaps they think of God as being angry and disappointed in them. They think He will never accept them. But, oh, how wrong they are! Even now a loving and caring Savior is knocking on the doors of millions of hearts, waiting for someone to open up and let Him in.

"Jumper Update"

In an earlier entry I told of an inmate who tried to kill himself by jumping from the top tier of his cell block. He plunged at least thirty feet and slammed against the concrete floor, but he survived and is still recuperating.

Depressed and lonely, hearing voices, his life was spinning out of control, and he saw no hope for his situation. Suicide seemed an acceptable end to a life of mental illness and deep inner pain. Now he has been transferred from the prison's infirmary, where he had been confined to an isolation room and kept under constant watch, to the Central New York Psychiatric Center in the town of Marcy. He will remain there until the mental health staff determines that he can be sent back to a regular maximum security prison. While I may never see this man again, I will continue to pray for him. Jesus Christ loves him, so much, in fact, that He died for him.

In this prison environment Satan uses many devices to bring men to ruin. He whispers that life is not worth living, that there is no hope, and that death is the only answer. How he lies! Christ is fully capable of redeeming anyone, regardless of the crime that resulted in incarceration. God can and will pull all who ask out of Satan's grip, bringing spiritual freedom to hungry hearts. I pray this troubled man finds this freedom and peace with Jesus.

"A Pearl of Great Price"

It was on this day thirty-six years ago that my mother died. I still miss her very much, and not a day goes by that I do not think of her. I deeply regret my rebellion toward the authority of my parents. I was a wild fourteen-year-old when my mother passed away. Sadly she experienced a lot of grief and shed many tears over my bad behavior. I know I put my mom through a lot of pain when I got into trouble at school and also in my neighborhood. But we had many good times, too, and I prefer to focus on the latter. I miss my mother's companionship and care, her cooking and her love, and the passing of time has not dimmed my memory of how beautiful she was, both inside and out.

It just doesn't seem that long ago that I sat at our little kitchen table on the sixth floor of our Bronx tenement, eating her chiffon cake and drinking a glass of ice cold milk. Mom was always there waiting for me to come home from school. Our apartment was warm and cozy, and an assortment of pleasant cooking odors would greet me as I walked in the door. Our home was also filled with plants, as this was one of my mom's special hobbies. She loved plants and had them throughout our living room, as well as on the fire escape during the summer.

Rightfully, my mom's name was Pearl. She was generous, kind, and giving. A simple homemaker, she was indeed a Pearl of great price.

"Not Forgotten"

"God setteth the solitary in families."

—Psalm 68:6a

I thank God that He hasn't allowed me to be buried alive behind these bars and walls. Though seldom voiced, one of the biggest fears a prisoner has is that he will be forgotten by those on the outside. As time passes, family members die or move on with their lives. Friends do the same, sometimes never to be heard from again. At some point a prisoner discovers that the world doesn't stop for anyone, and that family and friends can get along without him. As the months march into years and the years become decades, a prisoner finds himself alone and increasingly cut off from the outside world. To be forgotten is a scary, lonely feeling. It's like being alive but dead at the same time.

> *Though seldom voiced, one of the biggest fears a prisoner has is that he will be forgotten by those on the outside.*

Yet by God's grace this hasn't happened to me. I have been incarcerated for twenty-six years now, but I still have my father, although he's in his nineties. Other close family members have died since I came to prison, but the Lord in His mercy has not allowed me to be forgotten. He has given me devoted Christian friends, and we have become like family.

God has been faithful to meet my needs, and God's family is very big. I am thankful to be a part of it, and I pray I will never disappoint those who love me.

"No Perfect Church"

During the past week I have had to help resolve a serious situation in my church. Along with two other elders from the congregation, Edwin and Alan, I had to be a mediator and peacemaker between two groups of Christians who were at odds with each other. This was a role I did not care for, in part because I can sometimes be guilty of having an idealistic view of Christ's Church. I do not like to see things that are wrong and then have to confront them. At the same time, it is a blessing to be used by God to be an instrument of peace and reconciliation.

Edwin, Alan, and I had several meetings with the quarreling parties. We prayed with them and examined scriptures about love and unity, which, by God's grace, resulted in a tremendous amount of forgiveness and healing. I was encouraged to see the progress that was made. Now genuine love and concern is flowing again in our fellowship. The brothers are back to embracing one another, and our congregation is moving forward.

And yet our prison church is no different from any other congregation. We have occasional problems that crop up among the brothers, such as bickering, jealousy, envy, disappointments, or some kind of dispute. In spite of these things, however, through love and patience we are endeavoring to keep the unity of the Spirit in the bond of peace (see Ephesians 4:3). There are no perfect churches on this side of eternity. The only perfect congregation is the one that is already formed in heaven.

> *There are no perfect churches on this side of eternity. The only perfect congregation is the one that is already formed in heaven.*

"Toilet Water"

I have known many instances where deep-seated anger and prolonged bitterness have caused people to become psychotic. I am sure there have been other factors in their lives that contributed to their mental illness, but my feeling is that anger and bitterness were huge parts of it.

Earlier today an inmate in the Intermediate Care Program was very agitated about something. When I came to work at 8:30 he was already carrying on and yelling. Later, when I passed by his cell and stopped to say good morning to him, he tossed a cup of toilet water at me. I saw it coming and quickly sprang out of the way, but he ended up dousing another inmate who was just walking by and minding his business. The man who got splashed is also mentally ill and has a habit of walking in circles in front of the cells of the other prisoners, often in a daze, which is why he was not able to duck in time. The inmate who tossed the dirty water from his twelve-ounce cup, however, wasn't really angry at me. He has a history, during his many years of incarceration, of suffering from delusions, often followed by outbursts of anger.

> *Deep-seated anger and prolonged bitterness have caused people to become psychotic.*
>
> *It is an understatement, I suppose, to say that prisons are not happy places.*

Without daily doses of psychotropic drugs, some of these prisoners will begin to deteriorate emotionally and get out of control. I have had men scream curses at me, and even hiss at me while in their unmedicated and delusional state. It has been a challenge, I confess, to smile back and speak kindly to someone who just yelled every cuss word imaginable at me, sometimes mixed with spit and threats.

It is an understatement, I suppose, to say that prisons are not happy places.

"Mental Illness"

It is not a secret anymore. Correctional facilities are filling up with the mentally ill. In the 1980s, as states began to look for ways to cut their ballooning budgets, psychiatric hospitals and mental institutions were among the first to close their doors. Patients were sent to outpatient facilities. Many ended up wandering the streets, delusional, disturbed, and far from cured. In New York State the mentally ill were basically dumped into the streets. Now they make up a large portion of New York's prison population.

> It is not a secret anymore. Correctional facilities are filling up with the mentally ill.

I just finished reading an enlightening editorial in the *New York Times* for Sunday, November 2, 2003, titled, "Treating Mental Illness in Prison." According to the editors, "Two new reports from prison study groups suggest that mentally ill inmates are prime candidates not just for recidivism, but for destructive behavior and suicide when prisons fail to handle them properly."

Having been incarcerated for more than twenty-six years, I know that, for the most part, prisons are primarily for punishment and not for treatment. This current system is not designed to be kind to the mentally ill. Of course, over the years I have met many dedicated and concerned correctional employees as well as many from the civilian staff, the latter group having been specifically trained to work with the mentally disturbed. I also know a number of psychiatrists, psychologists, social workers, therapists, and counselors who do all they can with limited resources. Still, the negative pull of the prison setting, especially in walled maximum security facilities where most inmates who suffer from some form of mental illness are housed, offsets whatever positive therapies a mental health worker can provide.

According to the *Times* editorial, "Nearly 45 percent of the prisoners in the New York study reported that they had tried suicide, more than a third reported self-mutilation and 20 percent had been previously admitted to a psychiatric hospital." It went on to say, "When their prison terms are finished, these inmates are dumped onto the streets, where they become a hazard to themselves and to their community." I have known this for years. I have seen the same faces come back into the system, some for parole violations, others for new crimes. It is good, however, that the public is becoming more aware of this. These reports, quoted in the *Times* editorial, were done by Human Rights Watch and the Correctional Association of New York, both of which are alert, legitimate, and credible organizations.

> *I view prisons as wide open mission fields full of broken, damaged, and hurting men and women who need a touch of love from the Lord.*

As a Christian I view prisons as wide open mission fields full of broken, damaged, and hurting men and women who need a touch of love from the Lord, as well as many words of forgiveness, hope, and healing.

"Charlie's Dead!"

Within the space of a few hours the news began to circulate throughout the prison. Charlie Wesson was found dead in his cell. He was forty-eight years old, though he looked much older, and it appears that he suffered a massive heart attack or a stroke. Charlie was a thin black man who had been in prison for twenty-seven years. His health was poor, and he was a heavy smoker. In fact, he was the man who recently tossed toilet water at me during an episode of psychotic rage.

For about two weeks during the second half of October, Charlie was unapproachable. He cursed and snarled at anyone who happened to walk in front of his cell. He also had a history of verbally and violently lashing out at inmates and staff. However, when Charlie was stable he was very pleasant. Over the years he and I had many good conversations. He followed the Muslim religion, but he told me his only close family members, a sister and a niece, are Christians. Sometimes when I went to work

> *I spent about two hours with the guys, some of whom were clearly grieving.*

in the E-North cell block I brought him a handful of Lipton teabags and packets of sugar, which he loved. Charlie couldn't write very well, and he was partially crippled in one arm, so about every other month he asked me to write a letter to his sister for him. We would sit at a table in the recreation area of the cellblock, and he would dictate while I wrote. His letters were short and simple, as he never had much to say. Now he's gone, suddenly and unexpectedly.

Friday afternoon was the last time I saw Charlie alive. We talked for several minutes, and he seemed fine. Then shortly after Saturday's lunch meal, Charlie lay down on his bunk to take a nap. He never woke up. An officer making his rounds saw Charlie lying on his bunk, not breathing. The officer immediately used his walkie-talkie to call in a Code Blue, but the medical team from the prison's hospital could not revive him.

This morning, being a Sunday, I requested and received special permission from the area sergeant to go to E-North to visit the residents. I am not assigned to report for work on weekends, but the sergeant thought it was a good idea if I spent time with the men before I had to leave for this morning's chapel service at ten. I spent about two hours with the guys, some of whom were clearly grieving. I had brought along four sympathy cards for them to sign as a group, and they all wrote special messages to Charlie's family. On Monday the civilian counselor for E-North will mail the cards to Charlie's sister. I know she will be touched that he had so many friends.

Charlie grew up poor in a housing project in the Bronx. He died poor in a prison cell.

"Memories of Charlie"

When I returned to work this morning and began my rounds I was uncomfortable at the thought of having to walk past Charlie Wesson's cell. I knew it would be hard not to look into what had been his little living space and not half expect to see him sitting on his bunk, smoking one of his hand-rolled cigarettes. Of course, I knew that wouldn't happen. Charlie's cell is empty now, except for his personal property, which will soon be packed up by the corrections officers. Everything Charlie owned, which wasn't much, will be packed into canvas bags and then itemized in the office of the prison's personal property clerk. The bags will then be stored for about thirty days to give his family time to come for them. If they don't pick them up within the specified time, all the items, including family photos, will be discarded in the trash.

Then, by tomorrow afternoon or the following day, what was once Charlie's cell will be occupied by another prisoner. The only remaining memories of Charlie will be in the heads and hearts of those who knew him.

"Education"

I thank God that when I was attending public school and having problems concentrating, learning, and exercising self-control, my parents made every effort to help me. My dad tutored me in math as we sat together at our kitchen table, and my mom kept after me to do my homework.

After my mother passed away my dad tried his best to raise me. He often had to lecture me about staying in school, as I had begun to cut classes and play hooky. My dad was very upset and disappointed about that, but he refused to give up on me. With his ongoing support and encouragement, I managed to graduate high school in 1971.

> *Sadly, I have met hundreds of inmates here who can barely read or write. They simply do not have the means to get a decent job and get ahead in this world.*

Sadly, I have met hundreds of inmates here who can barely read or write. They simply do not have the means to get a decent job and get ahead in this world. When it is time for them to leave prison, they need an education if they are going to have any chance of making it on the outside. The prison system offers inmates the opportunity to learn a lot of trades, or at the very least to get a General Educational Development (GED). The tragedy is that many prisoners do not take advantage of this opportunity, either because they don't see the importance of it or because they lack self-discipline and/or are unable to apply themselves because of learning disabilities.

Whatever the reasons, many of these men have trouble writing a simple, legible letter. What chance will they have once they are released and sent back into such a technologically advanced world?

"Woe!"

The Word of the Lord which came unto Zephaniah…. I will utterly consume all things from off the land…. And them that are turned back from the Lord; and those that have not sought the Lord, nor inquired for Him.

Zephaniah 1:1, 1:6

There is a magnificent snowstorm rolling through much of the northeastern part of the United States right now. My area may get more than a foot of snow. Yet it looks so beautiful as millions of snowflakes cascade downward, covering the roofs of buildings as well as the hills outside my window. As I watched this storm increase in intensity, the Lord gave me a message about not giving up as we wait on Him. Unfortunately there have been too many casualties in the spiritual war that rages around us, particularly in the Body of Christ. The Christian journey is a blend of pain and triumph, and if we as individual Christians are not prepared for these periods of pain, we will not endure long enough to experience the blessed pleasures of peace and joy that come when the victory arrives and our seasons of pain finally end. I believe I can better appreciate the times of calm in my life because of the terrible spiritual storms I have endured in the past. Likewise I can better appreciate my seasons of peace after I have been through many fierce wars.

God is not pleased when we turn our backs on Him. He never said we would not go through storms, but rather that He would provide peace in the midst of the storms, as we trust and remain steadfast in Him.

"Saving a Life"

He showed many of the signs of someone who was suicidal. In fact, he was not acting like himself at all. Steven is in his early twenties, and he is several years into a twelve-year sentence for shooting a man multiple times with a handgun as they argued on a Bronx street. Fortunately Steven's victim did not die. He just staggered away with three bullet wounds in his torso. If the man had died, Steven would be facing twenty-years-to-life instead of what he "copped out" to in court. As is often the case these days, Steven's crime revolved around drugs. With so many young inner city men packing guns, the days of resolving disputes with clenched fists are pretty much over.

When I saw Steven earlier this afternoon he looked awful. He was sitting on his bunk, looking dejected and defeated. His head was hanging down, and he did not make eye contact with me as he usually did. He was using a small brush and some kind of ink to paint bright red crosses on the top of his right hand. He wore a large white crucifix, attached to a set of milky white rosary beads that encircled his neck. The white crucifix seemed to stand out even more because he had on a dark green sweatshirt.

I have seen that look before. When I asked Steven how he was doing, he just mumbled something I could not understand, as he continued to paint the crosses on his hand. I then asked a neighbor in the next cell if he had seen Steven giving away any of his possessions to the other inmates. He said he had.

I quickly realized what was up. I watched Steven for another minute or so, then went downstairs to the first floor of the cellblock and asked one of the corrections officers if I could speak with someone from E-North's mental health staff. The officer gave me the okay, and I immediately went and spoke to a counselor and a social worker about the situation. They made a phone call and requested that Steven be escorted to their office by a guard.

My job was done. Steven was examined and placed in the observation unit. Later in the day the social worker thanked me for letting her know about Steven's condition. She said I had made a good call and probably prevented Steven from hurting himself.

I thank God I was in the right place at the right time.

"The Best Blessing: Dying with and for Christ"

Anyone who watches Christian TV as their main source of spiritual food may think that God's whole purpose is to bless every Christian and make us all happy, and that our job as believers in Christ primarily comes from getting things, or by having certain prayers answered our way. But that is just not true. Our greatest joy as Christians should be in giving our lives to Jesus Christ to do as He will with each of us (see Romans 12:1, 12:2). Giving up our lives for Christ's sake is the greatest blessing any of us can ever receive.

This is why I find myself so humbled and astounded by my Christian brothers and sisters in Third World countries who suffer deprivations and beatings, even death because they chose to serve the Lord. These martyrs and "sold-out-for-God" servants are perhaps the most blessed of all Christians on the earth. They have the privilege of being partakers in Jesus' sufferings and of having a bond with the Lord that we in the United States have never fully experienced.

"For unto you it is given in the behalf of Christ, not only to believe on Him, but also to suffer for his sake."

—Philippians 1:29

"That I may know him, and the power of his resurrection, and the fellowship of his sufferings, being made comformable unto his death."

—Philippians 3:10

As I examine these scriptures and compare these words with our modern-day Christianity, I wonder if we are even practicing the same faith. The early Church, rather than praying for God to give them more material possessions, instead gave them away to others.

"And all that believed were together, and had all things in common;

And sold their possessions and goods, and parted them to all men, as every man had need."

—Acts 2:44-45

Sadly, much of North America's version of Christianity encourages craving and obtaining possessions. Then, if we do not get our prayers answered the way we think we should, we get angry at God and are ready to abandon the faith. Surely this is a different kind of Christianity than the faith displayed in the Bible. The Holy Scriptures reveal that being a believer in Jesus may sometimes result in the loss of all things.

"And others had trials of cruel mockings and scourgings, yea, moreover of bonds and imprisonment: They were stoned, they were sawn asunder, were tempted, were slain with the sword: they wandered about in sheepskins and goatskins; being destitute, afflicted, tormented; (Of whom the world was not worthy:) they wandered in deserts, and in mountains, and in dens and caves of the earth."

—Hebrews 11:36-38

I must confess that I know little of this kind of life or suffering. But according to Jesus' own words, how blessed are those men and women who experience such things for His sake.

Blessed are they which are persecuted for righteousness' sake: for theirs is the kingdom of heaven.

—Matthew 5:10

I shall always be deeply grateful to my suffering brothers and sisters for their good confession, and for their demonstration of genuine Christian faith. I am sure they have their times of doubt, struggle, and fear. They are not "super saints," of course. And I am not idolizing the Church's martyrs, nor am I placing persecuted Christians on a pedestal. But I do believe they have much to teach the Christians of North America. Therefore may our hearts be open to them as they lead by example and triumph over their trials. Let us remember their love and devotion to King Jesus. Daily they risk

> *I shall always be deeply grateful to my suffering brothers and sisters for their good confession, and for their demonstration of genuine Christian faith.*

everything to follow Him. Are we doing likewise?

My prayer for myself and for the Church is that we will live with eternity in mind, and that we will unite with our suffering brothers and sisters through our prayers and by supporting worthy evangelistic ministries. May we choose to do without various luxuries so that we may have more to give to missions, and may we give ourselves to intercessory prayers for the suffering Church. Their labors and our prayers will not be in vain.

"Joseph"

But as for you, ye thought evil against me; but God meant it unto good,
to bring to pass, as it is this day, to save much people alive.

—Genesis 50:20

Today I was thinking of the famous Bible character Joseph. At the age of seventeen he was thrown into a pit in the ground, and later he was thrown into a prison cell. Joseph was despised and rejected by his own brothers who were jealous of him. They sold young Joseph into slavery, separating him from his beloved father, Israel (Jacob), and ultimately robbing Joseph of his youthful years. But in the end all the suffering he went through was worth it. His trials helped to build his character, and they made him ready to be used by God. As events unfolded, Joseph was able to save the lives of his own family, as well as the lives of hundreds of thousands of people when a terrible seven-year famine descended upon the land.

God can take our worst predicaments and turn them into victories. He can take curses and turn them into blessings. And God can take everything Satan has meant for evil in our lives and turn it around for our good, for God is the God of all flesh, and nothing is too hard for Him.

"Ah Lord God! behold, thou hast made the heaven and the earth by
thy great power and stretched out arm, and there is nothing too hard
for thee."

—Jeremiah 32:17

With the New Year approaching, I will keep Joseph's story in mind. His saga was one of hope, and so is mine.

2004

"Another Code Orange"

In everything give thanks: for this is the will of God in Christ Jesus concerning you.

—1 Thessalonians 5:18

A new year has begun. I wish I could say I was awake and on my knees until the wee hours of the morning, spending New Year's Eve in fervent prayer, but I went to sleep early. I was very tired and actually slept through the usual jailhouse merriment of a handful of guys screaming "Happy New Year!" at the top of their lungs.

Generally there are few open displays of celebration in prison. Holidays such as Thanksgiving, Christmas, and even New Year's tend to be somewhat subdued, though not somber. In addition, because of the alleged reports of the increased possibility of a terrorist attack on United States soil, New York's prison system is back to a Code Orange alert. And like the last Code Orange, this facility closed its doors to all civilian volunteer ministers who normally come here to teach Bible classes or conduct worship services. As a result, almost all our daily chapel events have been cancelled.

I must admit that I don't understand the logic of this, but it has happened before, and the cancellations will continue until this Code Orange is back down to a "mellow yellow."

"Code Yellow"

Yesterday I heard on the news that the Code Orange terrorist alert was rescinded, and the nation is back down to the less ominous sounding Code Yellow. I don't suppose things will change much for most American citizens, as I doubt many people pay much attention to these alert levels anyhow. But personally I will rejoice that, little by little, the chapel worship services and Bible studies will return to their previous levels. On Monday morning my chaplain will probably begin to contact our volunteer ministers to inform them that it is now okay to return to the prison.

Things like this remind me how vulnerable we prisoners are to outside events and situations. Thankfully there were no terrorist attacks on the United States. But had something happened, even if it had occurred on the west coast, causing the nationwide alert code to be elevated to red, this entire prison might have gone into a lockdown mode. All the inmates would be in continuous cell confinement, and almost all activities inside the prison would come to a stop, perhaps for weeks or even months.

However, I have learned to be thankful for what I do have. It is like the story about the man who always complained that he had no shoes until he met a man who had no feet. The shoeless man was humbled as he realized how blessed he was to have feet. Like that man, we tend to think we are in terrible straits until we meet someone in a worse condition. While I do not like being in prison or having to be so vulnerable to outside situations, the truth is that things could be much worse. May I always be thankful for all God's blessings.

"Shot Dead"

But if our gospel be hid, it is hid to them that are lost: In whom the god of this world hath blinded the minds of them which believe not, lest the light of the glorious gospel of Christ, who is the image of God, should shine unto them.

—*2 Corinthians 4:3, 4:4*

I didn't really know him, though I often saw him walking the prison's corridors, or working out with weights in the gym. Many times I observed him in the recreation yard, hanging out with the Organized Crime guys, with whom he seemed to fit well. His name was Frank Dimarco, and he was shot to death on a street in Queens, New York, shortly after he was released from Sullivan Correctional Facility. Frank was fifty-two years old, and Sullivan was his last prison stop before his life came to a sudden end.

Like hundreds of convicts who pass through this facility, Frank was just another face in the crowd. I believe he was just released a few months ago. Since I didn't know him personally, I forgot about him. But over the weekend word spread quickly that a man who had once been here had been shot to death. Out of curiosity I asked one of Frank's friends if it was true, since I know that both bad news and false rumors spread fast in prison. But the inmate who had known Frank quickly confirmed the report by showing me the "NYPD Daily Blotter" section in the February 6 edition of the *New York Post*. This section lists some of the daily incidents of murder, mayhem, and crime in the "Big Apple." Here is what I read about Frank:

> *Frank was like so many of those in prison whom Satan has blinded. The chapel's doors were always open. But Frank was a blind man.*

Police yesterday identified a Long Island man shot and killed on a Cambria Heights street. Frank Dimarco, 52, of Westbury, was shot in the head for unknown reasons at 132nd Road and 219th Street around 10:30 p.m. Wednesday. Dimarco, who had 60 prior arrests, was taken to Mary Immaculate Hospital, where he died.

My heart was pricked. As a Christian I quickly bowed my head and offered a silent prayer for his suffering family, as I am sure he has loved ones who are grieving. I also thought of Frank. Sixty arrests! His friend told me that Frank had a penchant for robbing drug dealers. I'm not sure what Frank was doing time for when he was here. His friend didn't know either. Frank Dimarco had so many prior arrests and had done so much jail and prison time that even his best friend had lost track of his many offenses.

And, of course, I wondered if Frank knew Jesus Christ as his Savior. Like multitudes of inmates, he hung out with the guys, aimlessly passing the time, perhaps never thinking about God and never showing any interest in going to the chapel services. Frank was like so many of those in prison whom Satan has blinded. Christian inmates were all around him. The chapel's doors were always open. But Frank was a blind man. The "god of this world" had kept Frank under his power. The temptations of drugs and money and having a "good reputation" among thieves was of more value than his being in right standing with the Lord. Now, sadly, only a short time after Frank walked out the doors of this prison, his body was dropped by a bullet on a desolate street corner.

A lifetime of crime was what he chose. All that was left to mark his life was a tiny blurb written in a New York City newspaper about his murder. What a waste.

MARCH 6, 2004

"Nostrand Barton"

In the prison system there are no guarantees of how long an inmate will remain at a certain facility or when he will be transferred. Many times such transfers are not based on the man's behavior, good or bad. Often it is a lowering of one's security level classification. Most frequently, however, it is simply a "facility need" to bring in new men and move on those who have been at a certain prison for a while.

I have a handful of friends in my cellblock, and I usually sit with three of them during our mealtimes, as each table in the dining area seats four. One of these men is named Geronimo, a sixty-five-year-old Native American who is almost blind and has several serious medical problems, so he needs to be taken in a wheelchair when he leaves the cellblock.

The other two men are Taso, an Hispanic man in his thirties, and Nostrand Barton, who is sixty-three and completely blind and has to maneuver through the cellblock and prison with the help of a cane and another inmate who is trained as a "mobility guide."

Geronimo and Taso are doing life sentences. Nostrand, however, is doing only about five years for assault. As often happens, during a routine evaluation of Nostrand's progress here, the prison administration reclassified him at a "medium security" level rather than his original status of "maximum security." This reclassification almost always results in a transfer.

Nostrand wanted to stay with us, but an inmate never has a choice about such matters. Several days ago a corrections officer came to the front of Nostrand's cell and told him to gather his things. Geronimo, Taso, and I knew we would never see him again.

Nostrand is a black man who was born in South Carolina. He came to New York City as a teenager, along with his mother and grandmother and a bunch of siblings, all in search of a better life. He told me he did okay for a while, working at various unskilled labor jobs. But Nostrand had a pen-

268

chant for alcohol, marijuana, and eventually cocaine; he soon drifted from job to job, and finally into poverty. Nostrand once told me that his closest brother died from cirrhosis of the liver as a result of alcohol abuse, while Nostrand became an alcoholic living on Welfare.

The real turning point came when Nostrand, who had good vision, was drinking in his girlfriend's apartment and got into an argument with her about the television. When he fell asleep on the couch, his intoxicated girl-friend got a carving knife from the kitchen and stabbed him in both eyes.

I cannot imagine the pain and terror Nostrand experienced at that moment. Bleeding profusely from both eye sockets, he managed to scram-ble out of the apartment and into the building's hallway where someone called the police. From that point on life went from bad to worse for Nostrand. His girlfriend had a nervous breakdown and went to jail for a while, then moved to Mississippi to live with her family. Nostrand, in his thirties at the time, had to learn to live with his blindness. Through a New York City-based Social Services agency, he eventually got some help and was taught how to function with his condition.

I have looked into Nostrand's face a thousand times, and each time I am struck by the fact that he has no eyes. But he possesses a strong will to survive, and by God's grace he has endured more than thirty years without sight. Unfortunately, being blind did not end Nostrand's addictions. He was so angry about his misfortune that he began to use cocaine and ended up being homeless, panhandling on the subways and collecting coins and handouts from sympathetic passengers. In his favor was the fact that as a kid he had learned how to play the harmonica. Ironically Geronimo is also an accomplished harmonica player. On occasion they entertained the inmates during our mealtimes, at least until a guard would yell for them to stop.

Nostrand's hair was always unkempt, his clothing wrinkled, and he was missing several teeth. When I watched him play his harmonica, he remind-ed me of the legendary character "Mister Bojangles." But Nostrand also had a perpetual smile and a happy-go-lucky attitude, so he kept the rest of us laughing.

Needless to say, when the officer showed up to tell Nostrand the news about his transfer, we were all saddened. Later that day I watched as some of the inmate porters helped him pack his belongings. He didn't have much property to take with him, other than his state-issued clothing and his work uniforms, some hygiene articles, all his tobacco, and, of course, his little harmonica. Seeing him head out the front entrance of the housing unit the following day left me with an empty feeling. Fortunately for him, though, he will be out of prison in less than two years. If all goes well, some of his grown children may help him make the adjustment to life on the outside.

When I think of Nostrand Barton I know that, in spite of his cheerful attitude, he is a lonely man. He frequently talked about winning the lottery and going back to South Carolina to buy some land and build himself a home. I doubt that will happen, but I wouldn't be surprised if he returns to New York City, pulls his harmonica out of his pocket, plops down on a sidewalk with a little pail in front of him, and panhandles again.

> *Unfortunately, being blind did not end Nostrand's addictions.*

Nostrand, a genuine Mr. Bojangles, will go back to serenading the crowds, living off coins and handouts and Welfare.

"Transferred"

It is a fearful thing to fall into the hands of the living God.
—Hebrews 10:31

Danny, my next-door neighbor, was just transferred to another prison. I have known Danny for about five years. He was a member of our chapel congregation all the time he was here. But he was also a terror and a thorn to us with his continual bickering, murmuring, and ridiculing. He complained about our chaplain, the choir, and almost all the Christians who attend our services. This was a daily thing, and he was constantly sowing discord among us.

Danny is doing twenty-five-years-to-life for an exceptionally brutal murder that happened in Manhattan. While on a crack-induced rampage, he repeatedly stabbed a wheelchair-bound man for a small amount of money. Several years ago Danny's crime was briefly featured on Court TV.

> *His choice will be between the "world" and Jesus Christ.*

Danny was a tough case. Sometimes he drove me crazy with his constant cussing, lying, and smoking, plus he was so rambunctious. When he walked into the chapel or came into the cellblock it was as if a tornado had arrived.

I had many conversations with Danny, as did several other Christians. There were times Danny wanted to talk about God and the Bible, but there were more times when he tried to initiate a conversation of gossip.

Throughout his years at Sullivan Correctional Facility he received many warnings spoken in love, asking and admonishing him to stop attacking others with his tongue. He was repeatedly asked to start cooperating with the spiritual leaders of our congregation, and with the lay ministers and Bible teachers who came here to help us. It was all to no avail. Danny never listened to the elders of the church. He never listened to me. He never listened to anyone. He was as stubborn as a mule.

Then a corrections officer came to his cell and told him to pack his things because he was being transferred the following day. As soon as the officer walked away Danny began to cry. He then called to me and asked me to stop by his cell as soon as our doors opened again. He needed someone to talk to, as he was upset and unsettled by the news. He felt like the bottom had dropped out, for he had been told he was going to Sing Sing, one of the worst and most violent prisons in New York State.

The gangs at Sing Sing are vicious. Inmates get sliced and stabbed almost daily by fellow prisoners who use knives, razors, box cutters, and even finely sharpened can tops. On occasion men die from the violence; many are maimed for life and carry the scars of their battles on their faces, necks, and backs.

When Danny was on the streets living in his world of drugs and hustling, he was like a wild man surviving by his wits and sheer luck. I recall the worn and haggard look on his face when I saw him on the Court TV program, where he was being questioned by several NYPD detectives who eventually got a full confession from him.

Ironically, Danny comes from a family that is financially well off. But at some point in his early twenties he made the choice to sell drugs. He then got badly addicted from sampling his own supply. Over time the streets consumed him. Now the gangs of Sing Sing, like the Bloods and the Latin Kings, may consume him as well. There are also a lot of drugs and corruption in that place.

Sing Sing Correctional Facility is about thirty miles north of New York City in the town of Ossining in Westchester County. It is an old fortress-like facility on about fifty acres of choice real estate along the east bank of the Hudson River. The area surrounding the prison is picturesque. Inside the prison, however, hangs a pall of anger and fear.

Shortly before Danny's time to leave I told him that a line has been drawn at his feet. I ran my right foot across the floor of the tier for emphasis. I told him that as soon as he gets to his next facility, he is going to have to make a decision as to whether he will run with the gangs and troublemakers, or with the Christian inmates he would find there. His choice will be between the "world" and Jesus Christ.

Just then the officer called out Danny's name and told him it was time to go. I gave him a big brotherly hug and promised to keep him in my prayers.

"My Dad"

My father is a good man. He tried his best to raise me and help me under sometimes difficult circumstances. I was a problem child with many emotional and behavioral problems. But while I often perplexed and exacerbated my father, he and I had many good times together.

I grew up in New York City, and my dad and I had a lot of fun together. I remember going to the movies with him and laughing so hard as we watched "The Odd Couple," and "West Side Story" quickly became one of my favorite movies.

Over the years my dad took me to Shea Stadium to watch the New York Mets play, and we also went to Yankee Stadium. I will never forget the night when I was about eleven and my father took me to a night game to watch the Yankees play under the bright lights.

In spite of the bad turn my life took and even during the times of my tumultuous childhood, I believe my father and I had a good life together. God has blessed me with the privilege of knowing and having a great dad, and I am very thankful.

Once, before my mother died, the three of us went to the observation deck of the famed Empire State Building. The following year my parents and I journeyed by ferry to the Statue of Liberty, where my dad and I climbed into the crown of Lady Liberty's head. My mom, however, opted for the elevator. I didn't blame her, as it was quite a hike to the top. Another time we went to the Planetarium in Manhattan, where we viewed the solar system. On several occasions we visited the Museum of Natural History to see the fossils and dinosaur bones from ages past. The three of us often went to Bear Mountain State Park, where my dad and I hiked while Mom stayed at the inn. And for many consecutive summers, when my dad was able to close his little neighborhood hardware store for a week, my parents took me on vacations to Lake George in the Adirondack Mountains. Every summer we rented a bungalow cottage in the same little town called Bolton

Landing. I loved the lake and the beauty of the surrounding mountains, and I enjoyed swimming and getting splashed by the small waves from the speedboats and tour boats. Occasionally I fished from the side of a small pier, and Dad and I took a rowboat out onto the huge lake.

My father, an avid bowler, got me fitted for my first bowling ball, which he purchased for me as a birthday gift. He taught me the game, and also taught me how to ride a bicycle.

Of course, we had bad times as well. More than once my parents cried tears of grief because of my bizarre behavior and rebellious ways. Still, in my mind, the better days do stand out. Furthermore, I don't hold anything against my father for having to work six days a week, ten hours a day, as he struggled to make a living in his small store. He grew up during the Great Depression, so he knew what it was to be poor and have just enough to get by. Working all those hours was a labor of love for him, and I am grateful to have such a hard working father as a good example.

In the community he lives in today, many people know my dad for his gentle spirit, as well as his kindness and generosity. For many years he has been the president of the local tenant's association, and his neighbors look to him for wise advice and good leadership.

Of course when I was an emotionally immature adolescent I did not see all these qualities, but at some point in my life I awoke to the inner beauty of this fine man. In spite of the bad turn my life took and even during the times of my tumultuous childhood, I believe my father and I had a good life together. God has blessed me with the privilege of knowing and having a great dad, and I am very thankful.

"God at Work"

God is quietly working in the hearts of many prisoners. In correctional facilities all across America men and women are repenting of their sins and coming to Christ. Some are doing so out of desperation, but that's all right. Multitudes of prisoners feel they have hit bottom, and many find there is no place left to go but to Jesus, much like the story of the prodigal son in Luke 15. This wayward son was broke, busted, and disgusted, and he finally came to the realization that his life was a mess. He was homeless and living like a pig. He was at a dead end. In fact, he probably would have been dead in a few more days if he hadn't come to his senses and made his way back to his father's house.

> *God is quietly working in the hearts of many prisoners. In correctional facilities all across America men and women are repenting of their sins and coming to Christ.*

And God is indeed a loving heavenly Father who is waiting for each of us to come to our senses and come back to Him. He wants us to freely admit that we have sinned and done wrong, and that we cannot fix anything, not even our broken lives. Furthermore, the Father sent His Son, Jesus, to find us and carry us home, for we are too lost and injured to make it without His help.

Thankfully, Jesus Christ gently picks us up and, one by one, carries us home to God.

"Spring and Restoration"

And I will restore to you the years that the locust hath eaten, the cankerworm, and the caterpillar, and the palmerworm, my great army which I sent among you.

—Joel 2:25

With spring comes the hope of restoration. All that has been dry and dead, brittle and brown from winter's frigid cold now blooms back to life. Lush green grass fills the fields and hills. Life seems to begin anew.

As with nature, restoration is a blessing and a gift from God that human beings can also experience. Jesus focused much of His ministry on mending broken hearts, and bringing healing and forgiveness into lives that had been damaged by sin. God can even restore the years we have wasted. I know this to be true from personal experience, for He has been doing this very thing with me.

The God of restoration removes, remolds, reshapes, and rebuilds inside of us what other people, demonic entities, or even our own stupidity, self-destructive ways, and carelessness has ruined. He can make all things new, even broken relationships. Therefore, by faith, I believe the best days of my life are yet to come.

"The Trip"

On Tuesday morning I left the prison to go on a medical trip, which included a two-and-a-half-hour ride each way. This was my first time out of the facility in several years. I rode in a van with two correctional officers and an armed corrections sergeant. Because it was a small vehicle I was able to look out through the screened windows.

As is standard procedure when a prisoner is being transported, I had to be handcuffed at the wrists. I also had my feet shackled together with cuffs similar to handcuffs, but slightly larger. The trip was interesting, though uncomfortable because of the heavy steel cuffs, chains, and shackles. The officers were decent, though. The young guard who sat behind me was friendly and talkative, and asked me many questions about my faith in Christ. It was one of the most encouraging conversations I have had in a while. This man was really listening

The hardest part of the trip was not all the heavy security hardware I had to wear, but seeing all the beauty outside the van's windows. As we drove through one town and then another I saw many lovely but simple homes. People were working in their gardens or walking about on a sunny and gorgeous day. I saw deer, too. And there were many rivers, creeks, and streams, all swollen with water after several days of very heavy rains.

The hospital, however, was crowded with people, most of whom were medical staff or other workers. With the officers in front and behind me, I shuffled up and down the long corridors wrapped in rattling chains and cuffs—not a pretty sight for anyone to see, I'm sure.

Fortunately very few people even bothered to look my way. They seemed more embarrassed than I at the situation. But I got the exam my doctor had insisted I take. I was anesthetized throughout most of the procedure, and I awoke on a portable bed, with the guards standing over me. A medical technician soon appeared to ask if I was okay and to let me know that a full report would be sent to the prison's doctor. Then it was time to get dressed and be tied up again in the security hardware for the return walk to the van and the scenic ride back to Sullivan.

I have been feeling a bit down today, but that is to be expected. Seeing yesterday's sights was a painful reminder of a world beyond these walls, a world where I cannot go and of which I can no longer be a part.

"Dad's Birthday"

I am weary with my groaning; all the night make I my bed to swim;
I water my couch with my tears.

—*Psalm 6:6*

My father turned ninety-four today. He has lived a healthy, full life, and is presently the patriarch of our family. Strong, smart, and confident, my dad is one in a million. Yet while I am glad he is doing so well, inside my heart there is an acute ache, a gnawing pain in my soul that never goes away. It is not a physical pain in the sense of being ill or injured. Rather, it is the anguish and despair of not being able to be with my father. I miss him, and I wish I could hug him.

Fortunately, just before leaving my cellblock to attend this morning's chapel service, I was able to get to a telephone. I called my dad to wish him a happy birthday, and we spoke for almost eight minutes.

As I have said so many times before, I would love to undo my horrible past and have the chance to relive my life, this time never doing wrong. If I had the chance to start my life over again, I would make sure that I honor my parents. I would never again be a source of grief and heartache for them. But, of course, I can't do that. So instead I will just say, "Happy birthday, Dad! I love you."

"Quiet Asset"

Earlier today I was talking with a corrections officer, and he made a comment that the inmates who attend the Christian services seem to be well behaved. According to his observation, these men do not get into the mischief that many of the other prisoners do. This officer also commented about the Christian family event that was held last summer in our large recreation yard. He said the atmosphere was different that day because the Christian prisoners and their families were respectful toward each other, as well as toward the staff. The officer heard no cussing or swearing, which is often the most frequent vocabulary of convicts. Months later this stuck in his mind.

> *Inmates who attend the Christian services seem to be well behaved.*
>
> *The chapel programs in thousands of correctional facilities are a quiet asset for both the inmates and staff.*

I believe views like the ones this officer expressed come about because the chapel programs in thousands of correctional facilities are a quiet asset for both the inmates and staff. In the fellowship I attend, for example, the men who are seriously trying to live as good Christians seldom break the rules. They no longer want to be troublemakers or remain in rebellion to authority. They have changed, and they are better men because of it.

Since I became a Christian, for example, I have received only one misbehavior report for a rule violation. That was in 1989 for disobeying a direct order. At the time I committed this infraction I was having difficulty understanding what the officer was telling me to do. In addition, this particular guard is known for writing up inmates at every opportunity.

Other than that one incident, however, for which I did indeed break a rule and subsequently received a punishment of fifteen days of confinement to my cell, my disciplinary record has been excellent, as have my work evaluations. This was not the case before I gave my life to Christ.

> *Prison administrations quietly and greatly benefit by having a variety of Christian programs available for those who are confined.*

Many of my fellow inmates have similar testimonies. They have managed to stay out of trouble because Jesus touched their lives and changed their hearts. While many negative comments are often made about "jailhouse religion" by obviously ignorant and misinformed people, prison administrations quietly and greatly benefit by having a variety of Christian programs available for those who are confined.

"Mothers and Sorrows"

Who can find a virtuous woman? for her price is far above rubies.
                                                                    —Proverbs 31:10

Today is Mother's Day. Consequently, a portion of this morning's worship service was devoted to talking about and honoring our mothers.

Shortly after our service began, the minister gave the opportunity for each of us to briefly say something about our mothers. Many of us shared how our mothers were a blessing to us and that we sorrow over not being able to be with them at this time. However, an almost equal number of men stood up, one by one, to express their sorrow and disappointment at never having loving and caring moms. For the latter group, feelings of bitterness and anger clearly surfaced as they talked about abusive, neglectful mothers, some of whom were drug addicts or alcoholics who abandoned their children completely.

A couple of prisoners spoke of being rejected by their maternal mothers, only to get passed around from one family to another in foster care. Several more told of being beaten and neglected. One man said his mother locked him out of their apartment during the nights she slept with different men. He would then wander the streets or sleep in deserted basements. Neither he nor his mother even knew his father's identity. Some of the men here grew up watching their parents shoot drugs into their veins, or saw their mothers vomit into sinks and toilets as they slowly drank themselves into oblivion, leaving behind emotionally damaged sons who now fill prison cells.

I heard a lot of sad stories today, but as I listened to those tales of woe God taught me that I need to be more sensitive and discerning so I can recognize and minister to those who are hurting. Many of these men have been attending our Christian fellowship for years, yet I never knew about their bad experiences or sensed the pain they were carrying around on the inside. Whether out of pride, fear, or denial, these men hid their hurts, keeping silent, as men often do. I realized my own mistakes in all this. Now I must begin to look beyond the superficial smiles and see the real persons in need of ministry.

Interestingly, I did not hear one man blame his parents for the crimes he has committed. But I do believe the misfortunes each man experienced during childhood helped to form at least a few pieces of the mosaic that makes him what he is today. It is therefore no surprise that boys who have been wounded early in life one day grow up to wound others. In addition, those who received very little love in their youth seldom learn how to love others unselfishly.

> *Many of us shared how our mothers were a blessing to us. An almost equal number of men stood up, one by one, to express their sorrow and disappointment at never having loving and caring moms.*

When our time of sharing was finished, the minister wisely asked us to pray for those who had experienced great pain through such abusive, neglectful relationships. In Jesus' name, we openly renounced all anger, animosity, and bitterness toward mothers who may have been cruel and irresponsible, and who failed in their role as a parent. For those of us who had or still have loving moms, we prayed they would forgive us for the hurt and pain we caused them by our own selfish actions. We also prayed for our wives, daughters, and grandmothers, as God touched many hearts today.

"A Visit from Death"

And as it is appointed unto men once to die, but after this the judgment....

—Hebrews 9:27

Death visited the prison yesterday evening. It was not the first time he was here, and it will not be the last. Almost always an unwanted guest, he seldom if ever announces his arrival. He just comes to take another soul, and he does his work quickly.

On May 21, shortly after 8:00 P.M., a man by the name of Leroy Green felt tightness in his chest as he was playing handball in the recreation yard. He found a corrections officer patrolling the yard and told him he needed to return to his cell to get his asthma pump, apparently assuming he was getting an asthma attack. When the officer granted Leroy his request, he made his way to his cell, where he laid down on his bunk and died. A guard making his rounds found him a short time later.

The other inmates in Leroy's housing unit were completely unaware of the situation. Most were watching television in the dayroom area when Leroy expired. They heard nothing. But when he was discovered a Code Blue was sounded. A team of officers carried Leroy to the Infirmary, and the nurse on duty asked that an Emergency Medical Unit be dispatched to the prison, which is routine procedure under such circumstances. But Leroy had already been dead for a while. Today, as expected, the entire prison was abuzz with the news of Leroy's passing. He had been in prison for a long time and was well known, though not necessarily well liked by everyone.

The thing that troubles me most about Leroy was that while he regularly attended our Sunday worship services, I do not know where his heart was concerning Jesus Christ. As my Christian friends and I discussed this unfortunate situation, we agreed that we liked Leroy, and he was even very close to some of us, but we were uneasy about his death.

Leroy was one of those men who lived a wild life, both in and out of prison. He loved to be involved in everything from the daily prison gossip to dealing in contraband, though nothing as serious as drugs or weapons. He was primarily a gambler and a cigarette hustler, buying and trading tobacco for gain. None of the dozens of sermons he heard over the years persuaded Leroy to change the direction of his life, and now he is dead.

My chaplain will conduct the traditional memorial service for Leroy, probably sometime next week. His body will be gone by then. Most likely it is already in the County Medical Examiner's Office right now, awaiting the standard autopsy as required by New York State law any time a person dies in a correctional facility. Fortunately Leroy has family on the outside who will claim his body, so he will not end up in our potter's field. But his soul? Only God knows where that is.

"Promotion"

For promotion cometh neither from the east, nor from the west, nor from the south. But God is the judge: he putteth down one, and setteth up another.

—Psalm 75:6-7

I did not previously write about a prophecy that had been made about me, as I thought it important to wait for it to come to pass. Now that it has, I will tell about it.

Back on March 14, Reverend Mackey, who visits this facility every second Sunday of the month, summoned me to the front of the chapel. As we stood before the entire congregation, he placed his hands on my head, looked at me, and spoke "words from the Lord." He said our current pastor, Brother Taylor, would soon be leaving, and that I was to be the next leader of our fellowship. I was quite surprised at his words and had mixed feelings about the news. Brother Taylor, an inmate, has been here fourteen years and, along with the chaplain, has been my mentor. Brother Taylor and I are very close, and I consider him a vital part of my life. We have been through all kinds of difficult situations together. We have prayed for each other and for our families countless times, and we have encouraged one another to go forward in our faith.

Now, however, Brother Taylor is moving on. He is serving a twenty-years-to-life sentence and has approximately two years remaining until he is eligible for parole. Earlier today the official order was given that he is to be transferred because his security classification has been lowered to medium level by the Department of Correction's Central Office in Albany. When he got the news about his transfer he had to gather his belongings and pack them for tomorrow's trip to another prison. I was expecting this to happen eventually, but the news hit me hard. Aside from being my pastor, this man is also my friend and confidant. By tomorrow he will be on a bus headed for a new place, and we probably will never see each other again until we get to heaven.

During this evening's Bible study, the approximately twenty-five men in attendance gathered around me. At Brother Taylor's direction, these men reached their hands towards me and prayed, officially anointing and appointing me as their new leader. I do not believe, however, that I will ever be able to fill Brother Taylor's shoes. He is an extremely gifted minister and preacher, and he is deeply loved by the men.

Yet during this time of prayer, Brother Taylor put his invisible spiritual mantle upon me and gave me his fullest blessing. And so begins still another chapter in my life, for I have just been promoted.

"Gone"

Yesterday I wrote about my friend and mentor Brother Taylor who, along with the Christians in my fellowship, appointed me to be the next pastor of our congregation. Today the time came for my pastor to board a prison bus that would carry him to his next facility. Now he is gone and I feel empty. After being close to Brother Taylor for fourteen years, it will take a while to get over such a loss. Our entire congregation is mourning, yet we know it is a necessary move if Brother Taylor is going to work his way toward release.

As for myself, I must confess that I do not want to be the pastor. I explained this to Brother Taylor before he left. He understood, of course, but it had been prophesied a few months earlier that this would come to pass, and it has. Now I must figure out how to manage pastoring a church of men with many needs, along with continuing my journal writing and handling my correspondence. In addition, being a pastor of a church behind prison walls is not recognized as a job assignment by the prison's administration, so I must continue to work at both my facility job assignments. During the mornings I am a mobility guide for the vision-impaired, and in the afternoons I help the men in the Intermediate Care Program.

Being a shepherd of a flock of Christians is nothing to take lightly. I want to be completely devoted to them because whatever I do, good or bad, can affect these men for all eternity. At this moment I am feeling completely overwhelmed by it all. For the past several weeks I have been feeling exhausted and was even planning to take a week off to get physically refreshed and spiritually revived. Now, however, I am being thrust forward to the very first position on the frontline in the battle for souls, and the corresponding battle against Satan and the powers of darkness that is being waged in this place. Becoming the pastor will mean that even more demands will be placed upon me, and my strength must come from Him alone. I pray, too, that my faith does not fail.

Above all, I am asking Jesus to humble my heart. I want to be the best I can be for the Lord and for my brethren. I am but a servant to all men.

"Fiery Trials"

That the trial of your faith, being much more precious than of gold
that perisheth, though it be tried with fire, might be found unto praise
and honour and glory at the appearing of Jesus Christ.

—*1 Peter 1:7*

I am thankful for the prayers people say on my behalf because the spiritual warfare against me has increased dramatically, especially since the Focus on the Family interview was aired this past March. The attacks seem to be coming from different areas all at once, and I do not believe this to be coincidence.

A few longtime friends have walked out of my life. All kinds of temptations have been assailing me. My mind has been overwhelmed with lustful thoughts, which I have been praying against in the name of Jesus. In addition, on May 21 there was the unexpected death of a member of my church. Then, on May 26, a friend and pastor, Brother Taylor, was informed that he was scheduled to be transferred to a different prison the following day, leaving

> *The spiritual warfare against me has increased dramatically.*

me to pastor and nurture the flock. He also left me with a mountain of responsibilities.

Furthermore, a mysterious woman, whom I believe may be involved in the occult, has been trying to gain entry into the facility to visit me. This woman first showed up on May 7. I was at work that Friday afternoon when an officer told me I had a visitor. I wasn't expecting anyone, so I immediately began to pray silently. I felt uneasy; something was not right.

I walked over to the officer's desk and explained my concern that someone had come to see me unannounced. He called the visiting room, which is at the opposite end of the prison, to get the person's name. It was a name I did not recognize. I sensed danger, so I told the officer at my work area that I would not be going to the visiting room. He in turn told this to the guard who was in charge of supervising the visiting area, and I went back to my job.

But this persistent person tried again. On Saturday, May 15, she returned to the facility and went into the visiting area. I was in my cellblock when, at approximately one o'clock in the afternoon, the officer in charge called out my name and said I had a visitor waiting for me. However, as before, I was not expecting anyone and again felt uneasy. This time, however, I went down to the visiting room. Without going inside, I explained my situation to the officer at the inmates' entry door. He was very understanding and told me the lady looked "unstable" and "seemed to be possessed by something." I am so glad God's Spirit guides my steps and that I have enough discernment to hear His voice!

> *I am so glad God's Spirit guides my steps and that I have enough discernment to hear His voice!*
>
> *Even with Stan's arrows flying at me from every direction, I can continue to walk with confidence and not be intimidated.*

Several days later my actions were confirmed as wise, for I was able to speak with two of the guards who saw this woman and spoke with her when she came to the visiting room. Both officers concurred that she did not appear to be mentally balanced. One of them even said she seemed to be "someone who is in the grip of a cult."

Situations like this put additional stress on me. Satan continues to try to make inroads into my life in order to distract, confuse, and weaken me, and his goal is to destroy my testimony. Without exaggeration, each day of my life as a Christian involves some form of spiritual warfare. Indeed I am walking through "the valley of the shadow of death." Yet God is with me. As Psalm 23 says, God's rod and staff are always present to comfort and sustain me. Even in the midst of many fiery trials and difficult situations, I possess God's peace that passes all human comprehension. Even with Satan's arrows flying at me from every direction, I can continue to walk with confidence and not be intimidated. The Lord is my protector, and He fights my battles. God is on my side; therefore, I will not fear what people can do to me.

"Parole Hearing"

Today I appeared before the New York State Parole Board for the second time. In accordance with the penal law I was sentenced under in 1978, I made my first appearance before the board in 2002.

I was not looking forward to this event. At approximately 8:15 this morning I was summoned to a small waiting area near the prison's visiting room. For one day each month the visiting room is closed to inmates and their families in order to accommodate a parole hearing. This is always a big event in every prison, as the inmates try to guess who will be granted parole, although almost no one ever gets it.

When I arrived at the waiting area there were nine other men scheduled for today's hearing. They hail from all walks of life, each with different crimes and varying lengths to their sentences. One man was so nervous his teeth were chattering. He made the rest of us a little more nervous than we already were by his continual pacing back and forth in such a tiny space. I was able to talk to him a bit and calm him down.

In my case, however, I was going into the room to appear before the commissioners simply to answer their questions, to apologize for my past criminal actions, and to show them the courtesy and respect due them as officials appointed by the governor, and as law enforcement personnel. I knew I would not be granted parole, and I was not seeking it. I was, however, hoping my hearing would be brief, and it was. When it was over I returned to my work assignment. The hearing was a small hurdle that had to be faced and overcome, and now it was done.

"Under Attack"

The Lord is my light and my salvation; whom shall I fear? the Lord is the strength of my life; of whom shall I be afraid?

—Psalm 27:1

What a bizarre day this has been for me. I awoke at about five o'clock this morning to have my time of prayer and Bible reading. At seven I decided to turn on my radio to listen to the news. To my surprise and dismay, one of the lead stories was about my "Forgiven for Life" Web site—and it was not a positive story.

I stood motionless in my prison cell as I listened intently to the report being given by the newscaster, who stated there was "outrage" over the Web site from some family members of the victims of my crimes. The coverage continued throughout the day, varying slightly each time it was repeated. I feel as if someone has kicked me in the stomach. I do not understand why the Web site with my testimony and journal, which has been in existence for six or seven years now, has suddenly become a major issue.

Although I had to work for about one hour this morning to help a visually-impaired inmate go to the infirmary to pick up his medications, I was originally planning to take the rest of the day off. I wanted to spend the morning listening to the funeral service for former President Ronald Reagan, and to spend time in reflection. Now I will also spend the remainder of the day thinking and praying about this Web site situation.

"Commotion"

O Lord my God, in thee do I put my trust: save me from all them that persecute me, and deliver me.

—Psalm 7:1

Yesterday I wrote about the media reports I heard concerning the "Forgiven for Life" Web site, and how some of the family members of the victims of my crimes are angry about it. Although I first learned of this situation when I happened to listen to the news on a New York City-based radio station, the originator of this story is the New York Daily News.

Earlier today a kindhearted guard gave me a copy of the June 11 edition so I could read for myself what the commotion is all about. This particular officer has known me for many years and could sense my pain and concern over what is now brewing. He also asked why the media would be fussing with me at this point in time. I told him I have no idea.

> *I feel it is important for me to explain what it is like to be a Christian serving God behind prison walls.*

Now, however, having read the headline story, I wish to apologize if the "Forgiven for Life" Web site has upset the two parties who voiced their complaints in the article. One person is Neysa Moskowitz, the mother of victim Stacy Moskowitz. The second party is Michael Lauria, whose daughter, Donna, perished by my hand. Both of these individuals have been angry and bitter toward me for many years, and I can certainly understand their feelings. After all, many years ago I caused them much pain and deprived them of their loved ones. They may never get over such a loss. The newspaper article, however, said I was flaunting my writings to the world, which is absolutely untrue. And one of yesterday's newscasters from the CBS radio station said in a sarcastic manner that I have now become a "cyber-celebrity."

The truth is that "Forgiven for Life" has existed for several years. I have never advertised it, nor have I tried to call attention to it. It is simply a Christian/spiritual Web site, owned and operated by my friends in California. Its main purpose is to honor and glorify Jesus Christ, and the main theme is forgiveness—how God can and will forgive all who call upon Him in faith. Also, in addition to writing about the love and mercy of God, I share my own story of redemption so others can draw hope and encouragement from it. I feel it is important for me to explain what it is like to be a Christian serving God behind prison walls. I write about an array of topics and subjects, especially about the lives of men who have committed crimes and how they struggle to survive in this often inhospitable and stressful environment. I explain how some of these men try to come to terms with what brought them to prison, and I share how they strive to make amends to their families as well as to a society that has, for the most part, rejected them. I tell stories about prisoners who seek forgiveness from their victims and from God. They want to change their lives, and they do not want to continue with self-destructive behavior patterns and in destructive lifestyles.

Over the years the responses to the Web page have been wonderful and positive. Furthermore, here in this correctional facility I am treated like any other inmate. I am afforded no special privileges, and I am doing my time in the general population. I am neither treated as a "celebrity" nor as a "little prince," as Mrs. Moskowitz said to the reporter who interviewed her for the article.

It is too bad the *Daily News* misled the public into thinking that "Forgiven for Life" is some kind of attention-seeking Web site, when it has been fairly low-key all these years, until the newspaper itself put the spotlight on it. My prayer is that this media firestorm quickly passes.

JULY 8, 2004

"Purpose-Driven Lives"

I recently came down with a bad case of the flu. The symptoms began the last few days of June. At first I thought it was only a summer cold, but it quickly escalated until I was very sick. I am just now getting over it at long last.

I have never before had the flu during the summer months. I think, however, that my immune system's resistance was down from the stresses I was under in June. Throughout the past month I had to deal with the parole hearing, followed by the media's criticisms of the Web site, which went on for several weeks. I also had an accumulation of pressures from having to be a full-time caregiver and pastoring a church. Now, thankfully, my strength is returning. God has been faithful, and His grace has once again proven to be sufficient. But I still feel tired and weak from the residue of this flu bug.

This evening I went to our regular Thursday night Bible study in the chapel. During tonight's class we have been studying from the popular book *The Purpose-Driven Life* by Rick Warren. An inmate named Brother Mike has been teaching from the book, and we have been trying to cover one chapter each week.

In today's class Mike asked each of us what we felt was our purpose in life—more specifically, what is our purpose within the Body of Christ, or the Church. I shared my view that our fullest purpose, according to God's plans, may not be completely achieved in this lifetime. I told the group that, while we as individual Christians do have our specific callings and functions within our respective fellowship and within the Church, there is a bigger picture to consider. I then read from John 14 where the Lord Jesus tells His disciples about the mansions He is preparing for us in heaven. I also shared a few passages that tell us our "citizenship" is already in heaven. I said that while God has already made us "complete" in Him, and while He has filled us with His Spirit and with joy, we have especially been created to live with

Him in eternity. Moreover, I explained that while the Lord is busy working in our lives, helping us to grow spiritually as well as preparing us for "works of service" now (see Ephesians 2:10), He is likewise preparing us for a place and a position in heaven.

I think this is an awesome concept, for we can live at present with a great hope and expectation, knowing that when we leave this earth the Lord has spectacular things planned for us. My heart, I told them, beats wildly with anticipation of what is ahead for all of us. In heaven there will be no taint of sin in our new bodies, and we shall never again experience pain or loss or disappointment. Jesus the Messiah has a place in heaven for those who, in this temporal life, are prisoners. Ahead is a far better life than we have ever known.

"The Adversary"

Be sober, be vigilant; because your adversary the devil, as a roaring lion, walketh about, seeking whom he may devour.

—1 Peter 5:8

Satan knows he has but a short time to finish his work of destruction, and he has declared an all-out war on the saints. The devil is busy trying to wear out the Church. He is always coming up with new schemes to harass and destroy God's faithful servants who, although far from perfect, desire to give their best to God. Satan tries to rob the Church of rest. Many Christians, however, know nothing of this level of warfare since they have never fully given their lives to the Lord.

> *The devil is busy trying to wear out the Church.*
>
> *Those who have set their hearts to serve the Lord and lay down their lives for the gospel's sake will suffer the most ferocious of trials.*

I don't think Satan is worried about Christians who are laid back, content to remain sitting in the pews or busying themselves with worldly affairs. But those who have set their hearts to serve the Lord and lay down their lives for the gospel's sake will suffer the most ferocious of trials, with all hell seemingly set against them. My message to these dedicated servants and saints is to arm yourselves and prepare to suffer. Keep on the full armor of God. Fight the good fight of faith. Pray fervently. Rejoice in your persecutions. Pray for your enemies and for those who lie and slander you. Give God the glory at all times, and give Him thanks for all things and in all circumstances, for it is only by His grace that we can endure to the end.

As the scripture says, "Nay, in all these things we are more than conquerors through him that loved us" (Romans 8:37; see also 1 Peter 4:1; 4:12-19; 5:8-10).

"Wonderful Day"

O come, let us sing unto the Lord: let us make a joyful noise to the rock of our salvation.

—Psalm 95:1

Today more than 180 men, women, and children gathered in Sullivan Correctional Facility's main recreation yard to praise the Lord and fellowship together. We made a joyful and loud noise unto the Lord, and we rejoiced at being able to sing to God and worship Him.

As the day began it appeared as if it might rain, but we prayed that it would not. The sun eventually came out, and from nine o'clock this morning until two-thirty this afternoon we had our annual Christian "Family Day" event. A number of the men from my fellowship had family members in attendance. We also had many of our regular volunteer ministers present. In addition, visiting with us were about twenty members from the Manhattan Grace Tabernacle Church in New York City, with their pastor, Luis Rivera, and his lovely wife, Debbie. Pastor Rivera's choir filled the yard with praise. Even the inmates in the cellblocks heard the music. Our inmate choir also sang many songs, and various ministers were able to give words of encouragement to the men and their families. I have no doubt that hearts were touched by all this.

The day before the event I had been part of an eighteen-man set-up detail. We went into the yard early Friday morning to lay out the tables and chairs, place garbage cans around the area, and help erect the heavy tents for everyone to sit and eat under. It was a lot of work, but it felt great to be out in the fresh air. We worked until afternoon. Then, on the day of the event, I helped serve the food, as well as greet many of our visitors and the inmates and their families. With a lot of kids running around it felt as if I were in a public park, far removed from prison life, at least until the event was over.

At exactly two-thirty a handful of corrections officers began to move through the crowd to announce that our time was up and everyone had to leave. Our family members and the ministry groups were escorted out of the yard first. When they were gone it was our turn to leave, a few men at a time, to be "strip-frisked" and searched, and then sent to our respective cellblocks.

It was hard to say goodbye to so many good friends.

"Big Decision"

This past week I had to make a major decision, and I had to be very careful to seek the Lord's counsel on the matter. I did, and He told me to make a change. Therefore, as of today, I have left my job at the Intermediate Care Program (ICP) in the afternoons.

This is a big change for me, as I have been going into this special unit for many years to help and encourage the inmates who have various mental and emotional problems. With my present workload, however, along with my many responsibilities as an elder in the church and all the writing I do, it has been too much for me. I was burning out. For many weeks I have been walking around in a state of semi-exhaustion, and the Lord had been trying to get my attention for a long time. After much prayer, I believe God directed me to leave my job at the mental health cellblock and to become a porter in my own cellblock during the afternoons.

This change takes effect today. In the mornings I will continue to do my work as a mobility guide to help the blind and visually-impaired, but in the afternoons I will be cleaning the building where I live. My janitorial work will allow me more time to pray and study my Bible, and I will still be able to go into the ICP Unit on occasion because Phil, who is blind, lives in this unit. I will therefore have the continued opportunity to minister to these men without having to spend as many hours in ICP as I once did.

"Talking to Teens"

I consider it a privilege to write serious and sobering messages for young persons to help them see life more clearly and think more intelligently about the choices they make, choices that may affect their lives for decades, maybe even forever. When I write my messages to teens I urge them to take life seriously. It is a blessing to be alive and healthy, not sick or crippled, in prison or dead.

I also want to tell teenagers, especially the guys who so often act impulsively and think they are invincible, that the road to manhood and getting respect should never involve violence. There is nothing more cowardly than stabbing someone with a knife, or slicing their face with a razor, or pointing a gun at an unarmed individual and shooting. There is nothing manly or cool about carrying a weapon, not even if you are trying to make the lame excuse that it's for "protection."

> *The prison I live in is full of men who have ruined their lives.*
>
> *The smartest and coolest people are those who come clean and come to Jesus Christ for forgiveness.*

The prison I live in is full of men who have ruined their lives. Many will swear that when they did their crime they never considered the consequences or thought about the families of the victims or how these people would suffer. Now it's just the opposite. These guys, who are locked up in cages like animals, think about their stupid crimes a lot, and the faces of their victims have come back to haunt them.

After personally spending more than twenty-seven years in prison, I believe the smartest and coolest people are those who come clean and come to Jesus Christ for forgiveness. They come to Him because they want to lead a better life and have a personal relationship with God. They are tired of doing wrong and want to live right.

For each one of them, Jesus Christ is and always will be the Best Choice. The next wise choice is to choose never again to commit a crime.

"Changing Seasons"

To every thing there is a season, and a time to every purpose under the heaven.

—Ecclesiastes 3:1

I always pay careful attention to the changing of the seasons and try to observe everything I can about nature. Now, as summer nears its end, several more trees have begun to make their transition from verdant greens to the brilliant brown and bronze of autumn. I have also been seeing more flocks of geese in the sky, crisscrossing over the prison en route to the many lakes that dot the countryside. Maybe they are trying to get their bearings before beginning their long journey south. In addition, an ever increasing number of sparrows seem to be using the thirty-foot triangular courtyard outside my window as a meeting place. Early in the morning they begin gathering in the concrete yard or on the rooftops of the buildings. I could spend hours watching them, as they bounce up and down on their little feet, then suddenly fly away as if being chased by some unseen predator.

However, as August comes to a close, I thank the Lord not only for the lovely displays of His creation, but also for a very spiritually prosperous and productive month. God has afforded me many opportunities to help the men and to share my testimony, but primarily I have been able to pray for them and give them words of encouragement from the Scriptures, much as the Lord encourages and strengthens me.

None of us knows how much longer we will be on this earth. The Lord's coming for His children could be soon, or possibly not for many more years. Either way, I want to be ready should the "midnight cry" come today. But while I am still on this earth I must give my heart to Christ each day, because I fall short in so many ways. I am still working on overcoming this lazy flesh that is so prone to sin. And while my carnal desires will never be completely eradicated in this lifetime, through the Holy Spirit's help and

His indwelling presence, I can live victoriously and not allow sin to rule me.

God is merciful. The Messiah's plan is for people to repent, to turn away from their sins, and to come to Him for forgiveness and salvation. May I never cease to proclaim the gospel.

"David's Face"

Instead of tombstones to mark the dead there were rows of faces. A few were smiling, but most were somber, staring into the camera with military-style bravado and machismo. These were the faces of soldiers ready for combat, though I am not sure how many were ready for death. Now none of them will get to hug their parents or pick up their kids or see their hometowns ever again.

It has been said that God works in mysterious ways. A few weeks ago I happened to come across a copy of the September 9 edition of the *New York Times*, which someone else had apparently left on a table in the dayroom. Though it was outdated, we inmates learn to make do with whatever periodicals and media we can find.

I took the paper to my cell and began to flip through the pages, reading only the articles that interested me. Then I came to the "National" section and found the "Roster of the Dead," the pictures of the men and women from the U.S. Military who have died in the latest conflict in Iraq. I immediately looked for a picture of David, my friend's son who died earlier this year.

Seeing his smiling face made me sad. He didn't look like a soldier, and he was too young to die. And yet I knew David was with Jesus, and his family takes great comfort in that. For Jesus Himself said, "And ye shall hear of wars and rumours of wars: see that ye be not troubled: for all these things must come to pass…" (Matthew 24:6).

Good will ultimately triumph over evil.

"My Tears"

And God shall wipe away all tears from their eyes.

—Revelation 21:4a

Today makes thirty-seven years since my mother left this world at the age of fifty-two, and I still miss her very much.

I vividly remember when I first learned she had died. A young man by the name of Mark Rubenstein, who was the son of my mother's best friend, Melba, was told by his mom to stand in front of our apartment building on Stratford Avenue and wait for me to come home from school at three o'clock. When Mark saw me coming down the street he began to walk in my direction. When we met, he told me my dad wanted me to call him at my Uncle Lou's house. As soon as Mark said those words, I knew my mom, who had been in the hospital for several months with terminal cancer, was dead.

> *We humans were never meant to die or to mourn.*
> *God created us to live forever.*

We humans were never meant to die or to mourn. The Bible makes it perfectly clear that God created us to live forever. But Adam and Eve sinned, and everything changed. With sin came death, and with death came grief for those left behind.

But that is not the end of the story. The Lord has promised that a day will come when there will no longer be any sin, death, or suffering. There will be only goodness in the new heaven and the new earth. One day God will wipe away all tears from the eyes of His children. How I long for that moment!

"Madman Made Free"

And he went his way, and published throughout the whole city how great things Jesus had done unto him.

—Luke 8:39b

The above Bible verse is a quote about the formerly demon-possessed man whom Jesus had set free from torment. According to the Scripture accounts in Mark 5 and Luke 8, wicked spirits had completely overwhelmed this poor man and taken over his life. They drove him into the wilderness and drove him insane. In fact, his condition got so bad the local townspeople often placed him in heavy chains in an effort to keep him under control. But through the power of those demons he broke all the chains, only to roam through the valleys in a rage, screaming and cutting himself with stones.

And then he had a sudden encounter with Jesus and was promptly delivered from his tormentors and his misery. In gratitude he asked Jesus if he could join His group and follow along with them. Instead the Lord told him to go back to his family and friends and tell everyone who would listen how God had mercy and compassion on him.

This grateful man did as Jesus told him. He returned home and began to tell everyone about the goodness and power of the Lord. And the Bible tells us that everyone marveled at his story.

I was like that lonely, tormented man whom the Son of God set free, and I am now on the same mission to proclaim the salvation and power of the Lord. I must share the message of forgiveness of sin through Jesus Christ to all who are perishing, to all who will hear.

"Freedom from Guilt"

Last night I answered a letter from a woman who had struggled with guilt after having an abortion. She spoke of having gone through an unbearable time, and said she had found it difficult to forgive herself. Now, however, she is doing well and is actively involved in a church. Best of all, through God's grace, she has finally come around to forgiving herself for what she believed to be a terrible wrong. I wrote to affirm her faith and told her how happy I am that she is now living with God's peace.

> *Freedom from Guilt*
> *I believe we can learn from our past sins.*
>
> *We do not have to wallow in guilt, self-pity, or despair.*

Many Christians are in great desperation because they believe they have fallen so far into sin that Jesus doesn't want them anymore, or else, after having committed certain sins, they cannot forgive themselves. Here is what I wrote to the woman who had struggled over just such a situation.

I am glad you have finally been able to forgive yourself. God's Word assures us that if we confess our sins to Him, He is faithful and just to forgive us of our sins and to cleanse us from all unrighteousness (1 John 1:9). The latter portion of this scripture verse deals with the aspect of cleansing not only God's record of our sins, but also the guilt we experienced after committing these sins. In addition, God also cleanses us from the bad memories that follow. Most often this kind of inner healing occurs gradually over time. Many Christians are pained by a guilty conscience, even long after the Lord has already forgiven them. I know this to be true from my own experience. It took several years after I got "saved" for me to finally realize I was indeed forgiven.

I believe we can learn from our past sins. We can suffer difficult consequences when we do wrong, and we can carry around the scars of such actions for a long time. But we do not have to wallow in guilt, self-pity, or despair. Through God's mercy we can confess our sins to Him, repent of them, and move on. Jesus Christ wants us to enjoy our relationship with Him. It is not His will for us to be in bondage to excessive feelings of sorrow for the things He has already forgiven—and paid for with His blood.

"Don't Trust in Wrong Things"

Thus saith the Lord; Cursed be the man that trusteth in man, and maketh flesh his arm, and whose heart departeth from the Lord.
—Jeremiah 17:5

The election is over and President Bush will remain in office. However, I don't want to have a false sense of security that our nation is safe because a professing Christian is in the White House. The terrorists are still out there, and they hate the United States of America.

Likewise the devil is still seeking souls to destroy. And millions continue to practice sin, giving no thought to the God of love and justice spoken of in the Bible.

I therefore say with both humility and boldness that trouble is ahead for the United States, and for the entire world. A period of tribulation is coming. Jesus Christ spoke of this future time concerning the end of the age. The book of Revelation discusses it. The ancient Hebrew prophets continue to shout their warnings from the pages of the Old Testament.

America, please listen! The drumbeats of a mighty demonic army are intensifying, and they will one day march across the earth, using the bodies of evil and ignorant men. Their weapons will be lies, hatred, fanaticism, and terrorism.

When will this happen? Only God knows. But it will occur just as the Bible predicts.

I give thanks to the Lord because He is still holding back this time of wrath, and for now there remains time to repent.

"Porter"

And whatsoever ye do in word or deed, do all in the name of the Lord Jesus, giving thanks to God and the Father by Him.

—Colossians 3:17

Today was officially my first day working as a full-time janitor. The prison's administration identifies my job as "porter," but janitor or custodian is more appropriate. Much of my work consists of washing and disinfecting the eating tables, sweeping the dayroom and other areas of the building, then mopping the steps and floors. I also do a lot of dusting. There are windows to wash, and five other men and I take turns cleaning the utility sink area. I don't mind, though, as I like working with my hands. But what I like best is that when I am done with my chores I can go back to my cell to pray, read, or write.

One of my early morning duties is to use a powerful disinfectant to sterilize the telephones. We have only two phones to share among sixty-eight men. I had long since taken the initiative on my own to clean the phones, wiping the entire booths with the disinfectant and a damp cloth. Over time many of the men have told me how much they appreciate this, as the receivers with their mouthpieces can be a serious source of germs.

Overall, being a porter can be monotonous, humbling work, as I have to clean up the messes that other people make. But as a Christian I am called to be a servant, so this job is good training.

"A Ticket"

The winter's first real snowfall began this morning. Several days ago there were flurries, along with a blustery wind. Now, however, large fat snowflakes have been spiraling downwards from the sky. But it is still too early for the snow to stay on the ground for very long.

Something else happened today that wasn't as nice as the snowfall. I was issued a misbehavior report for a rule violation: "113.15—Unauthorized Exchange." At approximately eight-thirty this morning the cellblock officer approached me while I was working and said someone had called for me from the disciplinary office and I had to report there immediately. I had no idea what it was about, as I was not conscious of breaking any rule.

When I entered the disciplinary area a guard showed me a report that had been filed against me the day before. According to procedure, I had to sign for my copy so I could review it. I was surprised to read that on November 11 at approximately 1620 hours (4:20 P.M.) I was written up by Correction Officer "G" in the following manner:

> On the above date and time, while packing cell IN #... [inmate's name was given], I found a prayer book with writing on the inside cover indicating it belongs to David Berkowitz.

The misbehavior report also mentioned that the book seized as "contraband" was given an identification number in the prison's evidence log. I knew it would then be placed in storage, under lock and key in an evidence locker where it will remain until the day of my disciplinary hearing. As a result of this report I was given a Tier II level "walking ticket," which is considered to be a serious level. But the lieutenant in charge of the disciplinary office did not deem it necessary for me to be confined to my cell until the hearing, so I am not under any restrictions. I can go about my business and continue to attend the chapel services and Bible studies. However, one day within the next two weeks I will have to appear before a lieutenant to answer for this violation.

I am very surprised that anyone would actually write up an inmate for giving another inmate a book about prayer. The inmate mentioned in the report in whose cell the book was found is an emotionally troubled individual with whom I have been sharing my faith.

Only the Lord knows what will become of this report and the future disciplinary hearing.

"Treasures in Prison"

This may sound offensive to some, but prisons contain many of God's children, for it is in places like this where the Lord has hidden some of His special treasures. Behind these walls are men and women who shine with the Holy Spirit. Unfortunately, society's inclination is to dismiss prisoners as unredeemable and incorrigible, with little worth and having no ability to contribute anything of value to the world. Even some Christians seem to hold this view, and many churches and ministries have tried to keep a safe distance from those who are incarcerated. They often do the same with those who have been released but remain branded by law enforcement and the criminal justice system as ex-cons, felons, or parolees.

> *Prisons contain many of God's children, for it is in places like this where the Lord has hidden some of His special treasures.*
>
> *With the Lord there is forgiveness, mercy, and hope.*

I must humbly say that Christians who hold these opinions and act like this are wrong. Yes, there are men and women in correctional facilities who have broken the law, though some may actually be innocent. Countless others are on parole. But God hasn't given up on them, just as He has never given up on me, for the Bible makes it clear that with the Lord there is forgiveness, mercy, and hope.

Of course we must all make our own choices. Some will reject the incarcerated, while others will be able to see what the Lord is doing in their lives. But I refer to John 3:16 as a reminder: "For God so loved the world, that he gave his only begotten Son, that whosoever believeth in him should not perish, but have everlasting life." Whosoever is a very big word, and it includes everyone!

"The Verdict"

This morning while doing my janitorial duties the cellblock officer informed me that I had to report to the disciplinary office immediately. I left what I was doing and promptly reported to the lieutenant on duty at disciplinary. I knew it was time to answer the ticket I had received on November 12 for an alleged violation of Rule 113.15, "Unauthorized Exchange." The prison administration has up to two weeks to call an inmate to answer to charges on a "Tier II" level misbehavior report. My being summoned today was within the allowable time limit, according to the State of New York Department of Correctional Services "Standards of Inmate Behavior for all Institutions" manual.

Here at Sullivan Correctional Facility, the disciplinary office is located near the front portion of the prison near the package room, visiting room, and a short distance from the infirmary. I had to walk down three long corridors and pass through a metal detector to get there. Once through the metal door at the entrance to the disciplinary office, I handed my pass to the officer on duty, who then directed me to a waiting room where I had to sit until I was called into the lieutenant's office.

The waiting room is a 15x15 foot windowless square with wooden benches placed against the side walls. Each bench is bolted to the floor. This morning the otherwise barren room was filled with several gloomy-faced men who, like me, awaited their turn to defend themselves.

My name was called at approximately 9:25. I entered the lieutenant's office, and my hearing officially commenced at 9:27. A small tape recorder sat on the desk between the lieutenant and me, as is the standard procedure for Tier II hearings. The charge was read, and then the hearing officer asked me how I was going to plead and if I had an explanation for my actions. I quickly discovered it was not a book about prayer that I was accused of giving to the other inmate, as the misbehavior report stated, but rather a little Gideon Pocket Testament, the same kind God had used to touch my heart about seventeen years ago.

I recognized the testament when the lieutenant showed it to me, so I humbly admitted that I had probably given it to the inmate mentioned in the report. I explained that it was my job as a program aide to go from cell to cell while I was working at the Intermediate Care Program and to minister to the residents. I told the lieutenant it was also my responsibility to look for signs of depression among the inmates, help them write letters home, pray for them when asked to do so, and give assistance any way I could. It seemed this would include giving a Bible to any prisoner who asked for one.

The lieutenant, after listening to my explanation, acknowledged that he knew of my faith and of my concern for the men. Then he reminded me that prison rules forbid me from giving anything to another inmate, even a Bible or a religious book, without first obtaining permission. He then acknowledged my good institutional record and the fact that I had not received a misbehavior "write-up" since 1989. (Some prisoners log a dozen or more misbehavior reports in a year's time!)

Nevertheless, I was found guilty of breaking rule 113.15, making an "unauthorized exchange." I was automatically fined five dollars, which is the required penalty for all Tier II misbehavior infractions. Fortunately, however, I was given no other penalties, such as confinement to my cell. The lieutenant counseled me not to break the rule again, and when the hearing was officially completed at 9:39 I was free to go back to my cellblock and return to work.

Later I told another officer, a man I've known for many years, that if inmates handed nothing but Christian books and Bibles to one another the guards wouldn't have anything to worry about. While I wasn't upset about getting a ticket for giving an inmate a Bible, I did feel foolish.

Overall the hearing went well. I spoke respectfully to the lieutenant, and all I had done was give a Bible to another prisoner. Other guys who are found guilty of making an "Unauthorized Exchange" have usually passed weapons or drugs or other forms of contraband. Later I told another officer, a man I've known for many years, that if inmates handed nothing but Christian books and Bibles to one another the guards wouldn't have anything to worry about. He laughed and admitted it was probably true.

While I wasn't upset about getting a ticket for giving an inmate a Bible, I did feel foolish. I'm fifty-one years old, and having to report to the disciplinary office and sit on a chair with my hands folded meekly in my lap while a sharply dressed lieutenant behind a big wooden desk eyeballs me suspiciously reminded me of being an adolescent in junior high school, getting summoned to the dean's office for a scolding.

I felt like a naughty little boy who got caught for putting a rotten egg on a hot radiator in a classroom, causing the room to stink.

The entire incident seemed pointless, but, of course, I kept this thought to myself.

"Thanks to the King"

O give thanks unto the Lord; for he is good: for his mercy endureth for ever.

—*Psalm 136:1*

I stand in humble gratitude and bow my heart before the King of Israel for His love and forgiveness, and for the wonderful things He has done in my life. I have absolutely no doubt that the Lord's hands of love and compassion have guided and protected me, and He has helped me through every problem. The Lord has removed every mountain of opposition from my path. I am also thankful for God's Word. Throughout the years so many passages from the Bible have brought me comfort, peace, and joy. His words have filled my heart with hope and encouragement.

And so, though my friends and loved ones are far away from me on this Thanksgiving Day, I have the Lord Jesus as my ever-present Companion. He has promised never to leave or forsake me, and I am complete in Him. I pray for all those who find themselves in adverse circumstances during this season. May God provide them with food, clothing, shelter, and a taste of His love.

"Plenty of Women"

A few weeks ago a friend handed me an article he thought I would be interested in reading. I put it in a folder and forgot about it until I came across it this morning. It is titled "More Women In Prison Than Ever, Report Finds." The Associated Press story, published on page 16 of the Times Herald Record on Monday, November 8, 2004, stated, "There are 101,179 women in prisons" in 2003, a "3.6 percent increase" from 2002.

Like death, incarceration is no respecter of persons. The article said that some of the biggest increases in female inmates in correctional facilities were in the states of North Dakota, Minnesota, Montana, Wyoming, and Hawaii, in that order. It also said there may be up to 80,000 more women in local jails that were not a part of the above count.

The federal prison system, according to the article, had a female population of 11,635 at the close of 2003. Texas had 13,487, while California had 10,656 at the end of last year. The numbers were rising in most states, though the incarceration rate for women actually went down in a dozen states.

I don't know all the reasons for such increases, but in many areas of the United States communities are losing ground to drugs. There has been a rise in the number of people addicted to methamphetamines, especially in the Midwest and in rural areas from Nebraska to North Dakota. Powerful mind-numbing drugs continue to destroy lives and damage families, yet these chemicals remain an escape mechanism for many. I believe drugs are used to seek solace from a world of pain, disappointment, and gnawing emptiness. Of course the end of an addiction is destruction. The drugs people take to stop their problems only end up causing more problems.

The article stated: "Expressed in terms of the population at large, this means that in 2003, one in every 109 U.S. men was in prison. For women the figure was one in every 1,613." Obviously many men and women are presently incarcerated in the United States. I believe a large part of the solution to rising incarceration rates and drug use is a spiritual awakening for our nation.

"Hidden Lives"

For ye are dead, and your life is hid with Christ in God.
—Colossians 3:3

During my interview with Focus on the Family I stated that the testimonies of men and women behind bars need to be heard. Such stories attest to the saving power of the gospel and how Jesus Christ can transform hearts and lives.

The public and media basically think most prisoners are incorrigible. Many inmates I have known—and I have met hundreds during my twenty-seven years of incarceration—freely admit they have done wrong and broken the law. They regret their criminal actions, as well as the pain they have inflicted on others and the damage they have done to themselves. Even the most seemingly hardened gang members and drug kingpins have soft spots. The Hollywood image of tough convicts devoid of any tender emotions is somewhat exaggerated.

> *The Testimonies of men and women behind bars need to be heard.*
>
> *Inmates who get radically changed by the Lord become some of the strongest Christians in America.*

The truth is that those inmates who get radically changed by the Lord become some of the strongest Christians in America. As the Lord Jesus said, "Those who have been forgiven for much, love much. Those who have been forgiven for little, love little" (Luke 7:47, personal paraphrase). Most Christian prisoners love God and others very much.

"The Harvest Field"

*Pray ye therefore the Lord of the harvest, that he will send forth labor-
ers into his harvest.*

—*Matthew 9:38*

I no longer see prison as a place of punishment. Yes, doing time is difficult
and inmates deal with many deprivations. But I see myself as a missionary serving God in a distant land. I also see my imprisonment as a training
ground to help me become a more mature Christian, and a man of strong
faith.

This is a place where I can get to know my Creator. I am learning to
love Jesus in ways and at levels that, if I were living as an ordinary guy with
a wife, kids, and a home in the suburbs, I might
never have experienced. Furthermore, prisons
contain many lonely, hurting, broken people.
These are my neighbors. I pass them in the hallways. I see them as they play basketball in the
recreation yard, or watch hours of television in
the dayrooms. I am fortunate that I don't have to
travel to the steaming jungles of Brazil or the
frozen steppes of Mongolia to find needy souls.

> *I see myself as a
> missionary serving God
> in a distant land.*
>
> *The prison is my
> mission field. In here
> is a ripe harvest of
> hungry hearts.*

All I have to do is stand in the chow line or sit in the dayroom of my cellblock. Lost and desperate souls are everywhere. I only have to open my
mouth and speak Christ's words of life.

This prison is my mission field. In here is a ripe harvest of hungry hearts.

"An Invitation"

This morning God blessed me when the counselor from E-North's Intermediate Care Program invited me to come and spend the afternoon with the mentally challenged men in the program. I was thrilled. Although I live in the general population I used to work in the Intermediate Care Program, and I am still one of the few inmates with the necessary clearance to go into that area of the facility. I have no doubt that God called me in this direction, because I have a heart for these men. I treat each one as special.

At twelve-thirty this afternoon, as soon as I finished my janitor's job, I headed to E-North. I was able to stay until three, and it was great being able to talk with these guys. They were glad to see me and asked when I was coming back to work in the Unit. I told them I would do so only if I sensed the Lord leading me to return.

There are about sixty-four men in E-North. Many suffer from depression and other mental and emotional ailments. Most are in touch with reality for much of the time, and almost all require some form of psychotropic medication to function well. Many, in my opinion, don't even belong in prison but in a psychiatric institution or something similar.

But today I simply came to these men as a friend, bringing God's compassion to the lonely, tormented, and hurting.

"Christmas Eve Service"

I know thy works, that thou hast a name that thou livest, and art dead.

—Revelation 3:1b

I just returned to my cell after attending the Christmas Eve service in the prison chapel. My chaplain is on vacation so I conducted the event. The Lord was with me, and it went very well.

For approximately one hour and forty-five minutes, which was our allotted time, the congregation was able to praise the Lord. Our choir led in the music and singing. We thanked Jesus our Savior for His love and mercy, and several men took turns telling how God had watched over them throughout the year.

With our chaplain absent it was up to me to preach the sermon. I took my text from Revelation 3, about the church in the ancient city of Sardis. It was not a typical Christmas message, yet I believe it was what God wanted us to hear. I spoke about the importance of getting right with God and seeking His forgiveness for all unconfessed sin. I talked about Jesus' message to Sardis about repentance, and explained that we are at a crucial stage as a body of believers because we can either neglect the things of God and spiritually wither away, or we can take hold of all the Lord has for us and flourish. I told the flock that just because we are a busy church does not mean God is automatically pleased with us.

> *There are many "works of the flesh" that appear spiritual, but God views such activities as mere human endeavors with no spiritual value.*

The church at Sardis was a busy congregation. They had a reputation in their community of being a lively and busy group. But as the passage from Revelation shows, Jesus saw them as being spiritually dead. They were doing many good works, and probably with the best of intentions, but without the Holy Spirit's guidance or direction. I asked the men if we might be guilty of doing the same.

I then went on to explain that there are many "works of the flesh" that appear spiritual, but God views such activities as mere human endeavors with no spiritual value. These carnal activities will turn out to be "wood, hay, and stubble" that will be consumed at the Judgment Seat of Christ. I also emphasized the importance of repentance. With a new year coming, it is a good time to "wipe the slate clean" with God. We should humbly confess our failings to Him and be ready to begin 2005 with a renewed love for Jesus and a fresh vision for our church.

Finally I confessed that being a pastor is very challenging. I must constantly examine myself to see where I am missing the mark. I admitted that I fall short of God's perfect standard, and I need His mercy and grace daily.

It was a good evening. I did, however, have a very difficult day. I have the flu again, and it has hit me hard. I also had to move to another cellblock shortly after breakfast this morning, and I have yet to unpack my things.

"Christmas Service"

I awoke this morning with the flu in full possession of my body. My throat was so sore I could barely speak or swallow. I had to push myself to get off my bunk and begin my prayers. Then I had to wash and get dressed. I knew this was going to be a long day and I would need divine assistance every step of the way.

Under other circumstances I would have tried to stay in bed. I was tempted to wrap myself in a blanket and go back to sleep. But today was the Christmas service (even though Christmas was yesterday), and I had to be present, especially in the chaplain's absence.

It had been planned well before my chaplain took his vacation that I would be in the chapel this Sunday to lead the service and make sure that all went well. The congregation and I were expecting our regular guests, a ministry group from Queens, New York, but they never showed up. Still, our service began promptly at ten. I opened in prayer and then called on different men to do their tasks, such as Scripture readings and announcements. Our choir then began to

> *I admonished and encouraged the men to look beyond the outward things like skin color to see the souls of others.*

lead us in worship. By eleven I realized that no one from the outside was coming. I began to pray and seek help from the Lord, as I was going to have to preach again, and I needed a message.

When the time came I stepped up to the podium and apologized that our guests were not here. The guys always look forward to people coming from the outside. But I assured the sixty or so prisoners in attendance that we were going to make the best of our situation, and that I would do my best to bring them a message.

Standing in the pulpit alone was difficult. I told the guys I had the flu. They saw my flushed face and raspy voice, and many of them prayed for me, which was a great encouragement. At some point, however, God's strength and presence overshadowed me. I began to feel stronger and my voice was coming back. My text was Acts 17:22-31. My message, although I touched on many different areas, was "We are all of different colors, but one blood and one Body in Christ."

I also read John 3:16 and preached on the love of Jesus the Messiah, who willingly took His place on the cross for us. I admonished and encouraged the men to look beyond the outward things like skin color to see the souls of others. I stressed that separating from others because of skin color, nationality, or even gang affiliations is not of God. The Lord has called us to be one Body in Christ, with all the members having the same care for one another.

Thanks to the Lord's faithfulness, everything went well at this Christmas service.

"Out of My Comfort Zone"

God knows how to keep me uncomfortable enough that I have to depend on Him for all my needs—not only physical but also for the spiritual needs of faith, peace, hope, and strength. God must have known I needed a change because I have now moved to a different cellblock and am no longer in what had become my comfort zone. The soul gets weak when a Christian gets too comfortable. I am now living in a tenser area of the prison, so more prayer is needed. This is a tough and hardened group, full of racism, anger, and bitterness, and even a handful of Santeria practitioners, whom I have nicknamed "The Voodoo Club."

I have my work cut out for me, but as I have often said, "The light of Jesus shines the brightest when the environment is the darkest." In addition, I am still working as a porter. When I got here I volunteered to take the least desirable of the custodial assignments, the showers. Every morning and afternoon from Monday through Friday I clean, scrub, and disinfect the shower stalls while they are not in use. I don a pair of Playtex gloves, grab a bucket and an assortment of brushes, disinfectant, and Ajax, and get to work. These are the tools of my trade. It is humbling work, but it is good for me.

"Bittersweet"

For we would not, brethren, have you ignorant of our trouble which came to us in Asia, that we were pressed out of measure, above strength, insomuch that we despaired even of life.

—*2 Corinthians 1:8*

I am staggering into the New Year, having been "pressed out of measure" by a seemingly endless string of trials. Weary and physically drained and still weak from the flu, I am going forward, knowing that God will see me through. I have no special plans for this year other than to continue to trust in the Lord and seek His face, for apart from Him I can do nothing (see John 15:5). God is my strength and my salvation, and He gives me a "song in the night" to keep me joyful and at peace. His grace is sufficient in my weakness, for when I am weak, Christ is strong (see 2 Corinthians 12:9, 12:10). I am learning to be thankful for the trials and tribulations, as they keep me on my knees, humble and completely dependent on the Lord.

With all this in mind I am closing out the year with both tears and joy. It has been bittersweet. Old friends have left, and new friends have come in. Satan has launched attacks to cause me hardship, but the Lord Jesus has remained a faithful companion who has not left me. He will see me through. Amen!

2005

"Moving Forward"

*"...forgetting those things which are behind, and reaching forth unto
those things which are before, I press toward the mark for the prize of
the high calling of God in Christ Jesus."*
— *Philippians 3:13, 3:14*

I am walking into this New Year weary but hopeful. In a world that groans
with war and tragedy, I have my own struggles and battles to fight. But
by the grace of God I am going to make it, for the joy of the Lord is my
strength.

I have been seeking the Lord's guidance about many things and am
now in a period of reflection and reevaluation. I believe I will soon be making
more changes. I may be taking a break from my journal writing, or
turning over the reins of ministry, at least for a few weeks, to some of the
more spiritually mature men. God is with them, just as He is with me, so I
know they will do a fine job of helping and teaching the flock.

This Christian journey, as I have said many times, is a walk of faith.
The steps ahead are not always visible, but with the Spirit of the Lord directing
my path, my steps will be solid and sure.

"Tsunami"

People everywhere are talking about the devastating tidal wave that struck nations in Asia and the South Pacific. India, Indonesia, Sri Lanka, and Thailand were especially hard hit, with more than 150,000 estimated to have been killed. The exact amount, of course, may never be known since many bodies were washed away into the ocean.

Yet as awful as this tsunami was, it was but another reminder that tomorrow is promised to no one. As the Lord Jesus said, "Except a man be born again, he cannot see the kingdom of God" (John 3:3). The Bible teaches that we must repent of our sin and receive Jesus as our Savior now, today, while we are still alive. This is the essential thrust of evangelism. Men are sinners who need salvation, and the time to place one's faith in Christ is at this very moment.

The tsunami tragedy, with its suddenness, should remind us of the brevity and uncertainty of life. Death stalks everyone. Its cold hands can strike one person or thousands in an instant. Second Corinthians 6:2 declares, "Now [today] is the day of salvation." Now, today, not tomorrow, because for some of us, there will be no tomorrow.

"The Hard Road"

And he [Jesus] said to them all, If any man will come after me, let him deny himself, and take up his cross daily, and follow me.

—Luke 9:23

We read the scriptures about denying ourselves and taking up our cross to follow Christ, and it is easy to give mental assent to these passages as we sit on our comfortable sofas at home or in the cozy and familiar setting of the local church. But when it comes to the reality of it all, few want to voluntarily undergo such hardship. In the United States, for example, where wealth, pleasure-seeking, and a desire for many hours of personal leisure time abound, which of us will choose the path of suffering and self-denial? Maybe if I were a Christian living in Afghanistan, but here in America?

Such things are nice spiritual ideals to read about and even discuss, but to live them out in our daily lives is another story. After all, the Lord says that those who follow Him will be hated by the world. The Bible also tells us that if we suffer with Jesus we will also reign with Him. But do I actually want this? The reigning part, yes—the suffering part, no way!

It is much easier to read about the brutal beatings inflicted upon the apostle Paul than to take such blows upon my own body. True, not that many modern-day Christians will experience such a level of persecution, but we need to be ready for the type of suffering that total devotion to Christ may bring.

I need to be ready. I love the Lord and want to give my life for service to the Kingdom, to be used by Him as a living sacrifice, and for His divine purposes. But from the beginning the Lord Jesus told His disciples the road would be difficult. It is also inconvenient, for to follow Jesus I must put the things of God and my concern for others above my own wants and needs.

The promise of God's all-sufficient grace should be enough to inspire me to seek a deeper spiritual life, to welcome self-denial, and to continue to put my own selfish desires to death.

"A Hard Lesson"

Be ye not unequally yoked together with unbelievers...

—2 Corinthians 6:14a

I made a big mistake and now I am paying for it. Amos 3:3 asks, "Can two walk together, except they be agreed?" By implication, the answer is no. God's Word is filled with good advice, if only we would heed it.

A little more than two years ago I was befriended by an attorney who wanted to involve me in a youth mentoring program. Everything he said sounded good, but he was not a Christian. I know God's Word says not to partner with such a person, but I tried to reason it out. As a result, I teamed up with this man. My motives were good, and I wanted to do the right thing. But because I did not follow the Bible's instructions, I went off course. After two years I realized my error. I was devastated when the attorney made off with hundreds of my belongings, including childhood and Bar Mitzvah photos, pictures of my parents, hundreds of letters, my college transcripts, personal and legal documents, and much more. It wasn't until November of last year that I discovered this man's true motives, which were to use me and to cash in on our casual relationship. I learned a powerful lesson by getting burned, and I pray I will never make that mistake again.

Nevertheless, the Lord chastened me through my blunder. He did not let me off the hook, for God is no respecter of persons. He had to discipline me, and there were times I felt His displeasure because of my poor choices. I have been going through a grieving process over this, but I am also on the road to recovery. At one point I had even considered stepping down from my position as pastor of this prison congregation because I had become uncertain of my ability to hear from the Lord. I do not dare stand behind a pulpit to preach to others if I cannot discern what God is speaking at any given moment. Too many souls can get hurt by a minister who speaks from his flesh, and not from God's Spirit.

But God has strengthened and encouraged my heart through this experience, though I am still grieving. I suffered personal loss, and I suppose my ego has been hurt. After all, it was painful and embarrassing to realize I had been duped and deceived, and that a con man had somehow penetrated my defenses and played me for a fool. Yet the Lord has been a patient teacher. I am wiser now and much more cautious, and I will forever be more discerning. I will also continue to be forgiving.

"Growing Old"

There is a frightening and unsettling aspect to prison life that has nothing to do with living among potentially violent men, or getting beat up, raped, slashed with a razor, or stabbed in the eye with a spike. It is growing old.

While the aging process affects everyone, growing old in prison is an exceptional hardship, and inmates seldom talk about it. For those like me who are doing long sentences and have already been incarcerated for many years, there is the dread of the world going on without us. Many of us are stuck in the past. The world seems to have stopped for us. I am computer illiterate, and I have no opportunities to learn how to use one. I have never operated a CD player or used a cell phone. When I was on the outside there were no cable TV stations or VCRs, let alone DVDs. It is almost as if I am living in a time warp. The world has become much more technologically advanced than when I knew it. In a sense, I feel as if I am still living in the 1970s.

As time goes on the people who were once in a prisoner's life often drift away. Some stay, but many do not. Family members die. Others realize they can get along fine without their loved one who is in prison. Visits become less frequent. A crushing loneliness settles in when you begin to realize that you are at the mercy of your keepers. In such a stark situation some men search for God. Others stew in anger or drown themselves in a sea of regret. Imprisonment plays heavily on a man's mind.

In the more than twenty-seven years I have been behind prison walls, I know of many who have never received a visit in five, ten, fifteen, twenty or more years. Some don't even get letters. If not for the fact that their names and identification numbers appear on the Department of Correction's public access Web site, they would exist in almost total obscurity. This is scary. It is like being suspended between the living and the dead—alive within the little world of the prison system, but dead in the minds of the masses.

Your space is a small cell, or a bunk and a footlocker. Your future, if you have to spend the remainder of your life behind bars, is an eventual trip to the local potter's field, which here at this prison is hidden on a desolate hill on state-owned land where no one from the general public can go.

Day after day it goes through your mind that the world has already forgotten you. You wonder if someone will claim your body when you die. Most of all you wonder if anyone even cares.

"Time Out"

For our light affliction, which is but for a moment, worketh for us a far more exceeding and eternal weight of glory.

—2 Corinthians 4:17

The apostle Paul, who penned this verse, probably suffered more than any Christian who has ever lived. The world despised him, while many in the Church either loved or were indifferent to this saint whom God used to shake a continent with the gospel and to encourage Christians from all walks of life. The torturous abuses Paul experienced are written about in the Bible, yet he shocks the Church with his understatement that all he went through were but "light afflictions." I suppose Paul referred to his trials in that manner because he was comparing them to that of the Savior, who was Paul's example of suffering.

The beloved Son of God endured the cross and all the pain and shame that went with it—the beatings, abuse, spitting, and a crown of stinging thorns that covered His face with His blood. The crowds cheered for His death, yet the Lord stood strong through His great afflictions, while Paul, through Christ's imparted strength, withstood his "light" ones.

As for myself, I have been through even lighter trials, yet they have hurt and wearied me, and my body and spirit have been begging for a rest. So a rest it shall be. I will not be writing in my journal for a while. I have several important matters to attend to, and I have responsibilities as the inmate pastor. I also need a time for refocusing, recuperation, and refreshing.

"Late Responses"

I thought yesterday's journal entry might be my last for a while, but I received some good news today. So with only a few hours left in the month of January, there is time for one more entry. But before I share the news, I will tell how a short while ago my cellblock was evacuated for our monthly fire drill. Every inmate, whether in his cell or in the dayroom, had to leave the building. A fire drill is always a hassle because we have to drop what we are doing and file out the main door of the unit. We are then required to line up for approximately ten minutes in a crowded corridor, about sixty men standing shoulder to shoulder, until the "all clear" is given.

Now I am back in my cell, and I want to attest to the faithfulness of the Lord. For a period of time I have been feeling as if I am in some kind of "spiritual slump" where nothing seems to be happening. Then yesterday, and again today, some unexpected blessings came my way. During this afternoon's mail call I received two late responses from people who were touched by the Focus on the Family radio interview which, as I mentioned last month, was reaired December 8-10. A woman from New York City wrote to say that while she was listening to one of the segments she felt compelled to confess her sins to the Lord, repent of her backsliding, and recommit her life to Christ. And then a man from Grand Island, New York, wrote a very encouraging letter telling me how much my words had inspired him. This was all the Lord's doing, of course, but their letters brought me great joy. God has indeed been good to me!